ISIS UNVEILED

ISIS UNVEILED

Secrets of the Ancient Wisdom Tradition

Madame Blavatsky's First Work

HELENA P. BLAVATSKY

A New Abridgment for Today

by Michael Gomes

Quest Books

Theosophical Publishing House

Wheaton, Illinois ♦ Chennai (Madras), India

First Edition 1997

Quest Books
Theosophical Publishing House
PO Box 270
Wheaton, IL 60187-0270

www.questbooks.com

Library of Congress Cataloging-in-Publication Data

Blavatsky, H. P. (Helena Petrovna), 1831–1891.
Isis unveiled: secrets of the ancient wisdom tradition, Madame
Blavatsky's first work / Helena P. Blavatsky; a new abridgment for
today by Michael Gomes.—1st Quest ed.
          p.   cm.
"Quest Books"
"A publication supported by the Kern Foundation."
Includes bibliographical references and index.
ISBN 978-0-8356-0729-2
1. Theosophy. I. Gomes, Michael, 1951– . II. Kern Foundation.
III. Title.
BP561.17 1997
299'.934—dc21   97-17867
                                                                        CIP

Printed in the United States of America

15 14 13 12 * 20 21 22 23

Contents

Publisher's Foreword   ix

Foreword   xi

Preface   xv

PART ONE: SCIENCE

1. Old Things with New Names   3

2. Phenomena and Forces   17

3. Theories Respecting Psychic Phenomena   24

4. The Ether or "Astral Light"   29

5. Psychophysical Phenomena   38

6. The Elements, Elementals, and Elementaries   47

7. Some Mysteries of Nature   55

8. Cyclic Phenomena   66

9. The Inner and Outer Man   83

10. Psychological and Physical Marvels   92

11. The "Impassable Chasm"   100

12. Realities and Illusion   106

13. Egyptian Wisdom   115

14. India: The Cradle of the Race   123

PART TWO: RELIGION

15. The Church: Where Is It?   135
16. Christian Crimes and Heathen Virtues   145
17. Divisions among the Early Christians   155
18. Oriental Cosmogonies and Bible Records   169
19. Mysteries of the Kabbala   177
20. Esoteric Doctrines of Buddhism Parodied in Christianity   184
21. Early Christian Heresies and Secret Societies   193
22. Jesuitry and Masonry   202
23. The Vedas and the Bible   211
24. The Devil Myth   221
25. Comparative Results of Buddhism and Christianity   231
26. Conclusions and Illustrations   240

Index   261

Publisher's Foreword

This abridged edition of Helena P. Blavatsky's first major work is offered as a way of approaching her seminal and influential writings. It is not intended to replace the text of the original edition (1877) or the excellent critical edition prepared by Boris de Zirkoff (Wheaton, IL: Theosophical Publishing House, 1972, 1994). This edition is rather an introduction to *Isis Unveiled* that the publishers hope will inspire readers to go on to the full and original text.

Michael Gomes has made a sensitive and intelligent abridgment of the book, highlighting the work's central theme by omitting the frequent digressions to which Blavatsky's fertile mind leaped from whatever topic she was considering. In addition, the publishers have modernized the punctuation, spelling, and in some cases the grammatical constructions and wording in an effort to make the text more accessible to a present-day reader. These changes have been made with an eye to clarifying the meaning of the text. I hope that we have nowhere distorted or modified that meaning.

We produce this edition in the spirit in which the original was prepared. *Isis Unveiled* is basically the work of H. P. Blavatsky, assisted by whatever sources she drew upon. But the published text shows the assistance of several others who edited her work and in some cases under her supervision wrote parts of it themselves. Chief among those was Henry Steel Olcott, but Alexander Wilder and others also participated in the work. In her later years, Blavatsky herself showed dissatisfaction with the state of the text, recognizing the flaws in the original.

We cannot hope to have amended the flaws that Blavatsky saw, but we have tried to produce a version that can serve for some readers as an entrée to her amazingly active mind and far-ranging thought. For those admirers of H. P. Blavatsky who prefer to have no such modifications made to her text, we paraphrase the advice Geoffrey Chaucer gave to those of his readers who found some of his works not to their liking: And if anyone finds anything here that displeases them, they should not attribute what they do not like here to ill will on our part, but only to our lack of skill.

Foreword

"Is it too much to believe that man should be developing new sensibilities and a closer relation with nature?" H. P. Blavatsky asked the reader in the preface to her first volume of *Isis Unveiled*. Over 1200 pages were devoted in her quest to answer this and other questions relating to "the mysteries of ancient and modern science and theology." She assembled a distinguished array of authorities who gave eloquent testimony of an ancient, universal world view; the myths and legends of humanity were sifted; the science of her time was pitted against the discoveries of antiquity in her attempt "to aid the student to detect the vital principles which underlie the philosophical principles of old"— concepts which at the time of the book's publication in 1877 were forgotten in the West and, as some measure of the work's influence, have reemerged in contemporary culture.

The first volume of *Isis Unveiled*, titled *Science*, addressed the capability of the ancients, based on their views of humanity and the universe, to anticipate modern science, while the second volume, dedicated to *Theology*, dealt with the rise of Christianity and the subsequent suppression of rival groups like the Mystery Schools. Her discussion of the Gnostics was quite ahead of its time and based in part on her contact with the descendants of early Christian groups such as the Druzes during her travels in Palestine and Egypt.

The work itself is a remarkable effort from one who had begun writing in English only three years before its debut, and who, by her own admission, had never been to any college or studied any branch of science. In spite of this, reviews at the time of its publication indicate that the book was regarded as one of great erudition and not just a literary curiosity. Public response was equally high: two months after its appearance in September 1877, a second printing of *Isis Unveiled* was required, and it has remained in print ever since.

Blavatsky drew on a wide range of writers, from classical authors, especially Plato and the Neoplatonists (perhaps an influence of her editor, Prof. Alexander Wilder), to Darwin and Huxley and Max Müller. She introduced English readers to a number of European writers, including the French mage Éliphas Lévi. That she also had her own sources is evident from the eyewitness account of her colleague Henry S. Olcott: "Her pen would be flying over the page, when she would suddenly stop, look out into space with the vacant eye of the clairvoyant seer, shorten her vision as though to look at something held invisibly in the air before her, and begin copying on her paper what she saw. The quotation finished, her eyes would resume their natural expression, and she would go on writing until again stopped by a similar interruption." (Further background on the writing of *Isis Unveiled* is given in the first volume of H. S. Olcott's *Old Diary Leaves*, in my own *Dawning of the Theosophical Movement*, and in the introduction to Boris de Zirkoff's edition of *Isis*.)

But the sheer volume of the material presented to sustain her case sometimes overwhelmed her theme. Added to this were lengthy digressions on burning issues of the time, such as discussion of the numerous theories put forth to explain the phenomena of spiritualism, which had swept through Europe and America in the 1850s and 1860s. Her fertile mind seemed to have seized on every bit of evidence and anticipated every possible argument. The result is that *Isis Unveiled* survives like one of the neglected ancient sanctuaries described in the book: a relic to be marveled at but not explored.

If the structure could be cleared of extraneous matter, what wonders might be revealed? With the hope of making *Isis Unveiled* more accessible, the present abridgment has been undertaken. It is not an easy task to remove more than three-quarters of an author's work. Yet when lengthy quotations from other writers, frequent explanations on the names of the various deities, and repetitious commentary have been pruned away, a thread of continuity emerges with startling clarity through the labyrinth of words, highlighting the basic concepts that Blavatsky was trying to explain.

The author was certainly aware of the defects of her book and had intended to prepare a new edition of *Isis. The Secret Doctrine*, her second work, had initially been advertised as "a new version of *Isis Unveiled*." Her untimely death on May 8, 1891, at the age of 59, put an end to this possibility. While the present attempt may not be all that the author might have wished, it reveals the basic structure of the work. Nothing has been added or changed on my part, though a great deal has been taken out. (So much was eliminated from *Science* chapters 3 and 4, dealing with nineteenth-century theories on table turning and similar phenomena, that they have been merged.) Parenthetical matter in quoted works can be taken as being from H. P. Blavatsky. The spelling of Sanskrit and other terms has been standardized, and works cited in the footnotes follow current style.

Closing the introductory chapter of the first volume, the author explained the scope of her work as follows: "Its object is not to force upon the public the personal views and theories of its author; nor has it pretensions of a scientific work, which aims at creating a revolution in some department of thought. It is rather a brief summary of the religions, philosophies, and universal traditions of human kind, and the exegesis of the same, in the spirit of those secret doctrines, which none—thanks to prejudice and bigotry — have reached Christendom in so unmutilated a form, as to secure a fair judgment."

Michael Gomes
Editor

Preface

The work now submitted to public judgment is the fruit of a somewhat intimate acquaintance with Eastern adepts and study of their science. It is offered to such as are willing to accept truth wherever it may be found and to defend it, even looking popular prejudice straight in the face. It is an attempt to aid the student to detect the vital principles which underlie the philosophical systems of old.

The book is written in all sincerity. It is meant to do even justice, and to speak the truth without malice or prejudice. But it shows neither mercy for enthroned error nor reverence for usurped authority. It demands for a spoliated past that credit for its achievements which has been too long withheld. It calls for a restitution of borrowed robes and the vindication of calumniated but glorious reputations. Toward no form of worship, no religious faith, no scientific hypothesis has its criticism been directed in any other spirit. Men and parties, sects and schools are but the mere ephemera of the world's day. Truth, high-seated upon its rock of adamant, is alone eternal and supreme.

We believe in no magic which transcends the scope and capacity of the human mind nor in "miracle," whether divine or diabolical, if such imply a transgression of the laws of nature instituted from all eternity. Nevertheless, we accept the saying of the gifted author of *Festus* [Philip J. Bailey], that the human heart has not yet fully uttered itself, and that we have never attained or even understood the extent of its powers. Is it too much to believe that man should be developing new sensibilities and a closer relation with nature? The logic of evolution must teach as much, if carried to its legitimate conclusions. If, somewhere, in the line of ascent from vegetable or ascidian to the noblest man a soul was evolved, gifted with intellectual qualities, it cannot be unreasonable to infer and believe that a faculty of perception is also growing in man, enabling him to descry facts and truths even beyond our ordinary ken. Yet we do not hesitate to accept the assertion of Biffé that "the essential is forever the same. Whether we cut away the marble inward that hides the statue in the block, or pile stone upon stone outward till the temple is completed, our new result is only an old idea. The latest of all the eternities will find its destined other half-soul in the earliest."

When, years ago, we first traveled over the East, exploring the penetralia of its deserted sanctuaries, two saddening and ever-recurring questions oppressed our thoughts: Where, who, what is God? Who ever saw the immortal spirit of man, so as to be able to assure himself of man's immortality?

It was while most anxious to solve these perplexing problems that we came into contact with certain men, endowed with such mysterious powers and such profound knowledge that we may truly designate them as the sages of the Orient. To their instructions we lent a ready ear. They showed us that by combining science with religion, the existence of God and immortality of man's spirit may be demonstrated like a problem of Euclid. For the first time we received the assurance that the Oriental philosophy has room for no other faith than an absolute and immovable faith in the omnipotence of man's own immortal self. We were taught that this omnipotence comes from the kinship of man's spirit with the Universal Soul—God! The latter, they said, can never be demonstrated but by the former.

Man-spirit proves God-spirit, as the one drop of water proves a source from which it must have come. Tell one who had never seen water that there is an ocean of water, and he must accept it in faith or reject it altogether. But let one drop fall upon his hand, and he then has the fact from which all the rest may be inferred. After that he could by degrees understand that a boundless and fathomless ocean of water existed. Blind faith would no longer be necessary; he would have supplanted it with knowledge. When one sees mortal man displaying tremendous capabilities, controlling the forces of nature and opening up to view the world of spirit, the reflective mind is overwhelmed with the conviction that if one man's spiritual Ego can do this much, the capabilities of the Father Spirit must be relatively as much vaster as

xvi

the whole ocean surpasses the single drop in volume and potency. *Ex nihilo nihil fit*; prove the soul of man by its wondrous powers and you have proved God!

In our studies, mysteries were shown to be no mysteries. Names and places that to the Western mind have only a significance derived from Eastern fable were shown to be realities. Reverently we stepped in spirit within the temple of Isis; to lift aside the veil of "the one that is and was and shall be" at Sais; to look through the rent curtain of the Sanctum Sanctorum at Jerusalem; and even to interrogate within the crypts which once existed beneath the sacred edifice, the mysterious Bath-Kol. The *Filia Vocis*—the daughter of the divine voice—responded from the mercy-seat within the veil, and science, theology, every human hypothesis and conception born of imperfect knowledge, lost forever their authoritative character in our sight. The one living God had spoken through his oracle, man, and we were satisfied. Such knowledge is priceless; and it has been hidden only from those who overlooked it, derided it, or denied its existence.

Our work then, is a plea for the recognition of the Hermetic philosophy, the anciently universal Wisdom Religion, as the only possible key to the Absolute in science and theology.

The contest now going on between the party of public conscience and the party of reaction has already developed a healthier tone of thought. It will hardly fail to result ultimately in the overthrow of error and the triumph of truth. We repeat again—we are laboring for the brighter morrow.

And yet, when we consider the bitter opposition that we are called upon to face, who is better entitled than we upon entering the arena to write upon our shield the hail of the Roman gladiator to Caesar: MORITURUS TE SALUTAT!

New York, September, 1877

H. P. Blavatsky

Part One

SCIENCE

1

Old Things with New Names

There exists somewhere in this wide world an old book—so very old that our modern antiquarians might ponder over its pages an indefinite time and still not quite agree as to the nature of the fabric upon which it is written. It is the only original copy now in existence. The most ancient Hebrew document on occult learning—the *Sifra di-Tseniuta* [Book of Concealed Mystery]—was compiled from it, and that at a time when the former was already considered in the light of a literary relic. One of its illustrations represents the Divine Essence emanating from ADAM[1] like a luminous arc proceeding to form a circle; and then, having attained the highest point of its circumference, the ineffable Glory bends back again and returns to earth, bringing a higher type of humanity in its vortex. As it approaches nearer and nearer to our planet, the Emanation becomes more and more shadowy, until upon touching the ground it is as black as night.

A conviction, founded upon seventy thousand years of experience,[2] as they allege, has been entertained by Hermetic philosophers of all periods that matter has in time become, through sin, more gross and dense than it was at man's first formation; that, at the beginning, the human body was of a half-ethereal nature; and that, before the fall, mankind communed freely with the now unseen universes. But since that time matter has become the formidable barrier between us and the world of spirits. The oldest esoteric traditions also teach that, before the mystic Adam, many races of human beings lived and died out, each giving place in its turn to another.

As the cycle proceeded, man's eyes were more and more opened, until he came to know "good and evil" as well as the Elohim themselves. Having reached its summit, the cycle began to go downward.

3

When the arc attained a certain point which brought it parallel with the fixed line of our terrestrial plane, the man was furnished by nature with "coats of skin," and the Lord God "clothed them."

This same belief in the preexistence of a far more spiritual race than the one to which we now belong can be traced back to the earliest traditions of nearly every people. In the ancient Quiché manuscript—the *Popol Vuh*—the first men are mentioned as a race that could reason and speak, whose sight was unlimited, and who knew all things at once. According to Philo Judaeus [*De gigantibus* 2], the air is filled with an invisible host of spirits, some of whom are free from evil and immortal, and others are pernicious and mortal. "From the sons of EL we are descended, and sons of EL must we become again." And the unequivocal statement of the anonymous Gnostic who wrote the Gospel according to John (1.12) that "as many as received Him," i.e., who followed practically the esoteric doctrine of Jesus, would "become the sons of God" points to the same belief. "Know ye not, ye are *gods?*" exclaimed the Master. Plato describes admirably in *Phaedrus* [246C] the state in which man once was and what he will become again, before and after the "loss of his wings," when "he lived among the gods, a god himself in the airy world." From the remotest periods, religious philosophies taught that the whole universe was filled with divine and spiritual beings of diverse races. From one of these evolved, in the course of time, ADAM, the primitive man.

The discoveries of modern science do not disagree with the oldest traditions, which claim an incredible antiquity for our race. Within the last few years geology, which previously had only conceded that man could be traced as far back as the tertiary period, has found unanswerable proofs that human existence antedates the last glaciation of Europe—over 250,000 years! A hard nut, this, for patristic theology to crack, but an accepted fact with the ancient philosophers.

Moreover, fossil implements have been exhumed together with human remains, which show that man hunted in those remote times and knew how to build a fire. But the forward step has not yet been taken in this search for the origin of the race; science comes to a dead stop and waits for future proofs. Neither geologists nor archaeologists are able to construct, from the fragmentary bits hitherto discovered, the perfect skeleton of the triple man—physical, intellectual, and spiritual. Because the fossil implements of man are found to become

4

more rough and uncouth as geology penetrates deeper into the bowels of the earth, it seems a proof to science that the closer we come to the origin of man, the more savage and brutelike he must be. Strange logic! Does the finding of the remains in the cave of Devon prove that there were no contemporary races then who were highly civilized? When the present population of the earth have disappeared, and some archaeologist belonging to the "coming race" of the distant future shall excavate the domestic implements of one of our Indian or Andaman Island tribes, will he be justified in concluding that mankind in the nineteenth century was "just emerging from the Stone Age"?

Whether arrived at by the method of Aristotle, or that of Plato, we need not stop to inquire; but it is a fact that both the inner and outer natures of man are claimed to have been thoroughly understood by the ancient andrologists. Notwithstanding the superficial hypotheses of geologists, we are beginning to have almost daily proofs in corroboration of the assertions of those philosophers.

They divided the interminable periods of human existence on this planet into cycles, during each of which mankind gradually reached the culminating point of highest civilization and gradually relapsed into abject barbarism.[3] To what eminence the race in its progress had several times arrived may be feebly surmised by the wonderful monuments of old, still visible, and the descriptions given by Herodotus of other marvels of which no traces now remain. Even in his day the gigantic structures of many pyramids and world-famous temples were but masses of ruins. Scattered by the unrelenting hand of time, they are described by the Father of History as "these venerable witnesses of the long bygone glory of departed ancestors." He "shrinks from speaking of divine things" and gives to posterity but an imperfect description from hearsay of some marvelous subterranean chambers of the Labyrinth, where lay—and now lie—concealed the sacred remains of the King-Initiates.

The impenetrable veil of arcane secrecy was thrown over the sciences taught in the sanctuary. This is the cause of the modern depreciating of the ancient philosophies. Even Plato and Philo Judaeus have been accused by many a commentator of absurd inconsistencies, whereas the design which underlies the maze of metaphysical contradictions, so perplexing to the reader of the *Timaeus*, is but too evident.

The speculations of these philosophers upon matter were open to public criticism, but their teachings in regard to spiritual things were profoundly esoteric. Being thus sworn to secrecy and religious silence upon abstruse subjects involving the relations of spirit and matter, they rivaled each other in their ingenious methods for concealing their real opinions.

The doctrine of *metempsychosis* has been abundantly ridiculed by men of science and rejected by theologians, yet if it had been properly understood in its application to the indestructibility of matter and the immortality of spirit, it would have been perceived that it is a sublime conception. Should we not first regard the subject from the standpoint of the ancients before venturing to disparage its teachers? The solution of the great problem of eternity belongs neither to religious superstition nor to gross materialism.

If the Pythagorean metempsychosis should be thoroughly explained and compared with the modern theory of evolution, it would be found to supply every "missing link" in the chain of the latter.

There was not a philosopher of any notoriety who did not hold to the doctrine of metempsychosis, as taught by the Brahmans, Buddhists, and later by the Pythagoreans, in its esoteric sense, whether he expressed it more or less intelligibly. Origen and Clement Alexandrinus, Synesius and Chalcidius, all believed in it; and the Gnostics, who are unhesitatingly proclaimed by history as a body of the most refined, learned, and enlightened men, were all believers in metempsychosis. Socrates entertained opinions identical with those of Pythagoras; and both, as the penalty of their divine philosophy, were put to a violent death. The rabble has been the same in all ages. Materialism has been and will ever be blind to spiritual truths. These philosophers held with the Hindus that God had infused into matter a portion of his own Divine Spirit, which animates and moves every particle. They taught that men have two souls of separate and quite different natures: the one perishable—the astral soul, or the inner, fluidic body—the other incorruptible and immortal—the *augoeides*, or portion of the Divine Spirit; that the mortal or astral soul perishes at each gradual change at the threshold of every new sphere, becoming with every transmigration more purified. The astral man, intangible and invisible as he might be to our mortal, earthly senses, is still constituted of matter, though sublimated.

6

But the too great dependence upon physical facts led to a growth of materialism and a decadence of spirituality and faith. At the time of Aristotle, this was the prevailing tendency of thought. And though the Delphic commandment was not as yet completely eliminated from Grecian thought and some philosophers still held that "in order to know what man *is*, we ought to know what man *was*"—still materialism had already begun to gnaw at the root of faith. The Mysteries themselves had degenerated in a very great degree into mere priestly speculations and religious fraud. Few were the true adepts and initiates, the heirs and descendants of those who had been dispersed by the conquering swords of various invaders of old Egypt.

The time predicted by the great Hermes in his dialogue with Asclepius had indeed come: the time when impious foreigners would accuse Egypt of adoring monsters and naught but the letters engraved in stone upon her monuments would survive—enigmas incredible to posterity. Their sacred scribes and hierophants were wanderers upon the face of the earth. Obliged from fear of a profanation of the sacred mysteries to seek refuge among the Hermetic fraternities—known later as the Essenes—their esoteric knowledge was buried deeper than ever. The triumphant brand of Aristotle's pupil [Alexander the Great] swept away from his path of conquest every vestige of a once pure religion, and Aristotle himself, the type and child of his epoch, though instructed in the secret science of the Egyptians, knew but little of this crowning result of millenniums of esoteric studies.

As well as those who lived in the days of the Psammetichus, our present-day philosophers "lift the Veil of Isis"—for Isis is but the symbol of nature. But they see only her physical forms. The soul within escapes their view, and the Divine Mother has no answer for them.

Our modern science acknowledges a Supreme Power, an Invisible Principle, but denies a Supreme Being, or Personal God. Logically, the difference between the two might be questioned; for in this case, the Power and the Being are identical. Human reason can hardly imagine to itself an Intelligent Supreme Power without associating it with the idea of an Intelligent Being. The masses can never be expected to have a clear conception of the omnipotence and omnipresence of a Supreme God, without investing a gigantic projection of their own personality with those attributes. But the kabbalists have never looked upon the invisible EN-SOF otherwise than as a Power.

7

Very few Christians understand, if indeed they know anything at all, of Jewish theology. The Talmud is the darkest of enigmas even for most Jews, while those Hebrew scholars who do comprehend it do not boast of their knowledge. Their kabbalistic books are still less understood by them; for in our days more Christian than Jewish students are engrossed in the elucidation of their great truths. How much less is definitely known of the Oriental, or the universal Kabbala! Its adepts are few, but these heirs-elect of the sages who first discovered "the starry truths which shone on the great Shemaia of the Chaldean lore"[4] have solved the "absolute" and are now resting from their grand labor. They cannot go beyond that which is given to mortals of this earth to know; and no one, not even these elect, can trespass beyond the line drawn by the finger of the Divinity itself.

Travelers have met these adepts on the shores of the sacred Ganges, brushed against them in the silent ruins of Thebes and in the mysterious deserted chambers of Luxor. Within the halls upon whose blue and golden vaults the weird signs attract attention, but whose secret meaning is never penetrated by the idle gazers, they have been seen but seldom recognized. Historical memoirs have recorded their presence in the brilliantly illuminated salons of European aristocracy. They have been encountered again on the arid and desolate plains of the great Sahara, as in the caves of Elephanta. They may be found everywhere, but make themselves known only to those who have devoted their lives to unselfish study and are not likely to turn back.

Thoroughly acquainted with all the resources of the vegetable, animal, and mineral kingdoms, experts in occult chemistry and physics, psychologists as well as physiologists—why wonder that the graduates or adepts instructed in the mysterious sanctuaries of the temples could perform wonders which even in our days of enlightenment would appear supernatural? It is an insult to human nature to brand magic and the occult science with the name of imposture. To believe that, for so many thousands of years, one-half of mankind practiced deception and fraud on the other half is equivalent to saying that the human race was composed only of knaves and incurable idiots. Where is the country in which magic was not practiced? At what age was it wholly forgotten?

In the oldest documents now in our possession—the Vedas and the older laws of Manu—we find many magical rites practiced and

8

permitted by the Brahmans. Tibet, Japan, and China teach in the present age that which was taught by the oldest Chaldeans. The clergy of these respective countries prove, moreover, what they teach: namely that the practice of moral and physical purity and of certain austerities develops the vital soul-power of self-illumination. Affording to man control over his own immortal spirit gives him truly magical powers over the elementary spirits inferior to himself.

In the West we find magic of as high an antiquity as in the East. The Druids of Great Britain practiced it in the silent crypts of their deep caves; and Pliny (*Natural History* 29.12, 30.4, etc.) devotes many a chapter to the "wisdom" of the leaders of the Celts. The Semothees— the Druids of the Gauls—expounded the physical as well as the spiritual sciences. They taught the secrets of the universe, the harmonious progress of the heavenly bodies, the formation of the earth, and above all the immortality of the soul. Into their sacred groves—natural academies built by the hand of the Invisible Architect—the initiates assembled at the still hour of midnight to learn about what man once was and what he will be. They needed no artificial illumination to light up their temples, for the chaste goddess of night beamed her most silvery rays on their oak-crowned heads; and their white-robed sacred bards knew how to converse with the solitary queen of the starry vault.

On the dead soil of the long bygone past stand their sacred oaks, now dried up and stripped of their spiritual meaning by the venomous breath of materialism. But for the student of occult learning, their vegetation is still as verdant and luxuriant, and as full of deep and sacred truths, as at that hour when the archdruid performed his magical cures and, waving the branch of mistletoe, severed with his golden sickle the green bough from its mother oak tree.

Magic is as old as man. It is as impossible to name the time when it sprang into existence as to indicate on what day the first man himself was born. Whenever a writer has started with the idea of connecting its first foundation in a country with some historical character, further research has proved his views groundless. Odin, the Scandinavian priest and monarch, was thought by many to have originated the practice of magic some seventy years B.C. But it was easily demonstrated that the mysterious rites of the priestesses called *Völvas, Valas,* were greatly anterior to his age. Some modern authors were bent on proving that

9

Zoroaster was the founder of magic because he was the founder of the Magian religion. Ammianus Marcellinus, Arnobius, Pliny, and other ancient historians demonstrated conclusively that he was but a reformer of magic as practiced by the Chaldeans and Egyptians.[5]

The greatest teachers of divinity agree that nearly all ancient books were written symbolically and in a language intelligible only to the initiated. The biographical sketch of Apollonius of Tyana affords an example. As every kabbalist knows, it embraces the whole of the Hermetic philosophy, being a counterpart in many respects of the traditions left us of King Solomon. It reads like a fairy story but, as in the case of the latter, sometimes facts and historical events are presented to the world under the colors of a fiction. The journey to India represents allegorically the trials of a neophyte. His long discourses with the Brahmans, their sage advice, and the dialogues with the Corinthian Menippus would, if interpreted, give the esoteric catechism. His visit to the empire of the wise men and interview with their king Iarchas, the oracle of Amphiaraus, explain symbolically many of the secret dogmas of Hermes. They would disclose, if understood, some of the most important secrets of nature.

No subsequent people has been so proficient in geometry as the builders of the pyramids and other titanic monuments, antediluvian and postdiluvian. On the other hand, none has ever equaled them in the practical interrogation of nature. An undeniable proof of this is the significance of their countless symbols. Every one of these symbols is an embodied idea—combining the conception of the Divine Invisible with the earthly and visible. The former is derived from the latter strictly through analogy according to the Hermetic formula—"as below, so it is above." Their symbols show great knowledge of natural sciences and a practical study of cosmical power.

Despite their apparent polytheism, the ancients—those of the educated class at all events—were entirely monotheistical; and this, too, ages upon ages before the days of Moses. In the *Ebers Papyrus* this fact is shown conclusively in the following words, translated from the first four lines of plate 1: "I came from Heliopolis with the great ones from Het-aat, the Lords of Protection, the masters of eternity and salvation. I came from Sais with the Mother-goddesses, who extended to me protection. The Lord of the Universe told me how to free the gods from all murderous diseases." Eminent men were called gods by

10

the ancients. The deification of mortal men and supposititious gods is no more a proof against their monotheism than the monument building of modern Christians, who erect statues to their heroes, is proof of their polytheism. Americans of the present century would consider it absurd in their posterity 3,000 years hence to classify them as idolaters for having built statues to their god Washington. So shrouded in mystery was the Hermetic philosophy that Volney asserted that the ancient peoples worshipped their gross material symbols as divine in themselves, whereas these were only considered as representing esoteric principles.

Magic was considered a divine science which led to a participation in the attributes of Divinity itself. "It unveils the operations of nature," says Philo Judaeus (*De specialibus legibus* 3.18.100), "and leads to the contemplation of celestial powers." In later periods its abuse and degeneration into sorcery made it an object of general abhorrence. We must therefore deal with it only as it was in the remote past, during those ages when every true religion was based on a knowledge of the occult powers of nature. It was not the sacerdotal class in ancient Persia that established magic, as is commonly thought, but the Magi who derive their name from it. Magic appeared in the world with the earlier races of men.

The ancients knew more concerning certain sciences than our modern savants have yet discovered. Reluctant as many are to confess as much, it has been acknowledged by more than one scientist. "The degree of scientific knowledge existing in an early period of society was much greater than the moderns are willing to admit," says Dr. A. Todd Thomson, the editor of *The Occult Sciences* by Salverte; "but," he adds, "it was confined to the temples, carefully veiled from the eyes of the people and exposed only to the priesthood."[6]

In order to demonstrate that the notions which the ancients entertained about dividing human history into cycles were not utterly devoid of a philosophical basis, we will close this chapter by introducing to the reader one of the oldest traditions of antiquity as to the evolution of our planet.

At the close of each "great year," called by Aristotle—according to Censorinus—the greatest, which consists of six *sars* [cycles of eclipses],[7] our planet is subjected to a thorough physical revolution. The polar and equatorial climates gradually exchange places, the former moving slowly toward the Line, and the tropical zone, with its exuberant vegetation and swarming animal life, replacing the forbidding wastes of the icy poles. This change of climate is necessarily attended by cataclysms, earthquakes, and other cosmic throes. As the beds of the ocean are displaced, at the end of every decimillennium and about one neros, a semi-universal deluge like the legendary Noachian flood is brought about. This year was called the *heliacal* by the Greeks, but no one outside the sanctuary knew anything certain either as to its duration or particulars. The winter of this year was called the Cataclysm or the Deluge; the summer, the Ecpyrosis. The popular traditions taught that at these alternate seasons the world was in turn burned and deluged.

The neroses, the brihaspati, or the periods called yugas or kalpas, are life problems to solve. The Satya-yuga and Buddhistic cycles of chronology would make a mathematician stand aghast at the array of ciphers. The Maha-kalpa embraces an untold number of periods far back in the antediluvian ages. Their system comprises a kalpa or grand period of 4,320,000,000 years, consisting of seventy-one Maha-yugas, each divided into four lesser yugas, running as follows:

1st— Satya-yuga	1,728,000 years
2nd—Tretya-yuga	1,296,000 years
3rd— Dvapara-yuga	864,000 years
4th— Kali-yuga	432,000 years
Total	4,320,000

These make one divine age or Maha-yuga. Seventy-one Maha-yugas make 306,720,000 years, to which is added a sandhya (or the time when day and night border on each other, morning and evening twilight), equal to a Satya-yuga of 1,728,000 years, making a manvantara of 308,448,000 years.[8] Fourteen manvantaras make 4,318,272,000 years, to which must be added a sandhya to begin the kalpa, 1,728,000 years, making the kalpa or grand period of 4,320,000,000 years. As we are now only in the Kali-yuga of the twenty-eighth age of the seventh manvantara of 308,448,000 years, we have yet sufficient time before us to wait before we reach even half of the time allotted to the world.

These ciphers are not fanciful, but founded upon actual astronomical calculations, as has been demonstrated by S. Davis.[9] Many a scientist, Higgins among others, notwithstanding their researches, has been utterly perplexed as to which of these was the secret cycle. Bunsen has demonstrated that the Egyptian priests, who made the cyclic notations, kept them always in the profoundest mystery.[10] Perhaps their difficulty arose from the fact that the calculations of the ancients applied equally to the spiritual progress of humanity as to the physical.

It will not be difficult to understand the close correspondence drawn by the ancients between the cycles of nature and of mankind, if we keep in mind their belief in the constant and all-potent influences of the planets upon the fortunes of humanity. Higgins justly believed that the cycle of the Indian system, of 432,000, is the true key of the secret cycle. But his failure in trying to decipher it was made apparent; for as it pertained to the mystery of the creation, this cycle was the most inviolable of all. It was repeated in symbolic figures only in the Chaldean *Book of Numbers*, the original of which, if now extant, is certainly not to be found in libraries, as it formed one of the most ancient books of Hermes,[11] the number of which is at present undetermined.

As our planet revolves once every year around the sun and at the same time turns once in every twenty-four hours upon its own axis, thus traversing minor circles within a larger one, so is the work of the smaller cyclic periods accomplished and recommenced within the great saros.

The revolution of the physical world, according to the ancient doctrine, is attended by a like revolution in the world of intellect—the spiritual evolution of the world proceeding in cycles like the physical one.

Thus we see in history a regular alternation of ebb and flow in the tide of human progress. The great kingdoms and empires of the world, after reaching the culmination of their greatness, descend again in accordance with the same law by which they ascended; till, having reached the lowest point, humanity reasserts itself and mounts up once more, the height of its attainment being, by this law of ascending progression by cycles, somewhat higher than the point from which it had before descended.

The division of the history of mankind into Golden, Silver, Copper, and Iron Ages is not a fiction. We see the same thing in the literature of peoples. An age of great inspiration and unconscious productiveness is invariably followed by an age of criticism and consciousness. The one affords material for the analyzing and critical intellect of the other.

Thus all those great characters who tower like giants in the history of mankind, like Buddha-Siddhartha and Jesus in the realm of spiritual and Alexander the Macedonian and Napoleon the Great in the realm of physical conquests, were but reflexed images of human types which had existed ten thousand years before, in the preceding decimillennium, reproduced by the mysterious powers controlling the destinies of our world. There is no prominent character in all the annals of sacred or profane history whose prototype we cannot find in the half-fictitious and half-real traditions of bygone religions and mythologies. As the star, glimmering at an immeasurable distance above our heads in the boundless immensity of the sky, reflects itself in the smooth waters of a lake, so does the imagery of men of the antediluvian ages reflect itself in the periods we can embrace in a historical retrospect.

"As above, so it is below. That which has been, will return again. As in heaven, so on earth."

Too many of our thinkers do not consider that the numerous changes in language, the allegorical phraseology, and the evident secretiveness of old mystic writers, who were generally under an obligation never to divulge the solemn secrets of the sanctuary, might have sadly misled translators and commentators. The phrases of the medieval alchemist they read literally, and even the veiled symbology of Plato is commonly misunderstood by the modern scholar. One day they may learn to know better and so become aware that the method of extreme necessarianism was practiced in ancient as well as in modern philosophy; that from the first ages of man, the fundamental truths of all that we are permitted to know on earth was in the safe keeping of the adepts of the sanctuary; that the difference in creeds and religious practice was only external; and that those guardians of the primitive divine revelation, who had solved every problem that is within the grasp of human intellect, were bound together by a universal freemasonry of science and philosophy, which formed one unbroken chain around the globe. It is for philology and psychology to find the end of the thread. That done, it will then be ascertained that, by relaxing one single loop of the old religious systems, the chain of mystery may be disentangled.

The moment is more opportune than ever for the review of old philosophies. Archaeologists, philologists, astronomers, chemists, and physicists are getting nearer and nearer to the point where they will be forced to consider them. Physical science has already reached its limits of exploration; dogmatic theology sees the springs of its inspiration dry. Unless we mistake the signs, the day is approaching when the world will receive the proofs that only ancient religions were in harmony with nature and ancient science embraced all that can be known. Secrets long kept may be revealed; books long forgotten and arts long lost may be brought out to light again; papyri and parchments of inestimable importance will turn up in the hands of men who pretend to have unrolled them from mummies or stumbled upon them in buried crypts; tablets and pillars, whose sculptured revelations will stagger theologians and confound scientists, may yet be excavated and interpreted. Who knows the possibilities of the future? An era of disenchantment and rebuilding will soon begin—nay, has already begun. The cycle has almost run its course; a new one is about to begin, and the future pages of history may contain full evidence and convey full proof that

> If ancestry can be in aught believed,
> Descending spirits have conversed with man,
> And told him secrets of the world unknown.

Notes

1. The name is used in the sense of the Greek word *anthropos*. [Although the note indicates that here ADAM signifies mankind, *The Mahatma Letters* (3rd. ed.), Letter 9, suggests that ADAM must be regarded as emanating from the Divine Essence.—ED.]
2. The traditions of the Oriental Kabbalists claim their science to be older than that. Modern scientists may doubt and reject the assertion. They *cannot* prove it false.
3. [Letter 16 of *The Mahatma Letters* recommends that "mankind" in this sentence be changed to "human races," and for "civilization" read "spiritual evolution of that particular race."—ED.]
4. Bulwer-Lytton, *Zanoni* bk. 3, ch. 5.

5. Ammianus Marcellinus, *Roman History* 23.6.32–33; [Arnobius, *Adversus Gentes* 1.5; Pliny, *Natural History* 30.2–3].

6. [(New York, 1847), preface, 1: xiii.]

7. Berosus, himself a Chaldean astrologer at the Temple of Belus at Babylon, gives the duration of the sar, or sarus, as 3,600 years; a neros, 600; and a sossus, 60. See I. P. Cory, *Ancient Fragments* (London, 1832), 29; Berosus (fragment from Abydenus), "Of the Chaldean Kings and the Deluge." See also Eusebius, *Chronicon* 1.6, and the fragment from Theon of Alexandria in MS. ex. cod. reg. Gall. gr. No. 2390, fol. 154 [in Cory, 329–30].

8. Charles Coleman, who makes this calculation [*Mythology of the Hindus* (London, 1832), xiii], allowed a serious error to escape the proofreader; the length of the manvantara is given at 368,448,000, which is just sixty million years too much.

9. Samuel Davis, "On the Astronomical Computations of the Hindus," in *Asiatic Researches* 2:175–226; and Godfrey Higgins, *Anacalypsis* (London, 1832), 1:176.

10. C. K. J. Bunsen, *Egypt's Place in Universal History* (London, 1848), 1:24.

11. The forty-two Sacred Books of the Egyptians, mentioned by Clement of Alexandria as having existed in his time, were but a portion of the books of Hermes. Iamblichus, on the authority of the Egyptian priest Abammon, attributes 1200 of such books to Hermes, and Manetho 36,000. But the testimony of Iamblichus as a Neoplatonist and theurgist is of course rejected by modern critics. [Blavatsky's editor, Alexander Wilder, in his translation of Iamblichus's *De mysteriis*, gives the figures of 2,000 for Hermes and 36,525 for Manetho.—ED.]

2

Phenomena and Forces

I s it enough for man to know that he exists? Is it enough to be formed a human being to enable him to deserve the appellation of *man*? It is our decided impression and conviction that to become a genuine spiritual entity, which that designation implies, man must first create himself anew, so to speak—i.e., thoroughly eliminate from his mind and spirit not only the dominating influence of selfishness and other impurity, but also the infection of superstition and prejudice. The latter is far different from what we commonly term *antipathy* or *sympathy*. We are at first irresistibly or unwittingly drawn within its dark circle by that peculiar influence, that powerful current of magnetism which emanates from ideas as well as from physical bodies. By this we are surrounded and finally prevented through moral cowardice—fear of public opinion—from stepping out of it. It is rare that men regard a thing in either its true or false light, accepting the conclusion by the free action of their own judgment. Quite the reverse: The conclusion is more commonly reached by blindly adopting the opinion current at the hour among those with whom they associate.

Many years of wandering among "heathen" and "Christian" magicians, occultists, mesmerizers, and the *tutti quanti* of white and black art ought to be sufficient, we think, to give us a certain right to feel competent to take a practical view of this doubted and very complicated question. We have associated with the fakirs, the holy men of India, and seen them when in intercourse with the *Pitris*. We have watched the proceedings and modus operandi of the howling and dancing dervishes; we have held friendly communications with the marabouts of European and Asiatic Turkey; and the serpent-charmers

17

of Damascus and Benares have but few secrets that we have not had the fortune to study.

In *Researches on the Phenomena of Spiritualism*, [(London, 1874), 98–100], William Crookes submits to the option of the reader eight theories "to account for the phenomena observed."

These theories run as follows:

First Theory.—The phenomena are all the result of tricks, clever mechanical arrangements, or legerdemain; the mediums are impostors, and the rest of the company fools.

Second Theory.—The persons at a seance are the victims of a sort of mania, or delusion, and imagine phenomena to occur which have no real objective existence.

Third Theory.—The whole is the result of conscious or unconscious cerebral action.

Fourth Theory.—The result of the spirit of the medium, perhaps in association with the spirits of some or all of the people present.

Fifth Theory.—The actions of evil spirits, or devils, personifying whom or what they please, in order to undermine Christianity, and ruin men's souls. (Theory of our theologians.)

Sixth Theory.—The actions of a separate order of beings living on this earth, but invisible and immaterial to us. Able, however, occasionally to manifest their presence, known in almost all countries and ages as demons (not necessarily bad), gnomes, fairies, kobolds, elves, goblins, Puck, etc. (One of the claims of the kabbalists.)

Seventh Theory.—The actions of departed human beings—the spiritual theory *par excellence*.

Eighth Theory.—(The psychic force) . . . an adjunct to the fourth, fifth, sixth, and seventh theories.

The first of these theories, having been proved valid only in exceptional though unfortunately still too frequent cases, must be ruled out as having no material bearing upon the phenomena themselves. The second and the third theories are the last crumbling entrenchments of the guerrilla of skeptics and materialists, and remain, as lawyers say, *Adhuc sub judice lis est*. Thus we can deal in this work only with the four remaining ones, the eighth theory being according to Mr. Crookes's opinion but "a necessary adjunct" of the others.

The recognized laws of physical science account for but a few of the more objective of the so-called spiritual phenomena. While proving the reality of certain visible effects of an unknown force, they have not thus far enabled scientists to control at will even this portion of the phenomena. The truth is that the professors have not yet discovered the necessary conditions of their occurrence. They must go as deeply into the study of the triple nature of man—physiological, psychological, and divine—as did their predecessors, the magicians, theurgists, and thaumaturgists of old.

Years ago the old German philosopher Schopenhauer disposed of this force and matter at the same time. Schopenhauer's doctrine is that the universe is but the manifestation of the will. Every force in nature is also an effect of will, representing a higher or lower degree of its objectiveness. It is the teaching of Plato, who stated distinctly that everything visible was created or evolved out of the invisible and eternal WILL and after its fashion. Our Heaven, he says, was produced according to the eternal pattern of the "Ideal World," contained, like everything else, in the dodecahedron, the geometrical model used by the Deity (*Timaeus* 28, 55C). With Plato, the Primal Being is an emanation of the Demiurgic Mind (*Nous*), which contains from eternity the "idea" of the "to be created world" within itself, which idea he produces out of himself. The laws of nature are the established relations of this idea to the forms of its manifestations; "these forms," says Schopenhauer, "are time, space, and causality. Through time and space the idea varies in its numberless manifestations."

The ancient philosophy affirmed that it is in consequence of the manifestation of that Will—termed by Plato *the Divine Idea*—that everything visible and invisible sprang into existence. As that Intelligent Idea, which, by directing its sole will power toward a center of localized forces, called objective forms into being, so can man, the microcosm of the great Macrocosm, do the same in proportion with the development of his will power. The imaginary atoms—a figure of speech employed by Democritus and gratefully seized upon by the materialists—are like automatic workmen moved inwardly by the influx of that Universal Will directed upon them, which, manifesting itself as force, sets them into activity. The plan of the structure to be erected is in the brain of the Architect and reflects his will; abstract as yet, from the instant of the conception it becomes concrete through these atoms which follow faithfully every line, point, and figure traced in the imagination of the Divine Geometer.

19

As God creates, so man can create. Given a certain intensity of will, the shapes created by the mind become subjective. Hallucinations, they are called, although to their creator they are real as any visible object is to anyone else. Given a more intense and intelligent concentration of this will, the form becomes concrete, visible, objective; the man has learned the secret of secrets; he is a Magician.

The materialist should not object to this logic, for he regards thought as matter. Conceding it to be so, the cunning mechanism contrived by the inventor, the fairy scenes born in the poet's brain, the gorgeous painting limned by the artist's fancy, the peerless statue chiseled in ether by the sculptor, the palaces and castles built in air by the architect—all these, though invisible and subjective, must exist, for they are matter, shaped and molded. Who shall say, then, that there are not some men of such imperial will as to be able to drag these air-drawn fancies into view, enveloped in the hard casing of gross substance to make them tangible?

Many of these mystics, by following what they were taught by some treatises secretly preserved from one generation to another, achieved discoveries which would not be despised even in our day of exact sciences.

Men possessed of such knowledge and exercising such powers patiently toiled for something better than the vain glory of a passing fame. Seeking it not, they became immortal, as do all who labor for the good of the race, forgetful of mean self. Illuminated with the light of eternal truth, these rich-poor alchemists fixed their attention upon the things that lie beyond the common ken, recognizing nothing inscrutable but the First Cause, and finding no question unsolvable. To dare, to know, to will, and to REMAIN SILENT was their constant rule; to be beneficent, unselfish, and unpretending were, with them, spontaneous impulses.

We are far from believing that all the spirits that communicate at circles are of the classes called "Elemental" and "Elementary." Many—especially among those who control the medium subjectively to speak, write, and otherwise act in various ways—are human, disembodied spirits. Whether the majority of such spirits are good or bad largely depends on the private morality of the medium, much on the circle present, and a great deal on the intensity and object of their purpose.

20

If this object is merely to gratify curiosity and to pass the time, it is useless to expect anything serious.

But, in any case, human spirits can *never* materialize themselves *in propria persona*. These can never appear to the investigator clothed with warm, solid flesh, sweating hands and faces, and grossly material bodies. The most they can do is to project their ethereal reflection on the atmospheric waves, and if the touch of their hands and clothing can become upon rare occasions objective to the senses of a living mortal, it will be felt as a passing breeze gently sweeping over the touched spot, not as a human hand or material body. It is useless to plead that the "materialized spirits" that have exhibited themselves with beating hearts and loud voices (with or without a trumpet) are human spirits. The voices—if such sound can be termed a voice at all—of a spiritual apparition once heard can hardly be forgotten. That of a pure spirit is like the tremulous murmur of an Aeolian harp echoed from a distance; the voice of a suffering, hence impure, if not utterly bad spirit, may be assimilated to a human voice issuing from an empty barrel.

We will now again assert that no spirit claimed by the spiritualists to be human was ever proved to be such on sufficient testimony. The influence of the disembodied ones can be felt and communicated subjectively by them to sensitives. They can produce objective manifestations, but they cannot produce themselves otherwise than as described above. They can control the body of a medium and express their desires and ideas in various modes well known to spiritualists; but not materialize what is matterless and purely spiritual—their *divine essence*.

Thus every so-called "materialization"—when genuine—is produced either (perhaps) by the will of that spirit whom the "appearance" is claimed to be but can only personate at best, or by the elementary goblins themselves, which are generally too stupid to deserve the honor of being called devils. Upon rare occasions the spirits are able to subdue and control these soulless beings, which are ever ready to assume pompous names if left to themselves, in such a way that the mischievous spirit "of the air," shaped in the real image of the human spirit, will be moved by the latter like a marionette and unable to either act or utter other words than those imposed on him by the "immortal soul." But this requires many conditions generally unknown to the

21

circles of even spiritualists most in the habit of regularly attending seances. Not every one who likes can attract human spirits. One of the most powerful attractions of our departed ones is their strong affection for those whom they have left on earth. It draws them irresistibly, by degrees, into the current of the astral light vibrating between the person sympathetic to them and the Universal Soul. Another very important condition is harmony and the magnetic purity of the persons present.

To these assertions may be opposed a fact well known among spiritualists: The writer has publicly certified to having seen such materialized forms. We have most assuredly done so and are ready to repeat the testimony. We have recognized such figures as the visible representations of acquaintances, friends, and even relatives. We have, in company with many other spectators, heard them pronounce words in languages unfamiliar not only to the medium and to every one else in the room except ourselves, but, in some cases, to almost if not quite every medium in America and Europe, for they were the tongues of Eastern tribes and peoples. At the time, these instances were justly regarded as conclusive proofs of the genuine mediumship of the uneducated Vermont farmer who sat in the "cabinet." But, nevertheless, these figures were not the forms of the persons they appeared to be. They were simply their portrait statues, constructed, animated, and operated by the elementaries.

Pausanias writes that four hundred years after the battle of Marathon, there were still heard in the place where it was fought the neighing of horses and the shouts of shadowy soldiers [*Description of Greece* 1.32.4]. Supposing that the specters of the slaughtered soldiers were their genuine spirits, they looked like "shadows," not materialized men. Who, then, or what produced the neighing of horses? Equine "spirits"? And if it be pronounced untrue that horses have spirits—which assuredly no one among zoologists, physiologists, psychologists, or even spiritualists can either prove or disprove—then must we take it for granted that it was the "immortal souls" of men which produced the neighing at Marathon to make the historical battle scene more vivid and dramatic?

The phantoms of dogs, cats, and various other animals have repeatedly been seen, and the worldwide testimony is as trustworthy upon this point as that with respect to human apparitions. Who or *what* personates, if we are allowed such an expression, the ghosts of departed animals? Is it, again, human spirits? As the matter now stands, there is no side issue; we have either to admit that animals have surviving spirits and souls as well as ourselves, or hold with Porphyry (*De abstinentia* 2.37–43) that there are in the invisible world a kind of tricky and malicious demons, intermediary beings between living men and "gods," spirits that delight in appearing under every imaginable shape, beginning with the human form, and ending with those of multifarious animals.

Christopher Columbus discovered America, and Amerigo Vespucci reaped the glory and usurped his dues. Theophrastus Paracelsus rediscovered the occult properties of the magnet—"the bone of Horus" which, twelve centuries before his time, had played such an important part in the theurgic mysteries—and he very naturally became the founder of the school of magnetism and of medieval magico-theurgy. But Mesmer, who lived nearly three hundred years after him and as a disciple of his school brought the magnetic wonders before the public, reaped the glory that was due to the fire-philosopher, while the great master died in a hospital!

So goes the world: new discoveries, evolving from old sciences; new men—the same old nature!

3

Theories Respecting Psychic Phenomena

I t is admitted on all hands that from time immemorial the distant
East was the land of knowledge. Not even in Egypt were botany and
mineralogy so extensively studied as by the savants of archaic Middle
Asia. And yet, notwithstanding this, whenever the subject of magic
is discussed, that of India has rarely suggested itself to anyone, for
of its general practice in that country less is known than among any
other ancient people. With the Hindus it was and is more esoteric, if
possible, than it was even among the Egyptian priests. So sacred was
it deemed that its existence was only half admitted, and it was only
practiced in public emergencies. It was more than a religious matter,
for it was considered divine.

The Egyptian hierophants, notwithstanding the practice of a stern
and pure morality, could not be compared for one moment with the
ascetical Hindu Gymnosophists, either in holiness of life or miraculous
powers developed in them by the supernatural adjuration of everything
earthly. By those who knew them well they were held in still greater
reverence than the magians of Chaldea. "Denying themselves the
simplest comforts of life, they dwelt in woods, and led the life of
the most secluded hermits,"[1] while their Egyptian brothers at least
congregated together.

Notwithstanding the slur thrown by history on all who practiced
magic and divination, it has proclaimed them as possessing the greatest
secret in medical knowledge and unsurpassed skill in its practice.
Numerous are the volumes preserved in Hindu convents in which are
recorded the proofs of their learning. To attempt to say whether these
Gymnosophists were the real founders of magic in India, or whether
they only practiced what had passed to them as an inheritance from

the earliest Rishis[2]—the seven primeval sages—would be regarded as mere speculation by exact scholars.

First of all, their cosmogony shows how erroneous has been the opinion prevalent among the civilized nations that Brahma was ever considered by the Hindus their chief or Supreme God. Brahma is a secondary deity and like Jehovah is "a mover of the waters." He is the *creating* god and has in his allegorical representations four heads, answering to the four cardinal points. He is the demiurge, the architect of the world. "In the primordial state of the creation," says Polier's *Mythologie des Indous* [(Paris, 1809), 1:163], "the rudimental universe, submerged in water, reposed in the bosom of the Eternal. Sprung from this chaos and darkness, Brahma (the architect of the world), poised on a lotus leaf floated (moved?) upon the waters, unable to discern anything but water and darkness." This is as identical as possible with the Egyptian cosmogony, which shows in its opening sentence Hathor or Mother Night (which represents illimitable darkness) as the primeval element which covered the infinite abyss, animated by water and the universal spirit of the Eternal, dwelling alone in Chaos.

Wherever the mystic water lily (lotus) is employed, it signifies the emanation of the objective from the concealed or subjective, the eternal thought of the ever-invisible Deity passing from the abstract into the concrete or visible form.

The lotus is the product of fire (heat) and water, hence the dual symbol of spirit and matter. The God Brahma is the second person of the Trinity, as are Jehovah (Adam-Kadmon) and Osiris, or rather Pimander, or the Power of the Thought Divine, of Hermes; for it is Pimander who represents the root of all the Egyptian sun gods. The Eternal is the Spirit of Fire, which stirs up and fructifies and develops into a concrete form everything that is born of water or the primordial earth, evolved out of Brahma; but the universe is itself Brahma, and he is the universe. This is the philosophy of Spinoza, which he derived from that of Pythagoras; and it is the same for which Bruno died a martyr.

Bruno's and Spinoza's doctrines are nearly identical, though the words of the latter are more veiled and far more cautiously chosen than those to be found in the theories of the author of the *De la causa, principio e uno*, or *De l'infinito universo et mondi*. Both Bruno, who confesses that the source of his information was Pythagoras, and Spinoza, who, without acknowledging it as frankly, allows his philosophy to betray the secret, view the First Cause from the same standpoint. With them, God is an Entity totally *per se*, an Infinite Spirit, and the only Being utterly free and independent of either effects or other causes; who, through that same Will which produced all things and gave the first impulse to every cosmic law, perpetually keeps in existence and order everything in the universe. Like the Hindu Svabhavikas, erroneously called Atheists, who assume that all things, men as well as gods and spirits, were born from Svabhava, or their own nature,[3] both Spinoza and Bruno were led to the conclusion that God is to be sought for within nature and not without. For, creation being proportional to the power of the Creator, the universe as well as its Creator must be infinite and eternal, one form emanating from its own essence and creating in its turn another.

"What, then, is produced from death?" inquired Socrates of Cebes. "Life," was the reply (Plato, *Phaedo* 71D). "Can the soul, since it is immortal, be anything else than imperishable?" (*Phaedo* 106B). The "seed cannot develop unless it is in part consumed," says Prof. Le Conte; "it is not quickened unless it die," says St. Paul [1 Corinthians 15:36].

A flower blossoms, then withers and dies. It leaves a fragrance behind, which, long after its delicate petals are but a little dust, still lingers in the air. Our material sense may not be cognizant of it, but it nevertheless exists. Let a note be struck on an instrument, and the faintest sound produces an eternal echo. A disturbance is created on the invisible waves of the shoreless ocean of space, and the vibration is never wholly lost. Its energy, being once carried from the world of matter into the immaterial world, will live forever. And man, we are asked to believe, man, the living, thinking, reasoning entity, the indwelling deity of our nature's crowning masterpiece, will evacuate his casket and be no more! Would the principle of continuity which exists even for the so-called *inorganic* matter, for a floating atom, be denied to the spirit, whose attributes are consciousness, memory, mind, LOVE?

Why should it appear so impossible that when the spirit is once separated from its body, it may have the power to animate some evanescent form, created out of that magical "psychic" or "ectenic" or "ethereal" force, with the help of the elementaries who furnish it with the sublimated matter of their own bodies? The only difficulty is to realize the fact that surrounding space is not an empty void, but a reservoir filled to repletion with the models of all things that ever were, that are, and that will be, and with beings of countless races unlike our own.

It is not for the first time in the history of the world that the invisible world has to contend against the materialistic skepticism of soul-blind Sadducees. Plato deplored such an unbelief and refers to this pernicious tendency more than once in his works.

From Kapila, the Hindu philosopher, who many centuries before Christ demurred to the claim of the mystic Yogins that in ecstasy a man has the power of seeing Deity face to face and conversing with the "highest" beings, down to the Voltaireans of the eighteenth century, who laughed at everything that was held sacred by other people, each age had its unbelieving Thomases. Did they ever succeed in checking the progress of truth? No more than the ignorant bigots who sat in judgment over Galileo checked the progress of the earth's rotation. No exposures whatever are able to vitally affect the stability or instability of a belief which humanity inherited from the first races of men, those who—if we can believe in the evolution of spiritual man as in that of the physical one—had the great truth from the lips of their ancestors, the gods of their fathers, "that were on the other side of the flood." The fables of the mythopoeic ages will be found to have but allegorized the greatest truths of geology and anthropology. It is in these ridiculously expressed fables that science will have to look for her "missing links."

NOTES

1. Ammianus Marcellinus, *Rom. Hist.* 23.6.33.
2. The Rishis were seven in number and lived in days anteceding the Vedic period. They were known as sages and held in reverence like demigods. Haug (*Aitareya-Brahmanam* 2:479 fn.) shows that they occupy in the Brahmanical religion a position answering to that of the twelve sons of Jacob in the Jewish Bible. The Brahmans claim to descend directly from these Rishis.
3. Brahma does *not* create the earth, *Mrityuloka*, any more than the rest of the universe. Having evolved himself from the soul of the

world, once separated from the First Cause, he emanates in his turn all nature out of himself. He does not stand above it, but is mixed up with it; and Brahma and the universe form one Being, each particle of which is in its essence Brahma himself, who proceeded out of himself.

4

The Ether or "Astral Light"

There has been an infinite confusion of names to express one and the same thing. The Chaos of the ancients; the Zoroastrian sacred fire, or the *Atas-Behram* of the Parsis; the Hermes-fire; the St. Elmo's fire of the ancient Germans; the lightning of Cybele; the burning torch of Apollo; the flame on the altar of Pan; the inextinguishable fire in the temple on the Acropolis, and in that of Vesta; the fire-flame of Pluto's helm; the brilliant sparks on the hats of the Dioscuri, on the Gorgon head, the helm of Pallas, and the staff of Mercury; the Egyptian Ptah, or Ra; the Grecian *Zeus Kataibates* (the descending); the Pentecostal fire tongues; the burning bush of Moses; the pillar of fire of the Exodus, and the "burning lamp" of Abram; the eternal fire of the "bottomless pit"; the Delphic oracular vapors; the sidereal light of the Rosicrucians; the Akasa of the Hindu adepts; the astral light of Éliphas Lévi; the nerve-aura and the fluid of the magnetists; the *Od* of Reichenbach; the atmospheric magnetism of some naturalists; galvanism, and finally electricity are but various names for many different manifestations or effects of the same mysterious, all-pervading cause—the Greek *Archaeus*.

Those who have not given attention to the subject may be surprised to find how much was known in former days of that all-pervading, subtle principle which has recently been baptized the "universal ether."

The ancients called it Chaos; Plato and the Pythagoreans named it the Soul of the World. According to the Hindus, the Deity in the shape of Ether pervades all things. It is the invisible but, as we have said before, too tangible Fluid. Among other names this universal Proteus was termed by the theurgists "the living fire," the "Spirit of Light,"

29

and *Magnes*. This last appellation indicates its magnetic properties and shows its magical nature.

Now, what is this mystic, primordial substance? In the book of Genesis, at the beginning of the first chapter, it is termed the "face of the waters," said to have been incubated by the "Spirit of God." Job mentions in 26.5 that "dead things are formed from under the waters, and inhabitants thereof." In the original text, instead of "dead things," it is written dead *Rephaim* (giants, or mighty primitive men), from whom "evolution" may one day trace our present race. In the Egyptian mythology, Kneph the eternal unrevealed God is represented by a snake emblem of eternity encircling a water urn, with his head hovering over the waters, which he incubates with his breath. In this case the serpent is the Agathodaimon, the good spirit; in its opposite aspect it is the Kakodaimon—the bad one.

In the Scandinavian *Eddas*, the honey dew—the food of the gods and of the creative, busy Yggdrasil bees—falls during the hours of night, when the atmosphere is impregnated with humidity; and in the Northern mythologies, as the passive principle of creation, it typifies the creation of the universe out of water. This dew is the astral light in one of its combinations and possesses creative as well as destructive properties.

In the Chaldean legend of Berosus, Oannes or Dagon, the man-fish, instructing the people, shows the infant world created out of water and all beings originating from this *prima materia*. Moses teaches that only earth and water can bring a living soul; and we read in the Scriptures that herbs could not grow until the Eternal caused it to rain upon earth. In the Mexican *Popol Vuh* man is created out of mud or clay (*terre glaise*), taken from under the water. Brahma creates Lomasa, the great Muni (or first man), seated on his lotus, only after having called into being spirits, who thus enjoyed among mortals a priority of existence, and he creates him out of water, air, and earth.

Alchemists claim that primordial or pre-Adamic earth when reduced to its first substance is, in its second stage of transformation, like clear water, the first being the *alkahest*[1] proper. This primordial substance is said to contain within itself the essence of all that goes to make up man; it has not only all the elements of his physical being, but even the "breath of life" itself in a latent state, ready to be awakened. This it derives from the "incubation" of the Spirit of God upon the face of the waters—chaos; in fact, this substance is chaos itself. From this it was that Paracelsus claimed to be able to make his "homunculi"; and this is why Thales, the great natural philosopher, maintained that water was the principle of all things in nature.

What is the primordial Chaos but Aether? The modern Ether, not such as is recognized by our scientists, but such as was known to the ancient philosophers, long before the time of Moses; Ether, with all its mysterious and occult properties, containing in itself the germs of universal creation; Ether, the celestial virgin, the spiritual mother of every existing form and being, from whose bosom, as soon as "incubated" by the Divine Spirit, are called into existence Matter and Life, Force and Action. Electricity, magnetism, heat, light, and chemical action are so little understood even now that fresh facts are constantly widening the range of our knowledge. Who knows where ends the power of this protean giant, Ether, or whence its mysterious origin?—Who denies the spirit that works in it and evolves out of it all visible forms?

It is an easy task to show that the cosmogonical legends all over the world are based on a knowledge by the ancients of those sciences which have allied themselves in our days to support the doctrine of evolution and that further research may demonstrate that they were far better acquainted with the fact of evolution itself, embracing both its physical and spiritual aspects, than we are now. With the old philosophers, evolution was a universal theorem, a doctrine embracing the *whole*, and an established principle; while our modern evolutionists are enabled to present us merely with speculative theoretics; with *particular*, if not wholly negative theorems.

There is not a cosmogonical fragment, to whatever nation it may belong, but proves, by this universal allegory of water and the spirit brooding over it, that no more than our modern physicists did any of them hold the universe to have sprung into existence out of nothing; for all their legends begin with that period when nascent vapors and Cimmerian darkness lay brooding over a fluid mass ready to start on its journey of activity at the first flutter of the breath of Him who is the Unrevealed One. Him they felt, if they saw Him not. Their spiritual intuitions were not so darkened by the subtle sophistry of the forecoming ages as ours are now. If they talked less of the Silurian age slowly developing into the Mammalian, and if the Cenozoic time was only recorded by various allegories of the primitive man—the Adam of *our* race—it is but a negative proof after all that their "wise men" and leaders did not know of these successive periods as well as we do now. In the days of Democritus and Aristotle, the cycle had already begun to enter on its downward path of progress.

Éliphas Lévi, the modern magician, describes the astral light in the following sentence: "We have said that to acquire magical power, two things are necessary: to disengage the will from all servitude, and to exercise it in control."[2]

What is the will? Can "exact science" tell? What is the nature of that intelligent, intangible, and powerful something which reigns supreme over all inert matter? The great Universal Idea willed, and the cosmos sprang into existence. I *will*, and my limbs obey. I *will*, and my thought—traversing space, which does not exist for it—envelops the body of another individual who is not a part of myself, penetrates through his pores, and, superseding his own faculties, if they are weaker, forces him to a predetermined action. It acts like the fluid of a galvanic battery on the limbs of a corpse. The mysterious effects of attraction and repulsion are the unconscious agents of that will; fascination, such as we see exercised by some animals, by serpents over birds, for instance, is a conscious action of it, and the result of thought. Sealing wax, glass, and amber, when rubbed, i.e., when the latent heat which exists in every substance is awakened, attract light bodies; they unconsciously exercise *will*; for inorganic as well as organic matter possesses a particle of the divine essence in itself, however infinitesimally small it may be. And how could it be otherwise? Notwithstanding that in the progress of its evolution it may from beginning to end have passed through millions of various forms, it must ever retain its germ-point of that preexistent matter, which is the first manifestation and emanation of the Deity itself.

What is then this inexplicable power of attraction but an atomical portion of that essence that scientists and kabbalists equally recognize as the "principle of life"—the *akasa*? Granted that the attraction exercised by such bodies may be blind; but as we ascend higher on the scale of the organic beings in nature, we find this principle of life developing attributes and faculties which become more determined and marked with every rung of the endless ladder. Man, the most perfect of organized beings on earth, in whom matter and spirit—

i.e., *will*—are the most developed and powerful, is alone allowed to give a conscious impulse to that principle which emanates from him; and only he can impart to the magnetic fluid opposite and various impulses without limit as to the direction. "He wills," says Du Potet, "and organized matter obeys. It has no poles."

The divine light through which, unimpeded by matter, the soul perceives things past, present, and to come, as though their rays were focused in a mirror; the death-dealing bolt projected in an instant of fierce anger or at the climax of long-festering hate; the blessing wafted from a grateful or benevolent heart; and the curse hurled at an object—offender or victim—all have to pass through that universal agent, which under one impulse is the breath of God and under another—the venom of the devil. It was discovered (?) by Baron Reichenbach and called Od, whether intentionally or otherwise we cannot say, but it is singular that a name should have been chosen which is mentioned in the most ancient books of the Kabbala.

Our readers will certainly inquire what then is this invisible *all?* How is it that our scientific methods, however perfected, have never discovered any of the magical properties contained in it? To this we can answer that there is no reason, just because modern scientists are ignorant of them, that it should not possess all the properties with which the ancient philosophers endowed it. Science rejects many a thing today which she may find herself forced to accept tomorrow. A little less than a century ago the Academy denied Franklin's electricity, and at the present day we can hardly find a house without a conductor on its roof. Shooting at the barn door, the Academy missed the barn itself.

Emepht, the supreme, first principle, produced an egg; by brooding over it and permeating the substance of it with its own vivifying essence, the germ contained within was developed; and *Ptah,* the active, creative principle proceeded from it, and began his work. From the boundless expanse of cosmic matter, which had formed itself under his breath, or *will,* this cosmic matter—astral light, ether, fire-mist, principle of life, it matters not what we may call it—this creative principle, or, as our modern philosophy terms it, law of evolution, by setting in motion the potencies latent in it, formed suns and stars, and satellites, controlled their emplacement by the immutable law of harmony, and peopled them "with every form and quality of life."

In the ancient Eastern mythologies, the cosmogonic myth states that there was but water (the father) and the prolific slime (the mother, *Ilus* or *Hyle*), from which crept forth the mundane snake—matter. It was the god *Phanes*, the revealed one, the Word, or *logos*.

What modern cosmogonist could compress such a world of meaning within so simple a symbol as the Egyptian serpent in a circle? Here we have, in this creature, the whole philosophy of the universe: matter vivified by spirit, and the two conjointly evolving out of chaos (Force) everything that was to be. To signify that the elements are fast bound in this cosmic matter, which the serpent symbolizes, the Egyptians tied its tail into a knot.

There is one more important emblem connected with the sloughing of the serpent's skin, which so far as we are aware has never been heretofore noticed by our symbolists. As the reptile upon casting his coat becomes freed from a casing of gross matter, which cramped a body grown too large for it, and resumes its existence with renewed activity, so man, by casting off the gross material body, enters upon the next stage of his existence with enlarged powers and quickened vitality. Inversely, the Chaldean kabbalists tell us that primeval man, who contrary to the Darwinian theory was purer, wiser, and far more spiritual—as shown by the myths of the Scandinavian Buri, the Hindu Devatas, and the Mosaic "sons of God"—in short, of a far higher nature than the man of the present Adamic race—became *despiritualized* or tainted with matter, and then for the first time was given the fleshly body, which is typified in Genesis in that profoundly significant verse: "Unto Adam also and to his wife did the Lord God make coats of skin, and clothed them" (3.21). Unless the commentators would make of the First Cause a celestial tailor, what else can the apparently absurd words mean but that the spiritual man had reached, through the progress of involution, that point where matter, predominating over and conquering spirit, had transformed him into the physical man, or the second Adam, of the second chapter of Genesis?

Who can study carefully the ancient religious and cosmogonic myths without perceiving that this striking similitude of conceptions, in their exoteric form and esoteric spirit, is the result of no mere coincidence, but manifests a concurrent design? It shows that, already in those ages which are shut out from our sight by the impenetrable mist of tradition, human religious thought developed in uniform sympathy

34

in every portion of the globe. Christians call this adoration of nature in her most concealed verities "Pantheism." But if the latter—which worships and reveals to us God in space in His only possible objective form, that of visible nature—perpetually reminds humanity of Him who created it, and a religion of theological dogmatism only serves to conceal Him the more from our sight, which is the better adapted to the needs of mankind?

Modern science insists upon the doctrine of evolution; so do human reason and the Secret Doctrine, and the idea is corroborated by the ancient legends and myths, and even by the Bible itself when it is read between the lines. We see a flower slowly developing from a bud, and the bud from its seed. But whence the latter, with its predetermined program of physical transformation and its invisible and therefore spiritual forces which gradually develop its form, color, and odor? The word *evolution* speaks for itself. The germ of the present human race must have preexisted in the parent of this race, as the seed, in which lies hidden the flower of next summer, was developed in the capsule of its parent flower; the parent may be but slightly different, but it still differs from its future progeny. The antediluvian ancestors of the present elephant and lizard were, perhaps, the mammoth and the plesiosaurus; why should not the progenitors of our human race have been the "giants" of the Vedas, the *Völuspâ*, and the Book of Genesis?

Physical man, as a product of evolution, may be left in the hands of the man of exact science. None but he can throw light upon the physical origin of the race. But we must positively deny the materialist the same privilege as to the question of man's psychical and spiritual evolution, for he and his highest faculties *cannot* be proved on any conclusive evidence to be "as much products of evolution as the humblest plant or the lowest worm."[3]

Having said so much, we will now proceed to show the evolution hypothesis of the old Brahmans, as embodied by them in the allegory of the mundane tree. The Hindus represent their mythical tree, which they call *Asvattha*, in a way which differs from that of the Scandinavians. It is described by them as growing in a reversed position, the branches extending downward and the roots upward; the former typifying the external world of sense, i.e., the visible cosmical universe, and the latter the invisible world of spirit, because the roots have their genesis in the heavenly regions where, from the world's creation, humanity has placed its invisible deity. The creative energy having originated in the primordial point, the religious symbols of every people are so many illustrations of this metaphysical hypothesis expounded by Pythagoras, Plato, and other philosophers. "These Chaldeans," says Philo, "were of the opinion that the Kosmos, among the things that exist, is a single point, either being itself God (Theos) or that in it is God, comprehending the soul of all the things."[4]

The Egyptian pyramid also symbolically represents this idea of the mundane tree. Its apex is the mystic link between heaven and earth and stands for the root, while the base represents the spreading branches, extending to the four cardinal points of the universe of matter. It conveys the idea that all things had their origin in spirit— evolution having originally begun from above and proceeded down- ward, instead of the reverse, as taught in the Darwinian theory. In other words, there has been a gradual materialization of forms until a fixed ultimate of debasement is reached. This point is that at which the doctrine of modern evolution enters into the arena of speculative hypothesis.

Thus all the world mountains and mundane eggs, the mundane trees, and the mundane snakes and pillars may be shown to embody scientifically demonstrated truths of natural philosophy. All of these mountains contain, with very trifling variations, the allegorically expressed description of primal cosmogony; the mundane trees, that of subsequent evolution of spirit and matter; and the mundane snakes and pillars, symbolic memorials of the various attributes of this double evolution in its endless correlation of cosmic forces. Within the mysterious recesses of the mountain—the matrix of the universe—the gods (powers) prepare the atomic germs of organic life, and at the same time the life drink, which, when tasted, awakens in man-matter the man-spirit. The soma, the sacrificial drink of the Hindus, is that sacred beverage. For at the creation of the *prima materia*, while the grossest portions of it were used for the physical embryo-world, the more divine essence of it pervaded the universe, invisibly permeating and enclosing within its ethereal waves the newly born infant, developing and stimulating it to activity as it slowly evolved out of the eternal chaos.

NOTES

1. Alkahest, a word first used by Paracelsus to denote the menstruum or universal solvent that is capable of reducing all things.
2. [*Dogme et rituel de la haute magie* (Paris, 1856), 2:63.]
3. Lecture by T. H. Huxley, F.R.S., "Darwin and Haeckel," *The Popular Science Monthly* 6 (March, 1875), 593.
4. *De Migratione Abrahami* 32.179.

5

Psychophysical Phenomena

A work upon magico-spiritual philosophy and occult science would be incomplete without a particular notice of the history of animal magnetism, as it stands since Paracelsus staggered the schoolmen of the latter half of the sixteenth century with it.

We will observe briefly its appearance in Paris when imported from Germany by Anton Mesmer. Let us peruse with care and caution the old papers now moldering in the Academy of Sciences of that capital, for there we will find that, after having rejected in turn every discovery that was ever made since Galileo, the Immortals capped the climax by turning their backs upon magnetism and mesmerism. They voluntarily shut the doors before themselves, the doors which led to those greatest mysteries of nature, which lie hid in the dark regions of the psychical as well as the physical world.

The full views of Paracelsus on the occult properties of the magnet are explained partially in his famous book, *Archidoxa*, in which he describes the wonderful tincture, a medicine extracted from the magnet and called *Magisterium magnetis*, and partially in the *De ente Dei* and *De ente astrorum*, lib. 1.

He demonstrates further that in man lies hidden a "sidereal force," that emanation from the stars and celestial bodies of which the spiritual form of man—the astral spirit—is composed. This identity of essence, which we may term the spirit of cometary matter, always stands in direct relation with the stars from which it was drawn, and thus there exists a mutual attraction between the two, both being magnets. The identical composition of the earth and all other planetary bodies and man's terrestrial body was a fundamental idea in his philosophy. "The body comes from the elements, the (astral) spirit from the stars. . . . Man eats and drinks of the elements for the sustenance of his blood and flesh; from the stars are the intellect and thoughts sustained in his spirit."

And now we will notice how—when Mesmer had imported into France his *baquet* and system based entirely on the philosophy and doctrines of the Paracelsites—the great psychological and physiological discovery was treated by the physicians. It will demonstrate how much ignorance, superficiality, and prejudice can be displayed by a scientific body, when the subject clashes with their own cherished theories. It is the more important because the present materialistic drift of the public mind and certainly the gaps in the atomic philosophy, which we have seen its most devoted teachers confessing to exist, are probably due to the neglect of the committee of the French Academy of 1784.

The committee of 1784 comprised men of such eminence as Borie, Sallin, d'Arcet, and the famous Guillotin, to whom were subsequently added Franklin, Le Roy, Bailly, de Borg and Lavoisier. Borie died shortly afterward and Majault succeeded him. There can be no doubt of two things: that the committee began their work under strong prejudices and only because peremptorily ordered to do it by the king and that their manner of observing the delicate facts of mesmerism was injudicious and illiberal. Their report, drawn by Bailly, was intended to be a deathblow to the new science. It was spread ostentatiously throughout all the schools and ranks of society, arousing the bitterest feelings among a large portion of the aristocracy and rich commercial class, who had patronized Mesmer and been eyewitnesses of his cures.

Antoine L. de Jussieu, an academician of the highest rank who had thoroughly investigated the subject with the eminent court physician, d'Eslon, published a counter report drawn with minute exactness, in which he advocated the careful observation by the medical faculty of the therapeutic effects of the magnetic fluid and insisted upon the immediate publication of their discoveries and observations. His demand was met by the appearance of a great number of memoirs, polemical works, and dogmatical books developing new facts; and Thouret's work, entitled *Recherches et doutes sur le magnétisme animal*, displaying a vast erudition, stimulated research into the records of the past, and the magnetic phenomena of successive nations from the remotest antiquity were laid before the public.

The doctrine of Mesmer was simply a restatement of the doctrines of Paracelsus, Van Helmont, Santanelli, and Maxwell the Scotchman; he was even guilty of copying texts from the work of Bertrand and enunciating them as his own principles.

We find among the twenty-seven propositions laid down by Mesmer in 1775, in his "Letter to a Foreign Physician,"[1] the following:

1st. There exists a mutual influence between the heavenly bodies, the earth, and living bodies.

2nd. A fluid, universally diffused and continued, so as to admit no vacuum, whose subtility is beyond all comparison and which, from its nature, is capable of receiving, propagating, and communicating all the impressions of motion, is the medium of this influence.

3rd. This reciprocal action is subject to mechanical laws, unknown up to the present time.

4th. From this action result alternate effects which may be considered a flux and reflux.

5th. It is by this operation (the most universal of those presented to us by nature) that the relations of activity occur between the heavenly bodies, the earth, and its constituent parts.

There are two more which will be interesting reading to our modern scientists:

6th. The properties of matter, and of organized body, depend on this operation.

7th. The animal body experiences the alternate effects of this agent; and it is by insinuating itself into the substance of the nerves, that it immediately affects them.

There are two kinds of magnetization; the first is purely animal, the other transcendent and depending on the will and knowledge of the mesmerizer, as well as on the degree of spirituality of the subject and his capacity to receive the impressions of the astral light. Clairvoyance depends a great deal more on the former than on the latter. To the power of an adept, like Du Potet, the most positive subject will have to submit. If his sight is ably directed by the mesmerizer, magician, or spirit, the light must yield up its most secret records to our scrutiny; for, if it is a book which is ever closed to those "who see and do not perceive," on the other hand it is ever opened for

40

one who *wills* to see it opened. It keeps an unmutilated record of all that was, that is, or ever will be. The minutest acts of our lives are imprinted on it, and even our thoughts rest photographed on its eternal tablets. It is the book which we see opened by the angel in Revelations, "which is the Book of life, and out of which the dead are judged according to their works." It is, in short, the MEMORY of GOD!

"The oracles assert that the impression of thoughts, characters, men, and other divine visions appear in the aether. . . . In this the things without figure are figured," says an ancient fragment of the *Chaldean Oracles* of Zoroaster.[2]

Thus ancient as well as modern wisdom, vaticination, and science agree in corroborating the claims of the kabbalists. It is on the indestructible tablets of the astral light that is stamped the impression of every thought we think and every act we perform; and that future events—effects of long forgotten causes—are already delineated as a vivid picture for the eye of the seer and prophet to follow. Memory—the despair of the materialist, the enigma of the psychologist, the sphinx of science—is to the student of old philosophies merely a name to express that power which man unconsciously exerts and shares with many of the inferior animals—to look with inner sight into the astral light, and there behold the images of past sensations and incidents. Instead of searching the cerebral ganglia for "micrographs of the living and the dead, of scenes that we have visited, of incidents in which we have borne a part,"[3] they went to the vast repository where the records of every man's life as well as every pulsation of the visible cosmos are stored up for all eternity!

That flash of memory which is traditionally supposed to show a drowning man every long forgotten scene of his mortal life—as the landscape is revealed to the traveler by intermittent flashes of lightning—is simply the sudden glimpse which the struggling soul gets into the silent galleries where his history is depicted in imperishable colors.

The well-known fact—one corroborated by the personal experience of nine persons out of ten—that we often recognize as familiar to us scenes, landscapes, and conversations which we see or hear for the first time, and sometimes in countries never visited before, is a result of the same causes. Believers in reincarnation adduce this as an additional proof of our antecedent existence in other bodies. This recognition of men, countries, and things that we have never seen is attributed by them to flashes of soul-memory of anterior experiences. But the men of old, in common with medieval philosophers, firmly held to a contrary opinion.

They affirmed that though this psychological phenomenon was one of the greatest arguments in favor of immortality and the soul's preexistence, the latter being endowed with an individual memory apart from that of our physical brain, it is no proof of reincarnation. As Éliphas Lévi beautifully expresses it, "nature shuts the door after everything that passes, and pushes life onward" in more perfected forms. The chrysalis becomes a butterfly; the latter can never become again a grub.

In the stillness of the night hours, when our bodily senses are fast locked in the fetters of sleep and our elementary body rests, the astral form becomes free. It then oozes out of its earthly prison and, as Paracelsus has it, "confabulates with the outward world" and travels round the visible as well as the invisible worlds. "In sleep," he says, "the astral body (soul) is in freer motion; then it soars to its parents and holds converse with the stars." Dreams, forebodings, prescience, prognostications, and presentiments are impressions left by our astral spirit on our brain, which receives them more or less distinctly, according to the proportion of blood with which it is supplied during the hours of sleep.

The more the body is exhausted, the freer is the spiritual man and the more vivid the impressions of our soul's memory. After heavy and robust sleep, dreamless and uninterrupted, men may sometimes remember nothing upon awakening to outward consciousness. But the impressions of scenes and landscapes which the astral body saw in its peregrinations are still there, though lying latent under the pressure of matter. They may be awakened at any moment, and then, during such flashes of man's inner memory, there is an instantaneous interchange of energies between the visible and the invisible universes. Between the "micrographs" of the cerebral ganglia and the photo-scenographic galleries of the astral light, a current is established. And a man who knows that he has never visited in body nor seen the landscape and person that he recognizes may well assert that still he has seen and knows them, for the acquaintance was formed while traveling in "spirit."

No man, however gross and material he may be, can avoid leading a double existence; one in the visible universe, the other in the invisible. The life principle which animates his physical frame is chiefly in the astral body; and while the more animal portions of him rest, the more spiritual ones know neither limits nor obstacles. Some might object on the ground taken by theology that dumb brutes have no immortal souls, and hence can have no astral spirits; for theologians as well as laymen labor under the erroneous impression that soul and spirit are one and the same thing.

But if we study Plato and other philosophers of old, we may readily perceive that while the *"irrational* soul," by which Plato meant our astral body or the more ethereal representation of ourselves, can have at best only a more or less prolonged continuity of existence beyond the grave, the divine spirit—wrongly termed *soul* by the Church—is immortal by its very essence. (Any Hebrew scholar who comprehends the difference between the two words *ruah* and *nephesh* will readily appreciate the distinction.) If the life principle is something apart from the astral spirit and in no way connected with it, why is it that the intensity of the clairvoyant powers depends so much on the bodily prostration of the subject? The deeper the trance, the less signs of life the body shows, the clearer become the spiritual perceptions, and the more powerful are the soul's visions. The soul, disburdened of the bodily senses, shows activity of power in a far greater degree of intensity than it can in a strong, healthy body.

Such facts alone, once proved, ought to stand as invincible demonstrations of the continuity of individual life, at least for a certain period after the body has been left by us, either by reason of its being worn out or by accident. But though during its brief sojourn on earth our soul may be assimilated to a light hidden under a bushel, it still shines more or less bright and attracts to itself the influences of kindred spirits; and when a thought of good or evil import is begotten in our brain, it draws to it impulses of like nature as irresistibly as the magnet attracts iron filings. This attraction is also proportionate to the intensity with which the thought impulse makes itself felt in the ether; and so it will be understood how one man may impress himself upon his own epoch so forcibly that the influence may be carried—through the ever-interchanging currents of energy between the two worlds, the visible and the invisible—from one succeeding age to another, until it affects a large portion of mankind.

According to the kabbalistic doctrine, the future exists in the astral light in embryo, as the present existed in embryo in the past. While man is free to act as he pleases, the manner in which he *will* act was foreknown from all time—not on the ground of fatalism or destiny, but simply on the principle of universal, unchangeable harmony, just as it may be foreknown that, when a musical note is struck, its vibrations will not and cannot change into those of another note. Besides, eternity can have neither past nor future, but only the present—as boundless space, in its strictly literal sense, can have neither distant nor proximate places. Our conceptions, limited to the narrow area of our experience, attempt to fit if not an end, at least a beginning of time and space, but neither of these exist in reality; for in such case time would not be eternal, nor space boundless. The past no more exists than the future, as we have said; only our memories survive, and our memories are but the glimpses that we catch of the reflections of this past in the currents of the astral light, as the psychometrist catches them from the astral emanations of the object he holds.

The philosophers, and especially those who were initiated into the Mysteries, held that the astral soul is the impalpable duplicate of the gross external form which we call body. It is the *périsprit* of the Kardecists and the spirit-form of the spiritualists. Above this internal duplicate, and illuminating it as the warm ray of the sun illuminates the earth, fructifying the germ and calling out to spiritual vivification the latent qualities dormant in it, hovers the divine spirit. The astral périsprit is contained and confined within the physical body as ether is in a bottle, or magnetism in magnetized iron. It is a center and engine of force, fed from the universal supply of force and moved by the same general laws which pervade all nature and produce all cosmic phenomena. Its inherent activity causes the incessant physical operations of the animal organism and ultimately results in the destruction of the latter by overuse and its own escape. It is the prisoner, not the voluntary tenant, of the body. It has an attraction so powerful to the external universal force that after wearing out its casing it finally escapes to it. The stronger, grosser, more material its encasing body, the longer the term of its imprisonment.

44

Some persons are born with organizations so exceptional that the door which shuts other people in from communication with the world of the astral light can be easily unbarred and opened, and their souls can look into or even pass into that world and return again. Those who do this consciously, and at will, are termed magicians, hierophants, seers, adepts; those who are made to do it, either through the fluid of the mesmerizer or of "spirits," are "mediums." The astral soul, when the barriers are once opened, is so powerfully attracted by the universal, astral magnet that it sometimes lifts its encasement with it and keeps it suspended in midair, until the gravity of matter reasserts its supremacy, and the body redescends again to earth.

Every objective manifestation, whether it be the motion of a living limb or the movement of some inorganic body, requires two conditions: will and force—plus matter, or that which makes the object visible to our eye; these three are all convertible forces, or the force-correlation of the scientists. In turn they are directed or rather overshadowed by the divine intelligence which these men so studiously leave out of the account, but without which not even the crawling of the smallest earthworm could ever take place. The simplest as the most common of all natural phenomena—the rustling of the leaves which tremble under the gentle contact of the breeze—requires a constant exercise of these faculties. Scientists may well call them cosmic laws, immutable and unchangeable. Behind these laws we must search for the intelligent cause which, once having created and set these laws in motion, has infused into them the essence of its own consciousness. Whether we call this the first cause, the universal will, or God, it must always bear intelligence.

And now we may ask, how can a will manifest itself intelligently and unconsciously at the same time? It is difficult, if not impossible, to conceive of intellection apart from consciousness. By consciousness we do not necessarily imply physical or corporeal consciousness. Consciousness is a quality of the sentient principle or, in other words, the soul; and the latter often displays activity even while the body is asleep or paralyzed. When we lift our arm mechanically, we may imagine that we do it unconsciously because our superficial senses cannot appreciate the interval between the formulation of the purpose and its execution. Latent as it seemed to us, our vigilant will evolved force and set our matter in motion.

45

All the prophets of old—inspired sensitives—were said to be uttering their prophecies under the same conditions, either by the direct outward efflux of the astral emanation or a sort of damp fluxion, rising from the earth. It is this astral matter which serves as a temporary clothing of the souls who form themselves in this light.

Prophecies are delivered in two ways—consciously, by magicians who are able to look into the astral light, and unconsciously, by those who act under what is called inspiration. To the latter class belong the Biblical prophets and the modern trance speakers. So familiar with this fact was Plato, that of such prophets he says: "No man, when in his senses, attains prophetic truth and inspiration . . . but only when demented by some distemper or possession" (by a daimonion or spirit). "Some persons call them prophets; they do not know that they are only repeaters . . . and are not to be called prophets at all, but only transmitters of vision and prophecy," he adds (*Timaeus* 72A, B).

NOTES

1. ["Lettre à un médecin étranger," in *Le Nouveau Mercure* (Altona, January 5, 1775).]
2. Simplicius, *Physica* 144, 143; cited in Cory, *Ancient Fragments* 263.
3. J. W. Draper, *History of the Conflict between Religion and Science* (New York, 1875), 134.

6

The Elements, Elementals,
and Elementaries

Almost without exception, ancient and medieval scholars believed in the arcane doctrines of wisdom. These included alchemy, the Chaldeo-Jewish Kabbala, the esoteric systems of Pythagoras and the old Magi, and those of the later Platonic philosophers and theurgists. We also propose in subsequent pages to treat of the Indian gymnosophists and the Chaldean astrologers. We must not neglect to show the grand truths underlying the misunderstood religions of the past. The four elements of our fathers, earth, air, water, and fire, contain for the student of alchemy and ancient psychology—or, as it is now termed, *magic*—many things of which our philosophy has never dreamed. We must not forget that what is now called necromancy by the Church and spiritualism by modern believers—which includes the evoking of departed spirits—is a science that has, from remote antiquity, been almost universally diffused over the face of the globe.

Baptista Porta, the learned Italian philosopher, notwithstanding his endeavors to show to the world the groundlessness of their accusations of magic being a superstition and sorcery, was treated by later critics with the same unfairness as his colleagues. This celebrated alchemist left a work on *Natural Magic*,[1] in which he bases all of the occult phenomena possible to man upon the world soul, which binds all with all. He shows that the astral light acts in harmony and sympathy with all nature, that it is the essence out of which our spirits are formed, and that by acting in unison with their parent-source, our sidereal bodies are rendered capable of producing magic wonders. The whole secret depends on our knowledge of kindred elements. He believed in the philosopher's stone, "which the world hath so great an opinion of, which hath been bragged of in so many ages and happily attained unto by some." Finally, he throws out many valuable hints as to its "spiritual meaning."

In 1643, there appeared among the mystics a monk, Father Kircher, who taught a complete philosophy of universal magnetism. His numerous works embrace many of the subjects merely hinted at by Paracelsus. His definition of magnetism is very original, for he contradicted Gilbert's theory that the earth was a great magnet. He asserted that although every particle of matter and even the intangible, invisible "powers" were magnetic, they did not themselves constitute a magnet. There is but one MAGNET in the universe, and from it proceeds the magnetization of everything existing. This magnet is of course what the kabbalists term the central Spiritual Sun, or God. The sun, moon, planets, and stars he affirmed are highly magnetic; but they have become so by induction from living in the universal magnetic fluid—the spiritual light.

Kircher proves the mysterious sympathy existing between the bodies of the three principal kingdoms of nature, and strengthens his argument by a stupendous catalogue of instances. Many of these were verified by naturalists, but still more have remained unauthenticated; therefore, according to the traditional policy and very equivocal logic of our scientists, they are denied. For instance, he shows a difference between mineral magnetism and zoomagnetism, or animal magnetism. He demonstrates it in the fact that except in the case of the lodestone all the minerals are magnetized by the higher potency, the animal magnetism, while the latter enjoys it as the direct emanation from the first cause—the Creator. A needle can be magnetized by simply being held in the hand of a strong-willed man, and amber develops its powers more by the friction of the human hand than by any other object; therefore man can impart his own life to, and, to a certain degree, *animate* inorganic objects. This, "in the eyes of the foolish, is sorcery." "The sun is the most magnetic of all bodies," he says; thus anticipating the theory of General Pleasonton by more than two centuries. "The ancient philosophers never denied the fact," he adds, "but have at all times perceived that the sun's emanations were binding all things to itself, and that it imparts this binding power to everything, falling under its direct rays."

As a proof of it he brings the instance of a number of plants being especially attracted to the sun, showing their irresistible sympathy to it by following its course in the heavens, and others to the moon. The plant known as *Tithymallus*[2] faithfully follows its sovereign, even when it is invisible on account of the fog. The acacia uncloses its petals at its rising and closes them at its setting. So does the Egyptian lotus and the common sunflower. The nightshade exhibits the same predilection for the moon.

As examples of antipathies or sympathies among plants, he instances the aversion which the vine feels for the cabbage, and its fondness toward the olive tree; the love of the ranunculus for the water lily, and of the rue for the fig. The antipathy which sometimes exists even among kindred substances is clearly demonstrated in the case of the Mexican pomegranate, whose shoots, when cut to pieces, repel each other with the "most extraordinary ferocity."

Kircher accounts for every feeling in human nature as results of changes in our magnetic condition. Anger, jealousy, friendship, love, and hatred are all modifications of the magnetic atmosphere which is developed in us and constantly emanates from us. Love is one of the most variable, and therefore the aspects of it are numberless. Spiritual love, that of a mother for her child, of an artist for some particular art, and love as pure friendship are purely magnetic manifestations of sympathy in congenial natures. The magnetism of pure love is the originator of every created thing. In its ordinary sense love between the sexes is electricity, and he calls it *amor febris speciei*, the fever of species.

There are two kinds of magnetic attraction, sympathy and fascination: the one holy and natural, the other evil and unnatural. To the latter, fascination, we must attribute the power of the poisonous toad, which upon merely opening its mouth, forces the passing reptile or insect to run into it to its destruction. Deer as well as smaller animals are attracted by the breath of the boa and are made irresistibly to come within its reach. The electric fish, the torpedo, repels the arm with a shock that for a time benumbs it. To exercise such a power for beneficent purposes, man requires three conditions: (1) nobility of soul, (2) strong will and imaginative faculty, and (3) a subject weaker than the magnetizer, otherwise he will resist. A man free from worldly incentives and sensuality may cure in such a way the most "incurable" diseases, and his vision may become clear and prophetic.

It is especially in the countries unblessed with civilization that we should seek for an explanation of the nature and observe the effects of that subtle power which ancient philosophers called the "world's soul." In the East only, and on the boundless tracts of unexplored Africa, will the student of psychology find abundant food for his truth-hungering soul. The reason is obvious. The atmosphere in populous neighbor-hoods is badly vitiated by the smoke and fumes of factories, steam engines, railroads, and steamboats, and especially by the miasmatic exhalations of the living and the dead. Nature is as dependent as a human being upon conditions before she can work, and her mighty breathing, so to say, can be as easily interfered with, impeded, and arrested, and the correlation of her forces destroyed in a given spot, as though she were a man. Both climate and occult influences, daily felt, not only modify the physiopsychological nature of man, but even alter the constitution of so-called inorganic matter to a degree not fully realized by European science.

"Three spirits live and actuate man," teaches Paracelsus, "three worlds pour their beams upon him, but all three only as the image and echo of one and the same all-constructing and uniting principle of production. The first is the spirit of the elements (terrestrial body and vital force in its brute condition); the second, the spirit of the stars (sidereal or astral body—the soul); the third is the divine spirit (*augoeides*)."[3] Our human body being possessed of "primeval earth-stuff," as Paracelsus calls it, we may readily accept the tendency of modern scientific research "to regard the processes of both animal and vegetable life as simply physical and chemical." This theory only further corroborates the assertions of old philosophers and the Mosaic Bible that from the dust of the ground our bodies were made, and to dust they will return. But we must remember that

> "Dust thou art, to dust returnest"
> Was not spoken of the soul.[4]

Man is a little world—a microcosm inside the great universe. Like a fetus he is suspended, by all his three spirits, in the matrix of the macrocosmos. While his terrestrial body is in constant sympathy with its parent earth, his astral soul lives in unison with the sidereal *anima mundi*. He is in it, as it is in him, for the world-pervading element fills all space, and *is* space itself, shoreless and infinite. As to his third spirit, the divine, what is it but an infinitesimal ray, one of the countless radiations proceeding directly from the Highest Cause— the Spiritual Light of the World? This is the trinity of organic and inorganic nature—the spiritual and the physical, which are three in one, and of which Proclus says that "the first monad is the Eternal God; the second, eternity; the third, the paradigm, or pattern of the universe," the three constituting the Intelligible Triad. Everything in this visible universe is the outflow of this Triad and is a microcosmic triad itself. And thus they move in majestic procession in the fields of eternity, around the spiritual sun, as in the heliocentric system the celestial bodies move around the visible suns.

The Pythagorean *Monad*, which lives "in solitude and darkness," may remain on this earth forever invisible, impalpable, and undemonstrated by experimental science. Still the whole universe will be gravitating around it as it did from the "beginning of time," and with every second man and atom approach nearer to that solemn moment in eternity when the Invisible Presence will become clear to their spiritual sight. When every particle of matter, even the most sublimated, has been cast off from the last shape that forms the ultimate link of that chain of double evolution, which throughout millions of ages and successive transformations has pushed the entity onward, and when it shall find itself reclothed in that primordial essence, identical with that of its Creator, then this once impalpable organic atom will have run its race, and the sons of God will once more "shout for joy" at the return of the pilgrim.

"Man," says Van Helmont, "is the mirror of the universe, and his triple nature stands in relationship to all things." The will of the Creator, through which all things were made and received their first impulse, is the property of every living being. Man, endowed with an additional spirituality, has the largest share of it on this planet. It depends on the proportion of matter in him whether he will exercise its magical faculty with more or less success. Sharing this divine potency in common with every inorganic atom, he exercises it through the course of his whole life, whether consciously or otherwise. In the former case, when in the full possession of his powers, he will be the master, and the *magnale magnum* (the universal soul) will be controlled and guided by him. In the cases of animals, plants, minerals,

51

and even of the average of humanity, this ethereal fluid which pervades all things, finding no resistance and being left to itself, moves them as its impulse directs. Every created being in this sublunary sphere is formed out of the *magnale magnum* and is related to it. Man possesses a double celestial power, and is allied to heaven.

Healing, to deserve the name, requires either faith in the patient, or robust health united with a strong will, in the operator. With expectancy supplemented by faith, one can cure himself of almost any morbific condition. The tomb of a saint, a holy relic, a talisman, a bit of paper or a garment that has been handled by the supposed healer, a nostrum, a penance or a ceremonial, the laying on of hands, or a few words impressively pronounced—any of these will do. It is a question of temperament, imagination, and self-cure. In thousands of instances the doctor, the priest, or the relic has had credit for healings that were solely and simply due to the patient's unconscious will. The woman with the bloody issue who pressed through the throng to touch the robe of Jesus was told that her "faith" had made her whole.

But if the patient has no faith, what then? If he is physically negative and receptive and the healer is strong, healthy, positive, and determined, the disease may be extirpated by the imperative will of the operator, which consciously or unconsciously draws to and reinforces itself with the universal spirit of nature, and restores the disturbed equilibrium of the patient's aura.

In all these instances, the cure is radical and real, and without secondary ill-effects. But when one who is himself physically diseased attempts healing, he not only fails, but often imparts his illness to his patient, and robs him of what strength he may have. The decrepit King David reinforced his failing vigor with the healthy magnetism of the young Abishag (1 Kings 1.1–4); and the medical works tell us of an aged lady of Bath, England, who in the same way broke down the constitutions of two maids in succession. The old sages and also Paracelsus removed disease by applying a healthy organism to the afflicted part, and in the works of the above mentioned fire-philosopher their theory is boldly and categorically set forth. If a diseased person—medium or not—attempts to heal, his force may be sufficiently robust to displace the disease, to disturb it in the present place, and cause it to shift to another, where shortly it will appear, the patient meanwhile thinking himself cured.

But what if the healer be morally diseased? The consequences may be infinitely more mischievous, for it is easier to cure a bodily disease than cleanse a constitution infected with moral turpitude. In such a case, the healer conveys to his patient—who is now his victim—the moral poison that infects his own mind and heart. His magnetic touch is defilement; his glance, profanation. Against this insidious taint there is no protection for the passively receptive subject. The healer holds him under his power, spellbound and powerless, as the serpent holds a poor, weak bird. The evil that one such "healing medium" can effect is incalculably great; and such healers there are by the hundred.

The foregoing sketches are sufficient to show why we hold fast to the wisdom of the ages, respecting the laws of intermundane intercourse and the occult powers of man, in preference to any new theories that may have been hatched from the occurrences of our later days. While phenomena of a physical nature may have their value as a means of arousing the interest of materialists and confirming—if not wholly, at least inferentially—our belief in the survival of our souls and spirits, it is questionable whether, under their present aspect, the modern phenomena are not doing more harm than good. Many minds, hungering after proofs of immortality, are fast falling into fanaticism; and, as Stow remarks, "fanatics are governed rather by imagination than judgment."

We are at the bottom of a cycle and evidently in a transitory state. Plato divides the intellectual progress of the universe during every cycle into fertile and barren periods. In the sublunary regions, the spheres of the various elements remain eternally in perfect harmony with the divine nature, he says; "but their parts," owing to a too close proximity to earth and their commingling with the earthly (which is matter, and therefore the realm of evil), "are sometimes according and sometimes contrary to (divine) nature." When those circulations—which Éliphas Lévi calls "currents of the astral light"—in the universal ether, which contains in itself every element, take place in harmony with the divine spirit, our earth and everything pertaining to it enjoy a fertile period. The occult powers of plants, animals, and minerals magically sympathize with the "superior natures," and the divine soul of man is in perfect intelligence with these "inferior" ones. But during the barren periods, the latter lose their magic sympathy, and the spiritual sight of the majority of mankind is so blinded as to lose every notion of the superior powers of its own divine spirit. We are in a barren period: the eighteenth century, during which the malignant fever of skepticism broke out so irrepressibly, has entailed unbelief as a hereditary disease upon the nineteenth. The divine intellect is veiled in man; his animal brain alone philosophizes.

Formerly, magic was a universal science, entirely in the hands of the sacerdotal savant. Though the focus was jealously guarded in the sanctuaries, its rays illuminated the whole of mankind. Otherwise, how are we to account for the extraordinary identity of "superstitions," customs, traditions, and even sentences repeated in popular proverbs, so widely scattered from one pole to the other that we find exactly the same ideas among the Tatars and Laplanders as among the southern nations of Europe, the inhabitants of the steppes of Russia, and the aborigines of North and South America?

NOTES

1. *Magia naturalis* (Lugduni, 1569), bk. 1.
2. Kircher, *Magnes sive de arte magnetica* (Coloniae, 1643), lib. 3.4.
3. [*Opera omnia*, s.v. "The End of Birth, and Consideration of the Stars."]
4. [H. W. Longfellow, "A Psalm of Life."]

7

Some Mysteries of Nature

The radical element of the oldest religions was essentially *sabaistic*; we maintain that their myths and allegories, if once correctly and thoroughly interpreted, will dovetail with the most exact astronomical notions of our day. We will say more: there is hardly a scientific law—whether pertaining to physical astronomy or physical geography—that could not be easily pointed out in the ingenious combinations of their fables. They allegorized the most important as well as the most trifling causes of the celestial motions; the nature of every phenomenon was personified; and in the mythical biographies of the Olympic gods and goddesses, one well acquainted with the latest principles of physics and chemistry can find their causes, interagencies, and mutual relations embodied in the deportment and course of action of the fickle deities. The atmospheric electricity in its neutral and latent states is embodied usually in demigods and goddesses, whose scene of action is more limited to earth and who, in their occasional flights to the higher deific regions, display their electric tempers always in strict proportion with the increase of distance from the earth's surface: the weapons of Hercules and Thor were never more mortal than when the gods soared into the clouds.

The myth was less metaphysical and complicated but more truly eloquent as an expression of natural philosophy. Zeus, the male element of creation, with Chthonia-Vesta (the earth) and Metis (the water), the first of the Oceanides (the feminine principles), was viewed according to Porphyry and Proclus as the *zôon-ek-zôôn*, the chief of living beings. In the Orphic theology, the oldest of all, metaphysically speaking he represented both the *potentia* and *actus*, the unrevealed cause and the Demiurge, or the active creator as an emanation from the invisible potency. In the latter demiurgic capacity, in conjunction with his consorts, we find in him all the mightiest agents of cosmic evolution—chemical affinity, atmospheric electricity, attraction, and repulsion.

It is in following his representations in this physical qualification that we discover how well acquainted the ancients were with all the doctrines of physical science in their modern development. Later, in the Pythagorean speculations, Zeus became the metaphysical trinity: the monad evolving the active cause, effect, and intelligent will from its invisible Self, the whole forming the *Tetraktys*. Still later we find the earlier Neoplatonists leaving the primal monad aside on the ground of its utter incomprehensibleness to human intellect, speculating merely on the demiurgic triad of this deity as visible and intelligible in its effects—and thus the metaphysical continuation by Plotinus, Porphyry, Proclus, and other philosophers of this view of Zeus the father, Zeus *Poseidon*, or *dynamis*, the son and power, and the spirit or *nous*. This triad was also accepted as a whole by the Irenaeic school of the second century, the more substantial difference between the doctrines of the Neoplatonists and the Christians being merely the forcible amalgamation by the latter of the incomprehensible monad with its actualized creative trinity.

"Zeus," says an Orphic hymn, "is the first and the last, the head, and the extremities; from him have proceeded all things. He is a man and an immortal nymph (male and female element); the soul of all things; and the principal motor in fire; he is the sun and the moon; the fountain of the ocean; the demiurgus of the universe; one power, one God; the mighty creator and governor of the cosmos. Everything, fire, water, earth, ether, night, the heavens, Metis, the primeval architecturess (the Sophia of the Gnostics, and the Sephirah of the kabbalists), the beautiful Eros, Cupid, all is included within the vast dimensions of his glorious body!"[1]

This short hymn of laudation contains within itself the groundwork of every mythopoeic conception. The imagination of the ancients proved as boundless as the visible manifestations of the Deity itself which afforded them the themes for their allegories. Still the latter, exuberant as they seem, never departed from the two principal ideas which may ever be found running parallel in their sacred imagery: a strict adherence to the physical as well as moral or spiritual aspect of natural law. Their metaphysical researches never clashed with scientific truths, and their religions may be truly termed the psychophysiological creeds of the priests and scientists, who built them on the traditions of the infant world, such as the unsophisticated minds of the primitive races received them, and on their own experimental knowledge, hoary with all the wisdom of the intervening ages.

If their mode of impressing upon the popular minds the great astronomical truths differed from the "system of education" of our present century and appears ridiculous to some, the question still remains unanswered: which of the two systems was the best? With them science went hand in hand with religion, and the idea of God was inseparable from that of his works. And while in the present century there is not one person out of ten thousand who knows, if he ever knew the fact at all, that the planet Uranus is next to Saturn and revolves about the sun in eighty-four years, that Saturn is next to Jupiter and takes twenty-nine and a half years to make one complete revolution in its orbit, and that Jupiter performs his revolution in twelve years, the uneducated masses of Babylon and Greece, having impressed on their minds that Uranus was the father of Saturn, and Saturn that of Jupiter, considered them furthermore deities, as well as all their satellites and attendants. We may perhaps infer from this that while Europeans only discovered Uranus in 1781, a curious coincidence is to be noticed in the above myths.

How the ancients regarded the heavenly bodies is very hard to determine for one unacquainted with the esoteric explanation of their doctrines. While philology and comparative theology have begun the arduous work of analysis, they have as yet arrived at meager results. The allegorical form of speech has often led our commentators so far astray that they have confounded causes with effects and vice versa.

In the Hindu philosophy, "the souls issue from the soul of the world and return to it as sparks to the fire."[2] But in another place it is said that "the Sun is the soul of all things; all has proceeded out of it and will return to it,"[3] which shows that the sun is meant allegorically here and refers to the central, invisible sun, God, whose first manifestation was Sephirah, the emanation of EN-SOF—in short, Light.

If the limited space of the present work would permit, we might easily show that none of the ancients, the sun worshipers included,

57

regarded our visible sun otherwise than as an emblem of their metaphysical, invisible central sun god. Moreover, they did not believe what our modern science teaches us, namely, that light and heat proceed from our sun and that it is this planet which imparts all life to our visible nature. "His radiance is undecaying," says the Rig-Veda, "the intensely shining, all-pervading, unceasing, undecaying rays of Agni desist not, neither night nor day." This evidently related to the spiritual, central sun, whose rays are all-pervading and unceasing, the eternal and boundless life-giver. He is the Point; the center (which is everywhere) of the circle (which is nowhere); the ethereal, spiritual fire; the soul and spirit of the all-pervading, mysterious ether; and the despair and puzzle of the materialist, who will some day find that that which causes the numberless cosmic forces to manifest themselves in eternal correlation is but a divine electricity or rather galvanism, and that the sun is but one of the myriad magnets disseminated through space—a reflector, as General Pleasonton has it. That the sun has no more heat in it than the moon or the space-crowding host of sparkling stars; that there is no gravitation in the Newtonian sense, but only magnetic attraction and repulsion; and that it is by their magnetism that the planets of the solar system have their motions regulated in their respective orbits by the still more powerful magnetism of the sun, not by their weight or gravitation—this and much more they may learn. But until then we must be content with being merely laughed at, instead of being burned alive for impiety or shut up in an insane asylum.

Plato acknowledges man to be the toy of the element of necessity, which he enters upon in appearing in this world of matter; he is influenced by external causes, and these causes are *daimonia*, like that of Socrates. Happy is the physically pure man, for if his external soul (body) is pure, it will strengthen the second one (astral body), or the soul which is termed by him the *higher mortal soul*—which, though liable to err from its own motives, will always side with reason against the animal proclivities of the body. The lusts of man arise in consequence of his perishable material body, as do other diseases; but though he regards crimes as involuntary sometimes, for they result like bodily disease from external causes, Plato clearly makes a wide distinction between these causes. The fatalism which he concedes to humanity does not preclude the possibility of avoiding them;

for though pain, fear, anger, and other feelings are given to men by necessity, "if they conquered these they would live righteously, and if they were conquered by them, unrighteously" (*Timaeus* 42B). The dual man, i.e., one from whom the divine immortal spirit has departed, leaving but the animal form and astral body (Plato's higher mortal soul), is left merely to his instincts, for he was conquered by all the evils entailed on matter. Hence he becomes a docile tool in the hands of the invisibles—beings of sublimated matter, hovering in our atmosphere and ever ready to inspire those who are deservedly deserted by their immortal counselor, the Divine Spirit, called by Plato "genius" (*Timaeus* 90A).

The universal ether was not, in their eyes, simply a something stretching, tenantless, throughout the expanse of heaven; it was a boundless ocean peopled like our familiar seas with monstrous and minor creatures, and having in its every molecule the germs of life. Like the finny tribes which swarm in our oceans and smaller bodies of water, each kind having its habitat in some spot to which it is curiously adapted, some friendly and some inimical to man, some pleasant and some frightful to behold, some seeking the refuge of quiet nooks and landlocked harbors, and some traversing great areas of water, the various races of the elemental spirits were believed to inhabit the different portions of the great ethereal ocean, and to be exactly adapted to their respective conditions. If we will only bear in mind the fact that the rushing of planets through space must create as absolute a disturbance in this plastic and attenuated medium as the passage of a cannon shot does in the air or that of a steamer in the water, and on a cosmic scale, we can understand that certain planetary aspects, admitting our premises to be true, may produce much more violent agitation and cause much stronger currents to flow in a given direction than others. With the same premises conceded, we may also see why, by such various aspects of the stars, shoals of friendly or hostile "elementals" might be poured in upon our atmosphere, or some particular portion of it, and make the fact appreciable by the effects which ensue.

According to the ancient doctrines, the soulless elemental spirits were evolved by the ceaseless motion inherent in the astral light. Light is force, and the latter is produced by the will. As this will proceeds from an intelligence which cannot err—for it has nothing of the material organs of human thought in it, being the superfine pure emanation of the highest divinity itself (Plato's "Father")—it proceeds from the beginning of time, according to immutable laws, to evolve the elementary fabric requisite for subsequent generations of what we term human races. All of the latter, whether belonging to this planet or to some other of the myriads in space, have their earthly bodies evolved in the matrix out of the bodies of a certain class of these elemental beings which have passed away in the invisible worlds.

In the ancient philosophy there was no missing link to be supplied by what Tyndall calls an "educated imagination" and no hiatus to be filled with volumes of materialistic speculations made necessary by the absurd attempt to solve an equation with but one set of quantities; our "ignorant" ancestors traced the law of evolution throughout the whole universe. As by gradual progression from the star cloudlet to the development of the physical body of man, the rule holds good, so from the universal ether to the incarnate human spirit, they traced one uninterrupted series of entities. These evolutions were from the world of spirit into the world of gross matter, and through that back again to the source of all things. The "descent of species" was to them a descent from the spirit, primal source of all, to the "degradation of matter." In this complete chain of unfoldings the elementary, spiritual beings had as distinct a place, midway between the extremes, as Mr. Darwin's missing link between the ape and man.

In the following chapter we will contrive to explain some of the esoteric speculations of the initiates of the sanctuary, as to what man was, is, and may yet be. The doctrines they taught in the Mysteries—the source from which sprang the Old and partially the New Testament—belonged to the most advanced notions of morality and religious revelations. While the literal meaning was abandoned to the fanaticism of the unreasoning lower classes of society, the higher ones, the majority of which consisted of initiates, pursued their studies and their worship of the one God of Heaven in the solemn silence of the temples.

Plato's speculations in the *Symposium* on the creation of primordial men and his essay on Cosmogony in the *Timaeus* must be taken allegorically, if we accept them at all. It is this hidden Pythagorean meaning in *Timaeus*, *Cratylus*, *Parmenides*, and a few other trilogies and dialogues that the Neoplatonists ventured to expound, as far as the theurgical vow of secrecy would allow them. The Pythagorean doctrine that God is the universal mind diffused through all things and the dogma of the soul's immortality are the leading features in these apparently incongruous teachings. Plato's piety and the great veneration he felt for the Mysteries are sufficient warrant that he would not allow his indiscretion to get the better of that deep sense of responsibility which is felt by every adept. "Constantly perfecting himself in perfect Mysteries, a man in them alone becomes truly perfect," he says in the *Phaedrus* (249C).

He took no pains to conceal his displeasure that the Mysteries had become less secret than formerly. Instead of profaning them by putting them within the reach of the multitude, he would have guarded them with jealous care against all but the most earnest and worthy of his disciples. While mentioning the gods on every page, his monotheism is unquestionable, for the whole thread of his discourse indicates that by the term *gods* he means a class of beings far lower in the scale than deities and but one grade higher than men.

This doctrine of God as the universal mind diffused through all things underlies all ancient philosophies. The Buddhist tenets— which can never be better comprehended than when studying their faithful reflection, the Pythagorean philosophy—are derived from this source as well as the Brahmanical religion and early Christianity. The purifying process of transmigrations (the metempsychoses), however grossly anthropomorphized at a later period, must only be regarded as a supplementary doctrine, disfigured by theological sophistry with the object of getting a firmer hold upon believers through a popular superstition. Neither Gautama Buddha nor Pythagoras intended to teach this purely metaphysical allegory *literally*. Esoterically, it is explained in the "Mystery" of the *Kumbum*, and relates to the purely spiritual peregrinations of the human soul.

It is not in the dead letter of Buddhist sacred literature that scholars may hope to find the true solution of its metaphysical subtleties. The latter weary the power of thought by the inconceivable profundity of its ratiocination, and the student is never farther from truth than when he believes himself nearest its discovery. The mastery of every doctrine of the perplexing Buddhist system can be attained only by proceeding strictly according to the Pythagorean and Platonic method, from universals down to particulars. The key to it lies in the refined and mystical tenets of the spiritual influx of divine life.

"Whoever is unacquainted with my law," says Buddha, "and dies in that state, must return to the earth till he becomes a perfect Samanean. To achieve this object, he must destroy within himself the trinity of Maya.[4] He must extinguish his passions, unite and identify himself with the law (the teaching of the secret doctrine), and comprehend the religion of annihilation."

Here, annihilation refers but to matter, that of the visible as well as of the invisible body; for the astral soul is still matter, however sublimated. The same book says that what Fo (Buddha) meant to say was that "the primitive substance is eternal and unchangeable. Its highest revelation is the pure, luminous ether, the boundless infinite space, not a void resulting from the absence of forms, but on the contrary, the foundation of all forms, and anterior to them. But the very presence of forms denotes it to be the creation of Maya, and all her works are as nothing before the uncreated being, Spirit, in whose profound and sacred repose all motion must cease forever."

Thus *annihilation* means, in the Buddhist philosophy, only a dispersion of matter, in whatever form or semblance of form it may be; for everything that bears a shape was created, and thus must sooner or later perish, i.e., change that shape. Therefore, as something temporary, though seeming to be permanent, it is but an illusion, Maya; for, as eternity has neither beginning nor end, the more or less prolonged duration of some particular form passes, as it were, like an instantaneous flash of lightning. Before we have the time to realize that we have seen it, it is gone and passed away forever; hence, even our astral bodies, pure ether, are but illusions of matter so long as they retain their terrestrial outline. The latter changes, says the Buddhist, according to the merits or demerits of the person during his lifetime, and this is metempsychosis. When the spiritual entity breaks loose forever from every particle of matter, then only it enters upon the eternal and unchangeable Nirvana. He exists in spirit, in *nothing*, as a form, a shape, a semblance; he is completely annihilated, and thus will die no more, for spirit alone is no Maya, but the only reality in an illusionary universe of ever-passing forms.

"But what is that which has no body, no form; which is imponderable, invisible and indivisible; that which exists and yet is not?" ask the Buddhists. "It is Nirvana" is the answer. It is Nothing, not a region but a state. Once Nirvana is reached, man is exempt from the effects of the "four truths"; for an effect can only be produced through a certain cause, and every cause is annihilated in this state.

These "four truths" are the foundation of the whole Buddhist doctrine of Nirvana. They are, says the book of *Prajña Paramita* or *Perfection of Wisdom*, (1) the existence of pain, (2) the production of pain, (3) the annihilation of pain, and (4) the way to the annihilation of pain. What is the source of pain?—Existence. Since birth exists, decrepitude and death ensue; for wherever there is a form, there is a cause for pain and suffering. Spirit alone has no form, and therefore cannot be said to exist. Whenever man (the ethereal, inner man) reaches that point when he becomes utterly spiritual and thus formless, he has reached a state of perfect bliss. Man as an objective being becomes annihilated, but the spiritual entity with its subjective life will live forever, for spirit is incorruptible and immortal.

It is by the spirit of the teachings of both Buddha and Pythagoras that we can so easily recognize the identity of their doctrines. The all-pervading universal soul, the *Anima Mundi*, is Nirvana; and Buddha, as a generic name, is the anthropomorphized *monad* of Pythagoras. When resting in Nirvana, the final bliss, Buddha is the silent monad, dwelling in darkness and silence; he is also the formless Brahman, the sublime but unknowable Deity, which pervades invisibly the whole universe. Whenever it is manifested, desiring to impress itself upon humanity in a shape intelligent to our intellect, whether we call it an avatar, a King Messiah, a permutation of Divine Spirit, Logos, or Christos, it is all one and the same thing. In each case it is "the Father" who is in the Son, and the Son in "the Father." The immortal spirit overshadows the mortal man. It enters into him and, pervading his whole being, makes of him a god, who descends into his earthly tabernacle. Every man may become a Buddha, says the doctrine. And so throughout the interminable series of ages we find now and then men who more or less succeed in uniting themselves "with God," as the expression goes, with their *own spirit*, as we ought to translate. The Buddhists call such men *Arhat*. An Arhat is next to a Buddha, and none is equal to him either in infused science or miraculous powers.

Even the so-called fabulous narratives of certain Buddhist books, when stripped of their allegorical meaning, are found to be the secret doctrines taught by Pythagoras. In the Pali books called the *Jatakas*, the 550 incarnations or metempsychoses of Buddha are given. They narrate how he has appeared in every form of animal life and animated every sentient being on earth, from infinitesimal insect to the bird, the beast, and finally man, the microcosmic image of God on earth. Must this be taken literally? Is it intended as a description of the actual transformations and existence of one and the same individual, immortal, divine spirit, which by turns has animated every kind of sentient being? Ought we not rather to understand, with Buddhist metaphysicians, that though the individual human spirits are numberless, collectively they are one, just as every drop of water drawn out of the ocean, metaphorically speaking, may have an individual existence and still be one with the rest of the drops forming that ocean? For each human spirit is a scintilla of the one all-pervading light that animates the flower, the particle of granite on the mountain side, the lion, and the man.

Egyptian hierophants, like the Brahmans, the Buddhists of the East, and some Greek philosophers, maintained originally that the same spirit that animates the particle of dust, lurking latent in it, animates man, manifesting itself in him in its highest state of activity. The doctrine of a gradual refusion of the human soul into the essence of the primeval parent spirit was universal at one time. But this doctrine never implied annihilation of the higher spiritual ego—only the dispersion of the external forms of man after his terrestrial death, as well as during his abode on earth. Who is better fitted to impart to us the mysteries of after-death, so erroneously thought impenetrable, than those men who, having succeeded in uniting themselves with their "God" through self-discipline and purity of life and purpose, were afforded some glimpses, however imperfect, of the great truth.[5] And these seers tell us strange stories about the variety of forms assumed by disembodied astral souls, forms each one of which is a spiritual though concrete reflection of the abstract state of the mind and the thoughts of the once living man.

To accuse Buddhist philosophy of rejecting a Supreme Being, God, and the soul's immortality—of atheism, in short—on the grounds that according to their doctrines Nirvana means annihilation and *Svabhavat* is not a person, but nothing, is simply absurd. The En of the Jewish EN-SOF also means *nihil* or *nothing*, that which is not (*quo ad nos*); but no one has ever ventured to twit the Jews with atheism. In both cases the real meaning of the term *nothing* carries with it the idea that God is *not a thing*, not a concrete or visible Being to which a name expressive of any object known to us on earth may be applied with propriety.

Notes

1. Stobaeus, *Eclogues* [Cf. *Mystical Hymns of Orpheus*, trans. Thomas Taylor (London, 1824), 48].
2. M. Duncker, *Geschichte des Alterthums* 2:162.
3. A. Wuttke, *Geschichte des Heidenthum* 2:262.
4. "Illusion; matter in its triple manifestation in the earthly and the astral or fontal soul, or the body, and the Platonian dual soul, the rational and the irrational one."
5. Porphyry gives the credit to Plotinus, his master, of having been united with "God" six times during his life, and complains of having attained it but twice himself [*Plotini vita* 23].

8

———

Cyclic Phenomena

From the Platonic and Pythagorean views of matter and force, we will now turn to the kabbalistic philosophy of the origin of man, and compare it with the theory of natural selection enunciated by Darwin and Wallace. It may be that we shall find as much reason to credit the ancients with originality in this direction as in that which we have been considering. To our mind, no stronger proof of the theory of cyclical progression need be required than the comparative enlightenment of former ages and that of the Patristic Church, as regards the form of the earth and the movements of the planetary system. Even were other evidence wanting, the ignorance of Augustine and Lactantius, misleading the whole of Christendom upon these questions until the period of Galileo, would mark the eclipses through which human knowledge passes from age to age.

The "coats of skin," mentioned in the third chapter of Genesis as given to Adam and Eve, are explained by certain ancient philosophers to mean the fleshy bodies with which, in the progress of the cycles, the progenitors of the race became clothed. They maintained that the godlike physical form became grosser and grosser, until the bottom of what may be termed the last spiritual cycle was reached and mankind entered upon the ascending arc of the first human cycle. Then began an uninterrupted series of cycles, or *yugas*, the precise number of years of which each of them consisted remaining an inviolable mystery within the precincts of the sanctuaries and disclosed only to the initiates. As soon as humanity entered upon a new one, the Stone Age, with which the preceding cycle had closed, began to gradually merge into the following and next higher age. With each successive age, or epoch, men grew more refined, until the acme of perfection possible in that particular cycle had been reached.

Then the receding wave of time carried back with it the vestiges of human, social, and intellectual progress. Cycle succeeded cycle by imperceptible transitions; highly civilized, flourishing nations waxed in power, attained the climax of development, waned, and became extinct; and mankind, when the end of the lower cyclic arc was reached, was replunged into barbarism as at the start. Kingdoms have crumbled and nation succeeded nation from the beginning until our day, the races alternately mounting to the highest and descending to the lowest points of development. John W. Draper [author of *History of the Conflict between Religion and Science*] observes that there is no reason to suppose that any one cycle applied to the whole human race. On the contrary, while man in one portion of the planet was in a condition of retrogression, in another he might be progressing in enlightenment and civilization.

How analogous this theory is to the law of planetary motion, which causes the individual orbs to rotate on their axes, the several systems to move around their respective suns, and the whole stellar host to follow a common path around a common central center! Life and death, light and darkness, day and night on the planet, as it turns about its axis and traverses the zodiacal circle representing the lesser and the greater cycles.[1] Remember the Hermetic axiom: "As above, so below; as in heaven, so on earth."

While they made no attempt to calculate the duration of the "grand cycle," the Hermetic philosophers maintained that, according to the cyclic law, the living human race must inevitably and collectively return one day to that point of departure where man was first clothed with "coats of skin"; or, to express it more clearly, the human race must, in accordance with the law of evolution, be finally *physically* spiritualized.

It will be observed that this philosophy of cycles, which was allegorized by the Egyptian hierophants in the "circle of necessity," explains at the same time the allegory of the "fall of man." According to the Arabian descriptions, each of the seven chambers of the Pyramids—those grandest of all cosmic symbols—was known by the name of a planet. The peculiar architecture of the Pyramids shows in itself the drift of the metaphysical thought of their builders. The apex is lost in the clear blue sky of the land of the Pharaohs, and typifies the primordial point lost in the unseen universe whence started the first race of the spiritual prototypes of man.

Each mummy, from the moment that it was embalmed, lost its physical individuality in one sense; it symbolized the human race. Placed in such a way as was best calculated to aid the exit of the "soul," the latter had to pass through the seven planetary chambers before it made its exit through the symbolical apex. Each chamber typified, at the same time, one of the seven spheres and one of the seven higher types of physicospiritual humanity alleged to be above our own. Every 3,000 years, the soul, representative of its race, had to return to its primal point of departure before it underwent another evolution into a more perfected spiritual and physical transformation. We must go deep indeed into the abstruse metaphysics of Oriental mysticism before we can realize fully the infinitude of the subjects that were embraced at one sweep by the majestic thought of its exponents.

Starting as a pure and perfect spiritual being, the Adam of the second chapter of Genesis (Adam the second, the "man of dust"), not satisfied with the position allotted to him by the Demiurge (who is the eldest first-begotten, the Adam-Kadmon), strives in his pride to become Creator in his turn. Evolved out of the androgynous Kadmon, this Adam is himself an androgyne; for, according to the oldest beliefs presented allegorically in Plato's *Timaeus*, the prototypes of our races were all enclosed in the microcosmic tree which grew and developed within and under the great mundane or macrocosmic tree. Divine spirit being considered a unity, however numerous the rays of the great spiritual sun, man has still had his origin like all other forms (whether organic or otherwise) in this one Fount of Eternal Light.

Even if we were to reject the hypothesis of an androgynous man in connection with physical evolution, the significance of the allegory in its spiritual sense would remain unimpaired. So long as the first god-man, symbolizing the two first principles of creation, the dual male and female element, had no thought of good and evil, he could not hypostasize "woman," for she was in him as he was in her. It was only when, as a result of the evil hints of the serpent (matter), the latter condensed itself and cooled on the spiritual man in its contact with the elements, that the fruits of the man-tree—who is himself that tree of knowledge—appeared to his view. From this moment the

68

androgynal union ceased, and man evolved out of himself the woman as a separate entity. They have broken the thread between pure spirit and pure matter. Henceforth they will create no more spiritually; by the sole power of their will man has become a physical creator, and the kingdom of spirit can be won only by a long imprisonment in matter. The meaning of Gogard, the Mazdean tree of life, the sacred oak among whose luxuriant branches a serpent dwells and cannot be dislodged, thus becomes apparent. Creeping out from the primordial *ilus*, the mundane snake grows more material and waxes in strength and power with every new evolution.

The Adam Primus, or Kadmon, the Logos of the Jewish mystics, is the same as the Grecian Prometheus, who seeks to rival with the divine wisdom. He is also the Pimander of Hermes, or the Power of the Thought Divine in its most spiritual aspect, for he was less hypostasized by the Egyptians than the former two. These all create men but fail in their final object. Desiring to endow man with an immortal spirit, in order that by linking the trinity in one he might gradually return to his primal spiritual state without losing his individuality, Prometheus fails in his attempt to steal the divine fire and is sentenced to expiate his crime on Mount Kazbek. Prometheus is also the Logos of the ancient Greeks, as is Herakles.

All of these Logoi strove to endow man with the immortal spirit but failed, and nearly all are represented as being punished for the attempt by severe sentences. Those of the early Christian Fathers who like Origen and Clement Alexandrinus were well versed in pagan symbology, having begun their careers as philosophers, felt very much embarrassed. They could not deny the anticipation of their doctrines in the oldest myths. The latest Logos, according to their teachings, had also appeared in order to show mankind the way to immortality and, in his desire to endow the world with eternal life through the Pentecostal fire, had lost his life agreeably to the traditional program.

Adam the second, or the first-created race which Plato calls gods and the Bible the Elohim, was not triple in his nature like the earthly man, i.e., he was not composed of soul, spirit, and body but was a compound of sublimated astral elements into which the "Father" had breathed an immortal, divine spirit. The latter, by reason of its godlike essence, was ever struggling to liberate itself from the bonds of even that flimsy prison; hence the "sons of God," in their imprudent efforts, were the first to trace a future model for the cyclic law. But man must not be "like one of us," says the Creative Deity, one of the Elohim "intrusted with the fabrication of the lower animal."[2] And thus it was that, when the men of the first race had reached the summit of the first cycle, they lost their balance, and their second envelope, the grosser clothing (astral body), dragged them down the opposite arc.

Thus was set in motion the first cycle, which in its rotations downward brought an infinitesimal part of the created lives to our planet of mud. Arrived at the lowest point of the arc of the cycle, which directly preceded life on this earth, the pure divine spark still lingering in the Adam made an effort to separate itself from the astral spirit, for "man was falling gradually into generation," and the fleshy coat was becoming with every action more and more dense.

The whole Darwinian theory of natural selection is included in the first six chapters of the book of Genesis. The "Man" of chapter one is radically different from the "Adam" of chapter two, for the former was created "male and female"—that is, bisexed—and in the image of God; while the latter, according to verse seven, was formed of the dust of the ground and became "a living soul" after the Lord God "breathed into his nostrils the breath of life." Moreover, this Adam was a male being, and in verse twenty we are told that "there was not found a helpmeet for him." The Adonai, being pure spiritual entities, had no sex, or rather had both sexes united in themselves, like their Creator; and the ancients understood this so well that they represented many of their deities as of dual sex. The biblical student must either accept this interpretation, or make the passages in the two chapters alluded to absurdly contradict each other. It was such literal acceptance of passages that warranted the atheists in covering the Mosaic account with ridicule, and it is the dead letter of the old text that begets the materialism of our age. Not only are these two races of beings thus clearly indicated in Genesis, but even a third and a fourth one are ushered before the reader in chapter four, where the "sons of God" and the race of "giants" are spoken of.

One thing, at least, has been shown in the Hebrew text, viz., that there was one race of purely physical creatures and another purely spiritual. The evolution and "transformation of species" required to fill the gap between the two has been left to abler anthropologists. We can only repeat the philosophy of men of old, which says that the

70

union of these two races produced a third—the Adamite race. Sharing the natures of both its parents, it is equally adapted to an existence in the material and spiritual worlds. Allied to the physical half of man's nature is reason, which enables him to maintain his supremacy over the lower animals and to subjugate nature to his uses. Allied to his spiritual part is his conscience, which will serve as his unerring guide through the besetments of the senses; for conscience is that instantaneous perception between right and wrong which can only be exercised by the spirit and which, being a portion of the Divine Wisdom and Purity, is absolutely pure and wise. Its promptings are independent of reason, and it can only manifest itself clearly when unhampered by the baser attractions of our dual nature.

Reason being a faculty of our physical brain, one which is justly defined as that of deducing inferences from premises, and being wholly dependent on the evidence of other senses, cannot be a quality pertaining directly to our divine spirit. The latter *knows*—hence all reasoning which implies discussion and argument would be useless. So an entity, if it must be considered as a direct emanation from the eternal Spirit of wisdom, has to be viewed as possessed of the same attributes as the essence or the whole of which it is a part. Therefore it is with a certain degree of logic that the ancient theurgists maintained that the *rational* part of man's soul (spirit) never entered wholly into man's body, but only overshadowed him more or less through the *irrational* or astral soul, which serves as an intermediatory agent, or a medium between spirit and body. The man who has conquered matter sufficiently to receive the direct light from his shining *augoeides* feels truth intuitionally; he could not err in his judgment, notwithstanding all the sophisms suggested by cold reason, for he is illuminated. Hence, prophecy, vaticination, and the so-called Divine inspiration are simply the effects of this illumination from above by our own immortal spirit.

Where, then, lies the true, real secret so much talked about by the Hermetists? That there was and there is a secret, no candid student of esoteric literature will ever doubt. Men of genius—as many of the Hermetic philosophers undeniably were—would not have made fools of themselves by trying to fool others for several thousand consecutive years. That this great secret, commonly termed "the philosopher's stone," had a spiritual as well as a physical meaning attached to it was suspected in all ages. The author of *Remarks on Alchemy and the*

71

Alchemists very truly observes that the subject of the Hermetic art is man, and the object of the art is the perfection of man.[3] But we cannot agree with him that only those whom he terms "money-loving sots" ever attempted to carry the purely *moral* design of the alchemists into the field of physical science. The fact alone that man, in their eyes, is a trinity, which they divide into *Sol*, water of mercury, and sulfur, which is the secret fire—or, to speak plain, into body, soul, and spirit—shows that there is a physical side to the question. Man is the philosopher's stone spiritually—"a triune or trinity in unity," as Philalethes expresses it. But he is also that stone physically. The latter is but the effect of the cause, and the cause is the universal solvent of everything—divine spirit. Man is a correlation of chemical physical forces, as well as a correlation of spiritual powers. The latter react on the physical powers of man in proportion to the development of the earthly man.

Lowest in the scale of being are those invisible creatures called by the kabbalists the "elementary." There are three distinct classes of these. The highest in intelligence and cunning are the so-called terrestrial spirits, of which we will speak more categorically in other parts of this work. Suffice to say, for the present, that they are the *larvae* or shadows of those who have lived on earth, who have refused all spiritual light but remained and died deeply immersed in the mire of matter, and from whose sinful souls the immortal spirit has gradually separated.

The second class is composed of the invisible antitypes of the men *to be* born. No form can come into objective existence—from the highest to the lowest—before the abstract ideal of this form—or, as Aristotle would call it, the *privation* of this form—is called forth. Before an artist paints a picture every feature of it exists already in his imagination; to have enabled us to discern a watch, this particular watch must have existed in its abstract form in the watchmaker's mind. So with future men. Forms pass; ideas that created them and the material which gave them objectiveness remain. These models, as yet devoid of immortal spirits, are "elementals"—properly speaking, psychic embryos—which, when their time arrives, die out of the invisible world and are born into this visible one as human infants, receiving *in transitu* that divine breath called spirit which completes the perfect man. This class cannot communicate objectively with men.

72

The third class are the "elementals" proper, which never evolve into human beings but occupy, as it were, a specific step of the ladder of being. By comparison with the others, they may properly be called nature spirits or cosmic agents of nature, each being confined to its own element and never transgressing the bounds of others. These are what Tertullian called the "princes of the powers of the air."

This class is believed to possess but one of the three attributes of man. They have neither immortal spirits nor tangible bodies, but only astral forms, which partake in a distinguishing degree of the element to which they belong and also of the ether. They are a combination of sublimated matter and a rudimental mind. Some are changeless but still have no separate individuality, acting collectively, so to say. Others, of certain elements and species, change form under a fixed law, which kabbalists explain. The most solid of their bodies is ordinarily just immaterial enough to escape perception by our physical eyesight, but not so unsubstantial that they can be perfectly recognized by the inner, or clairvoyant vision.

They not only exist and can all live in ether, but can handle and direct it for the production of physical effects, as readily as we can compress air or water for the same purpose by pneumatic and hydraulic apparatus; in this occupation they are readily helped by the "human elementary." More than this, they can so condense it as to make to themselves tangible bodies, which by their Protean powers they can cause to assume such likeness as they choose, by taking as their models the portraits they find stamped in the memory of the persons present. It is not necessary that the sitter should be thinking at the moment of the one represented. His image may have faded many years before. The mind receives indelible impressions even from chance acquaintance or persons encountered but once. As a few seconds' exposure of the sensitized photograph plate is all that is requisite to preserve indefinitely the image of the sitter, so is it with the mind.

Éliphas Lévi expounds with reasonable clearness, in his *Dogme et rituel de la haute magie*, the law of reciprocal influences between the planets and their combined effect upon the mineral, vegetable, and animal kingdoms, as well as upon ourselves. He states that the astral atmosphere is as constantly changing from day to day and from hour to hour as the air we breathe. He quotes approvingly the doctrine of Paracelsus that every man, animal, and plant bears external and internal evidences of the influences dominant at the moment of germinal development. He repeats the old kabbalistic doctrine that nothing is unimportant in nature, and that even so small a thing as the birth of one child upon our insignificant planet has its effect upon the universe, as the whole universe has its own reactive influence upon him.

As to the human spirit, the notions of the older philosophers and medieval kabbalists, while differing in some particulars, agreed on the whole, so that the doctrine of one may be viewed as the doctrine of the other. The most substantial difference consisted in the location of the immortal or divine spirit of man. While the ancient Neoplatonists held that the augoeides never descends hypostatically into the living man, but only sheds more or less its radiance on the inner man (the astral soul), the kabbalists of the Middle Ages maintained that the spirit, detaching itself from the ocean of light and spirit, entered into man's soul, where it remained through life imprisoned in the astral capsule.

This difference was the result of the belief of Christian kabbalists, more or less, in the dead letter of the allegory of the fall of man. The soul, they said, through the fall of Adam, became contaminated with the world of matter or Satan. Before it could appear with its enclosed divine spirit in the presence of the Eternal, it had to purify itself of the impurities of darkness. They compared "the spirit imprisoned within the soul to a drop of water enclosed within a capsule of gelatin and thrown in the ocean; so long as the capsule remains whole, the drop of water remains isolated; break the envelope and the drop becomes a part of the ocean—its individual existence has ceased. So it is with the spirit. As long as it is enclosed in its plastic mediator, or soul, it has an individual existence. Destroy the capsule, a result which may occur from the agonies of withered conscience, crime, and moral disease, and the spirit returns back to its original abode. Its individuality is gone."

On the other hand, the philosophers who explained the "fall into generation" in their own way viewed spirit as something wholly distinct from the soul. They allowed its presence in the astral capsule only so far as the spiritual emanations or rays of the "shining one" were concerned. Man and soul had to conquer their immortality by ascending toward the unity with which, if successful, they were finally linked, and into which they were absorbed, so to say. The individualization of man after death depended on the spirit, not on his soul and body. Although the word "personality," in the sense in which it is usually understood, is an absurdity if applied literally to our immortal essence, still the latter is a distinct entity, immortal and eternal per se. As in the case of criminals beyond redemption, when the shining thread (which links the spirit to the soul from the moment of the birth of a child) is violently snapped and the disembodied entity is left to share the fate of the lower animals, to gradually dissolve into ether, and have its individuality annihilated— even then the spirit remains a distinct being. It becomes a planetary spirit, an angel; for the gods of the pagan or the archangels of the Christian, the direct emanations of the First Cause, notwithstanding the hazardous statement of Swedenborg, never were or will be men, on our planet at least.

The whole esoterism of the Buddhist philosophy is based on this mysterious teaching, understood by so few persons and so totally misrepresented by many of the most learned scholars. Even metaphysicians are too inclined to confound the effect with the cause. A person may have won his immortal life and remain the same inner-self he was on earth throughout eternity; but this does not imply necessarily that he must either remain the Mr. Smith or Brown he was on earth or lose his individuality. Therefore, the astral soul and terrestrial body of man may, in the dark hereafter, be absorbed into the cosmical ocean of sublimated elements, and cease to feel his ego, if this ego did not deserve to soar higher; and the divine spirit still remain an unchanged entity, though this terrestrial experience of his emanations may be totally obliterated at the instant of separation from the unworthy vehicle.

If the "spirit," the divine portion of the soul, is preexistent as a distinct being from all eternity, as Origen, Synesius, and other Christian fathers and philosophers taught, and if it is the same as and nothing more than the metaphysically objective soul, how can it be otherwise than eternal? And what does it matter in such a case whether man leads an animal or a pure life if, do what he may, he can never lose his individuality? This doctrine is as pernicious in its consequences as that of vicarious atonement. Had the latter dogma, in company with the false idea that we are all immortal, been demonstrated to the world in its true light, humanity would have been bettered by its propagation. Crime and sin would be avoided, not for fear of earthly punishment, or of a ridiculous hell, but for the sake of that which lies the most deeply rooted in our inner nature—the desire for an individual and distinct life in the hereafter, the positive assurance that we cannot win it unless we "take the kingdom of heaven by violence," and the conviction that neither human prayers nor the blood of another man will save us from individual destruction after death, unless we firmly link ourselves during our terrestrial life with our own immortal spirit—our God.

This doctrine of the possibility of losing one's soul, and hence individuality, militates against the ideal theories and progressive ideas of some spiritualists, though Swedenborg fully adopts it. They will never accept the kabbalistic doctrine which teaches that it is only through observing the law of harmony that individual life hereafter can be obtained and that the farther the inner and outer man deviate from this fount of harmony, whose source lies in our divine spirit, the more difficult it is to regain the ground.

But while the spiritualists and other adherents of Christianity have little if any perception of this fact of the possible death and obliteration of the human personality by the separation of the immortal part from the perishable, the Swedenborgians fully comprehend it. One of the most respected ministers of the New Church, the Rev. Chauncey Giles, D.D., of New York, recently elucidated the subject in a public discourse as follows: Physical death, or the death of the body, was a provision of the divine economy for the benefit of man, a provision by means of which he attained the higher ends of his being.

But there is another death which is the interruption of the divine order and the destruction of every human element in man's nature and every possibility of human happiness. This is the spiritual death which takes place before the dissolution of the body. "There may be a vast development of man's natural mind without that development being accompanied by a particle of love of God or of unselfish love of man." When one falls into a love of self and love of the world with its pleasures, losing the divine love of God and of the neighbor, he falls from life to death. The higher principles which constitute the essential elements of his humanity perish, and he lives only on the natural plane of his faculties. Physically he exists, spiritually he is dead. To all that pertains to the higher and the only enduring phase of existence he is as much dead as his body becomes dead to all the activities, delights, and sensations of the world when the spirit has left it.

76

This spiritual death results from disobedience of the laws of spiritual life, which is followed by the same penalty as the disobedience of the laws of natural life. But the spiritually dead still have their delights; they have their intellectual endowments and power and intense activities. All the animal delights are theirs, and to multitudes of men and women these constitute the highest ideal of human happiness. The tireless pursuit of riches and of the amusements and entertainments of social life, the cultivation of graces of manner, of taste in dress, of social preferment, and of scientific distinction intoxicate and enrapture these dead-alive; but, the eloquent preacher remarks, "these creatures, with all their graces, rich attire, and brilliant accomplishments, are dead in the eye of the Lord and the angels and, when measured by the only true and immutable standard, have no more genuine life than skeletons whose flesh has turned to dust." A high development of the intellectual faculties does not imply spiritual and true life. Many of our greatest scientists are but animate corpses—they have no spiritual sight because their spirits have left them. So we might go through all ages, examine all occupations, weigh all human attainments, and investigate all forms of society, and we would find these spiritually dead everywhere.

After the death of the depraved and the wicked, the critical moment arrives. If during life the ultimate and desperate effort of the inner self to reunite itself with the faintly glimmering ray of its divine parent is neglected and if this ray is allowed to be more and more shut out by the thickening crust of matter, the soul, once freed from the body, follows its earthly attractions and is magnetically drawn into and held within the dense fogs of the material atmosphere. Then it begins to sink lower and lower, until it finds itself, when returned to consciousness, in what the ancients termed *Hades*. The annihilation of such a soul is never instantaneous; it may last centuries, perhaps; for nature never proceeds by jumps and starts, and the astral soul being formed of elements, the law of evolution must bide its time. Then begins the fearful law of compensation, the *Yin-yuan* of the Buddhists.

This class of spirits is called the "terrestrial" or "earthly elementary," in contradistinction to the other classes. In the East they are known as the "Brothers of the Shadow." Cunning, low, vindictive, and seeking to retaliate upon humanity for their sufferings, they become, until final annihilation, vampires, ghouls, and prominent actors. These are the leading "stars" on the great spiritual stage of "materialization," which phenomena they perform with the help of the more intelligent of the genuine-born "elemental" creatures, which hover around and welcome them with delight in their own spheres. Henry Khunrath, the great German kabbalist, has representations of the four classes of these human "elementary spirits" on a plate of his rare work, *Amphitheatrum Sapientiae Aeternae.* Once past the threshold of the sanctuary of initiation, once an adept has lifted the "Veil of Isis," the mysterious and jealous goddess, he has nothing to fear; but till then he is in constant danger.

There is scarcely one phase of mediumship of either kind that we have not seen exemplified during the past twenty-five years in various countries. India, Tibet, Borneo, Siam, Egypt, Asia Minor, America (North and South), and other parts of the world have each displayed to us their peculiar phase of mediumistic phenomena and magical power. Our varied experience has taught us two important truths, viz., that for the exercise of the latter, personal purity and the exercise of a trained and indomitable will power are indispensable; and that spiritualists can never assure themselves of the genuineness of mediumistic manifestations, unless they occur in the light and under such reasonable test conditions as would make an attempted fraud instantly noticed.

For fear of being misunderstood, we would remark that while, as a rule, physical phenomena are produced by the nature spirits of their own motion and to please their own fancy, still good disembodied human spirits, under exceptional circumstances, such as the aspiration of a pure heart or the occurrence of some favoring emergency, can manifest their presence by any of the phenomena *except personal materialization.* But it must be a mighty attraction indeed to draw a pure, disembodied spirit from its radiant home into the foul atmosphere from which it escaped upon leaving its earthly body.

Magi and theurgic philosophers objected most severely to the "evocation of souls." "Bring her (the soul) not forth, lest in departing she retain something," says Psellus.[4]

> It becomes you not to behold them before your body is initiated,
> Since, by always alluring, they seduce the souls of the uninitiated . . .

says the philosopher Proclus, in another passage.[5]

They objected to it for several good reasons: (1) "It is extremely difficult to distinguish a good daemon from a bad one," says Iamblichus. (2) If a human soul succeeds in penetrating the density of the earth's atmosphere—always oppressive to her, often hateful—still there is a danger the soul is unable to come into proximity with the material world without contaminating her purity; "departing, she retains something," for which she has to suffer more or less after her departure. Therefore, the true theurgist will avoid causing any more suffering to this pure denizen of the higher sphere than is absolutely required by the interests of humanity. It is only the practitioner of black magic who compels the presence, by the powerful incantations of necromancy, of the tainted souls of such as have lived bad lives and are ready to aid his selfish designs.

That which survives as an individuality after the death of the body is the astral soul, which Plato, in the *Timaeus* and *Gorgias*, calls the *mortal soul*, for, according to the Hermetic doctrine, it throws off its more material particles at every progressive change into a higher sphere. Socrates narrates to Callicles (*Gorgias* 524) that this mortal soul retains all the characteristics of the body after the death of the latter, so much so, indeed, that a man marked with the whip will have his astral body "full of the prints and scars." The astral spirit is a faithful duplicate of the body, both in a physical and spiritual sense.

The Divine, the highest and immortal spirit, can be neither punished nor rewarded. To maintain such a doctrine would be at the same time absurd and blasphemous, for it is not merely a flame lit at the central and inexhaustible fountain of light, but actually a portion of it, and of identical essence. It assures immortality to the individual astral being in proportion to the willingness of the latter to receive it. So long as the double man, i.e., the man of flesh and spirit, keeps within the limits of the law of spiritual continuity and so long as the divine spark lingers in him, however faintly, he is on the road to an immortality in the future state. But those who resign themselves to a materialistic existence—shutting out the divine radiance shed by their spirit at the beginning of the earthly pilgrimage and stifling the warning voice of that faithful sentry, the conscience, which serves as a focus for the light in the soul—such beings as these, having left behind conscience and spirit and crossed the boundaries of matter, will of necessity have to follow its laws.

Matter is as indestructible and eternal as the immortal spirit itself, but only in its particles, and not as organized forms. When the body of so grossly materialistic a person as above described has been deserted by its spirit before physical death, the plastic material or astral soul, following the laws of blind matter, shapes itself thoroughly into the mold which vice has been gradually preparing for it through the earth life of the individual. Then, as Plato (*Timaeus* 42C) says, it assumes the form of that "animal to which it resembled in its evil ways" during life. "It is an ancient saying," he tells us (*Phaedo* 70C, 114B, C), "that the souls departing hence exist in Hades and return hither again and are produced from the dead. . . . But those who are found to have lived an eminently holy life, these are they who arrive at the pure abode ABOVE and DWELL ON THE UPPER PARTS of the earth" (the ethereal region). In *Phaedrus* (249B), again, he says that when man has ended his first life (on earth), some go to places of punishment beneath the earth. The kabbalists do not understand this region below the earth as a place inside the earth, but maintain it to be a sphere, far inferior in perfection to the earth and far more material.

Of all the modern speculators upon the seeming incongruities of the New Testament, the authors of *The Unseen Universe* alone seem to have caught a glimpse of its kabbalistic truths, respecting the gehenna of the universe.[6] This gehenna, termed by the occultists the eighth sphere (numbering inversely), is merely a planet like our own, attached to the latter and following it in its penumbra; a kind of dust hole, a "place where all its garbage and filth is consumed," to borrow an expression of the above-mentioned authors, and on which all the dross and scorification of the cosmic matter pertaining to our planet is in a continual state of remodeling.

The Secret Doctrine teaches that man, if he wins immortality, will remain forever the trinity that he is in life, and will continue so throughout all the spheres. The astral body, which in this life is covered by a gross physical envelope, becomes—when relieved of that covering by the process of corporeal death—in its turn the shell of another and more ethereal body. This begins developing from the moment of death, and becomes perfected when the astral body of the earthly form finally separates from it. This process, they say, is repeated at every new transition from sphere to sphere.

Let us advance another step in our argument. If there is such a thing as existence in the spiritual world after corporeal death, then it must occur in accordance with the law of evolution. It takes man from his place at the apex of the pyramid of matter and lifts him into a sphere of existence where the same inexorable law follows him. And if it follows him, why not everything else in nature? Why not animals and plants, which have a life principle and whose gross forms decay like his, when that life principle leaves them? If his astral becomes more ethereal upon attaining the other sphere, why not theirs?

If anthropologists, physiologists, and psychologists are equally perplexed by primal and final causes, and find in matter so much similarity in all its forms but in spirit such abysses of difference, it is perhaps because their inquiries are limited to our visible globe and they cannot, or dare not, go beyond. The spirit of a mineral, plant, or animal may begin to form here and reach its final development millions of ages hereafter on other planets, known or unknown, visible or invisible to astronomers. For who is able to controvert the theory previously suggested, that the earth itself, like the living creatures to which it has given birth, will ultimately, after passing through its own stage of death and dissolution, become an etherealized astral planet? "As above, so below": harmony is the great law of nature.

Harmony in the physical and mathematical world of sense is *justice* in the spiritual one. Justice produces harmony, and injustice, discord; and discord, on a cosmical scale, means chaos—annihilation.

If there is a developed immortal spirit in man, it must be in everything else, at least in a latent or germinal state, and it can only be a question of time for each of these germs to become fully developed. What gross injustice it would be for an impenitent criminal man, the perpetrator of a brutal murder in the exercise of his free will, to have an immortal spirit which in time may be washed clean of sin and enjoy perfect happiness, while a poor horse, innocent of all crime, should toil and suffer under the merciless torture of his master's whip during a whole life and then be annihilated at death? Such a belief implies a brutal injustice and is only possible among people taught the dogma that everything is created for man, that he alone is the sovereign of the universe, a sovereign so mighty that to save him from the consequences of his own misdeeds, it was not too much that the God of the universe should die to placate his own just wrath.

Notes

1. Orpheus is said to have ascribed to the grand cycle 120,000 years of duration, and Cassandrus 136,000. See Censorinus, *De die natali* 18.
2. See Plato, *Timaeus* 41, 42, 69.
3. E. A. Hitchcock (Boston, 1857), iv.
4. "Chaldean Oracles" 3; in Cory, *Ancient Fragments* 270.
5. *On the First Alcibiade*; in Cory, 270.
6. [Balfour Stewart and P. G. Tait], *The Unseen Universe* (New York, 1875), ch. 7.

9

The Inner and Outer Man

Whatever name the physicists may call the energizing principle in matter is of no account. It is a subtle something apart from the matter itself; and, as it escapes their detection, it must be something besides matter. If the law of attraction is admitted as governing the one, why should it be excluded from influencing the other? Leaving logic to answer, we turn to the common experience of mankind and there find a mass of testimony corroborative of the immortality of the soul, if we judge but from analogies. But we have more than that: we have the unimpeachable testimony of thousands upon thousands that there is a regular science of the soul, which, notwithstanding that it is now denied the right of a place among other sciences, *is* a science. This science, by penetrating the arcana of nature far deeper than our modern philosophy ever dreamed possible, teaches us how to force the invisible to become visible; the existence of elementary spirits; the nature and magical properties of the astral light; and the power of living men to bring themselves into communication with the former through the latter.

The existence of spirit in the common mediator, the ether, is denied by materialism, while theology makes of it a personal god. The kabbalist holds that both are wrong, saying that in ether the elements represent but matter—the blind cosmic forces of nature—and spirit, the intelligence which directs them. The Hermetic, Orphic, and Pythagorean cosmogonical doctrines, as well as those of Sanchoniathon and Berosus, are all based upon one irrefutable formula, viz., that the ether and chaos (or, in the Platonic language, mind and matter) were the two primeval and eternal principles of the universe, utterly independent of anything else. The former was the all-vivifying

83

intellectual principle; the chaos was a shapeless, liquid principle without "form or sense." From the union of these two, sprang into existence
the universe, or rather the universal world, the first androgynous
deity—the chaotic matter becoming its body, and ether the soul.
According to the phraseology of a Fragment of Hermias, "chaos, from
this union with spirit, obtaining sense, shone with pleasure, and thus
was produced the *Protogonos* (the firstborn) light." This is the universal
trinity based on the metaphysical conceptions of the ancients, who,
reasoning by analogy, made of man, who is a compound of intellect
and matter, the microcosm of the macrocosm or great universe.

This visible universe of spirit and matter, they say, is but the
concrete image of the ideal abstraction; it was built on the model
of the first divine Idea. Thus our universe existed from eternity in
a latent state. The soul animating this purely spiritual universe is
the central sun, the highest deity itself. It was not he who built the
concrete form of his idea, but his first-begotten; and it was constructed
on the geometrical figure of the dodecahedron (Plato, *Timaeus* 55C).

The ancients, who named but four elements, made of ether a fifth
one. On account of its essence being made divine by the unseen
presence, it was considered a medium between this world and the
next. They held that when the directing intelligences retired from
any portion of ether, one of the four kingdoms which they are bound
to superintend, the space was left in possession of evil. An adept
who prepared to converse with the "invisibles" had to know well his
ritual and be perfectly acquainted with the conditions required for the
perfect equilibrium of the four elements in the astral light. First of all,
he must purify the essence and, within the circle in which he sought
to attract the pure spirits, equilibrize the elements so as to prevent the
ingress of the elementaries into their respective spheres. But woe to the
imprudent inquirer who ignorantly trespasses upon forbidden ground;
danger will beset him at every step. He evokes powers that he cannot
control; he arouses sentries which allow only their masters to pass.

For, in the words of the immortal Rosicrucian, "Once that thou
hast resolved to become a cooperator with the spirit of the *living* God,
take care not to hinder Him in His work; for if thy heat exceeds the
natural proportion thou hast stirr'd the wrath of the *moyst* natures,[1]
and they will stand up against the central fire, and the central fire
against them, and there will be a terrible division in the chaos."[2]

The spirit of harmony and union will depart from the elements, disturbed by the imprudent hand; and the currents of blind forces will become immediately infested by numberless creatures of matter and instinct—the bad daemons of the theurgists, the devils of theology—and gnomes, salamanders, sylphs, and undines will assail the rash performer under multifarious aerial forms. Unable to invent anything, they will search your memory to its very depths; hence the nervous exhaustion and mental oppression of certain sensitive natures at spiritual circles. The elementals will bring to light long forgotten remembrances of the past: forms, images, sweet mementos, and familiar sentences long since faded from our own remembrance, but vividly preserved in the inscrutable depths of our memory and on the astral tablets of the imperishable "Book of Life."

Every organized thing in this world, visible as well as invisible, has an element appropriate to itself. The fish lives and breathes in the water; the plant consumes carbonic acid, which for animals and men produces death; some beings are fitted for rarefied strata of air; others exist only in the densest. Life, to some, is dependent on sunlight; to others, upon darkness; and so the wise economy of nature adapts to each existing condition some living form. These analogies warrant the conclusion that not only is there no unoccupied portion of universal nature, but also that for each thing that has life, special conditions are furnished, and, being furnished, they are necessary.

Now assuming that there is an invisible side to the universe, the fixed habit of nature warrants the conclusion that this half, like the other half, is occupied, and that each group of its occupants is supplied with the indispensable conditions of existence. It is as illogical to imagine that identical conditions are furnished to all as it would be to maintain such a theory respecting the inhabitants of the domain of visible nature. That there are spirits implies that there is a diversity of spirits; for men differ, and human spirits are but disembodied men.

To say that all spirits are alike, or fitted to the same atmosphere, or possessed of like powers, or governed by the same attractions—electric, magnetic, odic, astral, it matters not which—is as absurd as though one should say that all planets have the same nature, or that all animals are amphibious, or that all men can be nourished on the same food. It accords with reason to suppose that the grossest natures among the spirits will sink to the lowest depths of the spiritual atmosphere—

85

in other words, be found nearest to the earth. Inversely, the purest would be farthest away. In what, were we to coin a word, we should call the *Psychomatics* of occultism, it is as unwarrantable to assume that either of these grades of spirits can occupy the place or subsist in the conditions of the other, as in hydraulics it would be to expect that two liquids of different densities could exchange their markings on the scale of Baumé's hydrometer.

As the watch passes from hand to hand and room to room in a factory, one part being added here, and another there, until the delicate machine is perfected, according to the design conceived in the mind of the master before the work was begun; so, according to ancient philosophy, the first divine conception of man takes shape little by little, in the several departments of the universal workshop, and the perfect human being finally appears on our scene.

This philosophy teaches that nature never leaves her work unfinished; if baffled at the first attempt, she tries again. When she evolves a human embryo, the intention is that a man shall be perfected— physically, intellectually, and spiritually. His body is to grow mature, wear out, and die; his mind to unfold, ripen, and be harmoniously balanced; his divine spirit to illuminate and blend easily with the inner man. No human being completes its grand cycle, or the "circle of necessity," until all these are accomplished. As the laggards in a race struggle and plod in their first quarter while the victor darts past the goal, so, in the race of immortality, some souls outspeed all the rest and reach the end, while their myriad competitors are toiling under the load of matter, close to the starting point. Some unfortunates fall out entirely and lose all chance of the prize; some retrace their steps and begin again. This is what the Hindu dreads above all things— *transmigration* and *reincarnation*[3] in other inferior forms on this planet.

But there is a way to avoid it, and Buddha taught it in his doctrine of poverty, restriction of the senses, perfect indifference to the objects of this earthly vale of tears, freedom from passion, and frequent intercommunication with the Atma—soul-contemplation. The cause of reincarnation is ignorance of our senses and the idea that there is any reality in the world, anything except abstract existence. From the organs of sense comes the "hallucination" we call contact; "from contact, desire; from desire, sensation (which also is a deception of our body); from sensation, the cleaving to existing bodies; from this

86

cleaving, reproduction; and from reproduction, disease, decay, and death."

"Thus, like the revolutions of a wheel, there is a regular succession of death and birth, the moral cause of which is the cleaving to existing objects, while the instrumental cause is *karma* (the power which controls the universe, prompting it to activity, merit and demerit). It is therefore the great desire of all beings who would be released from the sorrows of successive birth to seek the destruction of the moral cause . . . the cleaving to existing objects, or evil desire. . . . They in whom evil desire is entirely destroyed are called *Arhats*. . . . Freedom from evil desire insures the possession of a miraculous power. At his death . . . the Arhat (is never reincarnated, for he) invariably attains Nirvana"[4]—a word, by the by, falsely interpreted by Christian scholars and skeptical commentators. Nirvana is the world of cause, in which all deceptive effects or delusions of our senses disappear. Nirvana is the highest attainable sphere. The *pitris* (the pre-Adamic spirits) are considered by the Buddhistic philosopher as reincarnated, though in a degree far superior to that of the man of earth. Do they not die in their turn? Do not their astral bodies suffer and rejoice, and feel the same curse of illusionary feelings as when embodied?

What Buddha taught in the sixth century B.C. in India, Pythagoras taught in the fifth in Greece and Italy. Gibbon shows how deeply the Pharisees were impressed with this belief in the transmigration of souls.[5] The Egyptian circle of necessity is ineffaceably stamped on the hoary monuments of old.

An Eastern artist has attempted to give pictorial expression to the kabbalistic doctrine of the cycles. The picture covers a whole inner wall of a subterranean temple in the neighborhood of a great Buddhist pagoda and is strikingly suggestive. Let us attempt to convey some idea of the design, as we recall it.

Imagine a given point in space as the primordial one; then with compasses draw a circle around this point. Where the beginning and the end unite, emanation and reabsorption meet. The circle is composed of innumerable smaller circles, like the rings of a bracelet, and each of these minor rings forms the belt of the goddess which represents that sphere. As the curve of the arc approaches the ultimate point of the semicircle—the nadir of the grand cycle—at which point the mystical painter placed our planet, the face of each successive goddess becomes more dark and hideous than European imagination is able to conceive. Every belt is covered with representations of plants, animals, and human beings belonging to the fauna, flora, and anthropology of that particular sphere. There is a certain distance between each of the spheres purposely marked; for after the accomplishment of the circles through various transmigrations, the soul is allowed a time of temporary nirvana, during which space of time the atma loses all remembrance of past sorrows. The intermediate ethereal space is filled with strange beings. Those between the highest ether and the earth below are the creatures of a "middle nature," nature spirits, or, as the kabbalists term them sometimes, the elementals.

This picture is either a copy of the one described for posterity by Berosus, the priest of the temple of Belus at Babylon, or the original. We leave it to the shrewdness of the modern archaeologist to decide. But the wall is covered with precisely such creatures as described by the semidemon or half-god Oannes, the Chaldean man-fish:[6] "hideous beings, which were produced of a twofold principle"—the astral light and the grosser matter.

We will now present a few fragments of this mysterious doctrine of reincarnation—as distinct from metempsychosis—which we have from an authority. Reincarnation, i.e., the appearance of the same individual, or rather of his astral monad, twice on the same planet is not a rule in nature; it is an exception, like the teratological phenomenon of a two-headed infant. It is preceded by a violation of the laws of harmony of nature and happens only when the latter, seeking to restore its disturbed equilibrium, violently throws back into earth life the astral monad which had been tossed out of the circle of necessity by crime or accident. Thus in cases of abortion, of infants dying before a certain age, and of congenital and incurable idiocy, nature's original design to produce a perfect human being has been interrupted. Therefore, while the gross matter of each of these several entities is suffered to disperse itself at death through the vast realm of being, the immortal spirit and astral monad of the individual—the latter having been set apart to animate a frame and the former to shed its divine light on the corporeal organization—must try a second time to carry out the purpose of the creative intelligence.

If reason has been so far developed as to become active and discriminative, there is no [immediate] reincarnation on this earth, for the three parts of the triune man have been united together, and he is capable of running the race. But when the new being has not passed beyond the condition of monad, or when, as in the idiot, the trinity has not been completed, the immortal spark which illuminates it has to reenter on the earthly plane as it was frustrated in its first attempt. Otherwise, the mortal or astral and the immortal or divine souls could not progress in unison and pass onward to the sphere above. Spirit follows a line parallel with that of matter, and the spiritual evolution goes hand in hand with the physical.

That is to say, the monad which was imprisoned in the elementary being—the rudimentary or lowest astral form of the future man—after having passed through and quitted the highest physical shape of a dumb animal (say an orangutan or again an elephant, one of the most intellectual of brutes) that monad, we say, cannot skip over the physical and intellectual sphere of the terrestrial man, and be suddenly ushered into the spiritual sphere above. What reward or punishment can there be in that sphere of disembodied human entities for a fetus or a human embryo which had not even time to breathe on this earth, still less an opportunity to exercise the divine faculties of the spirit? Or for an irresponsible infant whose senseless monad, remaining dormant within the astral and physical casket, could as little prevent him from burning himself as another person to death? Or for one idiotic from birth, the number of whose cerebral circumvolutions is only from twenty to thirty percent of those of sane persons and who therefore is irresponsible for either his disposition and acts or the imperfections of his vagrant, half-developed intellect?

Further, the same occult doctrine recognizes another possibility, albeit so rare and so vague that it is really useless to mention it. Even the modern Occidental occultists deny it though it is universally accepted in Eastern countries. When, through vice, fearful crimes, and animal passions, a disembodied spirit has fallen to the eighth sphere, the nearest to our earth—the allegorical Hades and the *gehenna* of the Bible—he can, with the help of that glimpse of reason and consciousness left to him, repent; that is to say, he can, by exercising the remnants of his will power, strive upward and, like a drowning man, struggle once more to the surface.

A strong aspiration to retrieve his calamities, a pronounced desire, will draw him once more into the earth's atmosphere. Here he will wander and suffer more or less in dreary solitude. His instincts will make him avidly seek contact with living persons. These spirits are the invisible but too tangible magnetic vampires, the subjective demons so well known to medieval ecstatics, nuns, and monks; to the "witches" made so famous in *The Witches' Hammer*;[7] and to certain sensitive clairvoyants, according to their own confessions. They are the blood-demons of Porphyry, the *larvae* and *lemures* of the ancients, the fiendish instruments which sent so many unfortunate and weak victims to the rack and stake. Origen held all the demons which possessed the demoniacs mentioned in the New Testament to be human "spirits." It is because Moses knew so well what they were and how terrible were the consequences to weak persons who yielded to their influence that he enacted the cruel, murderous law against such would-be "witches"; but Jesus, full of justice and divine love to humanity, healed instead of killing them. Subsequently our clergy, the pretended exemplars of Christian principles, followed the law of Moses, and quietly ignored the law of Him whom they call their "one living God" by burning dozens of thousands of such pretended "witches."

These demons seek to introduce themselves into the bodies of the simpleminded and idiots, and remain there until dislodged by a powerful and *pure* will. Jesus, Apollonius, and some of the apostles had the power to cast out devils by purifying the atmosphere within and around the patient, so as to force the unwelcome tenant to flight. Certain volatile salts are particularly obnoxious to them. Pure or even simply inoffensive human spirits fear nothing, for having rid themselves of terrestrial matter, terrestrial compounds can affect them in no wise; such spirits are like a breath. Not so with the earthbound souls and the nature spirits.

It is for these carnal terrestrial larvae, degraded human spirits, that the ancient kabbalists entertained a hope of reincarnation. But when, or how? At a fitting moment, and if helped by a sincere desire for his amendment and repentance by some strong, sympathizing person, or the will of an adept, or even a desire emanating from the erring spirit himself, provided it is powerful enough to make him throw off the burden of sinful matter. Losing all consciousness, the once bright monad is caught once more into the vortex of our terrestrial evolution, and it repasses the subordinate kingdoms and again breathes as a living child. To compute the time necessary for the completion of this process would be impossible. Since there is no perception of time in eternity, the attempt would be a mere waste of labor.

Notes

1. We give the spelling and words of this kabbalist who lived and published his works in the seventeenth century. Generally he is considered as one of the most famous alchemists among the Hermetic philosophers.
2. The most positive of materialistic philosophers agree that all that exists was evolved from ether; hence air, water, earth, and fire, the four primordial elements, must all proceed from ether and chaos, the first *Duad*; all the imponderables, whether now known or unknown, proceed from the same source. Now, if there is a spiritual essence in matter and that essence forces it to shape itself into millions of individual forms, why is it illogical to assert that each of these spiritual kingdoms in nature is peopled with beings evolved out of its own material?
3. [Originally the rest of this sentence read "only on other and inferior planets, never on this one." The author, however, later suggested that it should read as here, so the publishers have made the change as a more accurate statement of the Hindu view. See "Theories About Reincarnation and Spirits," *The Path* (New York, November 1886), 237.—Eds.]
4. R. Spence Hardy, *Eastern Monachism* (London, 1860), 6.
5. *Decline and Fall of the Roman Empire*, ch. 15.
6. Berosus, fragment preserved by Alexander Polyhistor, in Cory, *Ancient Fragments* 24.
7. [Jacob Sprenger, *Malleus maleficarum* (1487).]

10

___

Psychological and Physical Marvels

M usic is delightful to every person. Low whistling, a melodious chant, or the sounds of a flute will invariably attract reptiles in countries where they are found. We have witnessed and verified the fact repeatedly. In Upper Egypt, whenever our caravan stopped, a young traveler who believed he excelled on the flute amused the company by playing. The camel drivers and other Arabs invariably checked him, having been several times annoyed by the unexpected appearance of various families of the reptile tribe, which generally shirk an encounter with men. Finally our caravan met with a party, among whom were professional serpent charmers, and the virtuoso was then invited, for experiment's sake, to display his skill.

No sooner had he commenced than a slight rustling was heard, and the musician was horrified at suddenly seeing a large snake appear in dangerous proximity to his legs. The serpent, with uplifted head and eyes fixed on him, crawled slowly and as if unconsciously, softly undulating its body and following his every movement. Then appeared at a distance another one, then a third, and a fourth, which were speedily followed by others, until we found ourselves in quite a select company. Several of the travelers made for the backs of their camels, while others sought refuge in the cantinier's tent. But it was a vain alarm. The charmers, three in number, began their chants and incantations and, attracting the reptiles, were very soon covered with them from head to foot. As soon as the serpents approached the men, they exhibited signs of torpor and were soon plunged in a deep catalepsy. Their eyes were half closed and glazed, and their heads drooping.

There remained but one recalcitrant, a large and glossy black fellow with a spotted skin. This *mélomane* of the desert went on gracefully nodding and leaping as if it had danced on its tail all its life, keeping time to the notes of the flute. This snake would not be enticed by the "charming" of the Arabs, but kept slowly moving in the direction of the flute player, who at last took to his heels. The modern Psyllian then took out of his bag a half-withered plant, which he kept waving in the direction of the serpent. It had a strong smell of mint, and as soon as the reptile caught its odor, it followed the Arab, still erect upon its tail, but now approaching the plant. A few more seconds, and the "traditional enemy" of man was seen entwined around the arm of his charmer, became torpid in its turn, and the whole lot were then thrown together in a pool, after having their heads cut off.

Many believe that all such snakes are prepared and trained for the purpose and that they are either deprived of their fangs or have their mouths sewed up. There may doubtless be some inferior jugglers whose trickery has given rise to such an idea. But the genuine serpent charmer has too well established his claims in the East to resort to any such cheap fraud. They have the testimony on this subject of too many trustworthy travelers, including some scientists, to be accused of any such charlatanism. That the snakes, which are charmed to dance and to become harmless, are still poisonous is verified by Forbes. On "the music stopping too suddenly," says he, "or from some other cause," the serpent, which had been dancing within a circle of country people, darted among the spectators and inflicted a wound in "the throat of a young woman, who died in agony, in half an hour afterward."[1]

In India we have seen a small brotherhood of fakirs settled around a little lake, or rather a deep pool of water, the bottom of which was literally carpeted with enormous alligators. These amphibious monsters crawl out and warm themselves in the sun a few feet from the fakirs, some of whom may be motionless, lost in prayer and contemplation. So long as one of these holy beggars remains in view, the crocodiles are as harmless as kittens. But we would never advise a foreigner to risk himself alone within a few yards of these monsters.

When Iamblichus, Herodotus, Pliny, or some other ancient writer tells us of priests who caused asps to come forth from the altar of Isis, or of thaumaturgists taming with a glance the most ferocious animals, they are considered liars and ignorant imbeciles. When modern travelers tell us of the same wonders performed in the East, they are set down as enthusiastic jabberers or untrustworthy writers.

But despite materialistic skepticism, man does possess such a power as we see manifested in the above instances. When psychology and physiology become worthy of the name of sciences, Europeans will be convinced of the weird and formidable potency existing in the human will and imagination, whether exercised consciously or otherwise. And yet how easy to realize such power in spirit, if we only think of that grand truism in nature that every most insignificant atom in it is moved by spirit, which is one in its essence, for the least particle of it represents the whole; and that matter is but the concrete copy of the abstract idea, after all. In this connection, let us cite a few instances of the imperial power of even the unconscious will to create, according to the imagination or rather the faculty of discerning, images in the astral light.

The power of the imagination upon our physical condition, even after we arrive at maturity, is evinced in many familiar ways. In medicine, the intelligent physician does not hesitate to accord to it a curative or morbific potency greater than his pills and potions. He calls it the *vis medicatrix naturae,* and his first endeavor is to gain the confidence of his patient so completely that he can cause nature to extirpate the disease. Fear often kills, and grief has such a power over the subtle fluids of the body as not only to derange the internal organs but even to turn the hair white. The Renaissance Hermeticist Marsilio Ficino mentions the *signature* of the fetus with the marks of cherries and various fruits, colors, hairs, and excrescences, and acknowledges that the imagination of the mother may transform it into a resemblance of an ape, pig, dog, or any such animal.

Any anatomist who has made the development and growth of the embryo and fetus "a subject of special study" can tell, without much brain work, what daily experience and the evidence of his own eyes show him, viz., that up to a certain period the human embryo is a facsimile of a young batrachian in its first remove from the spawn—a tadpole. But no physiologist or anatomist seems to have had the idea of applying to the development of the human being—from the first instant of its physical appearance as a germ to its ultimate formation and birth—the Pythagorean esoteric doctrine of metempsychosis, so erroneously interpreted by critics. The meaning of the kabbalistic axiom, "A stone becomes a plant; a plant a beast; a beast a man," etc., was mentioned in another place in relation to the spiritual and physical evolution of man on this earth. We will now add a few words more to make the idea clearer.

What is the primitive shape of the future man? A grain or corpuscle, say some physiologists; a molecule, an ovum of the ovum, say others. If it could be analyzed—by the microscope or otherwise—of what might we to expect to find it composed? Analogically, we should say, of a nucleus of inorganic matter, deposited from the circulation at the germinating point and united with a deposit of organic matter. In other words, this infinitesimal nucleus of the future man is composed of the same elements as a stone—of the same elements as the earth, which the man is destined to inhabit. Moses is cited by the kabbalists as an authority for the remark that it required earth and water to make a living being, and thus it may be said that man first appears as a stone.

At the end of three or four weeks the ovum has assumed a plantlike appearance, one extremity having become spheroidal and the other tapering, like a carrot. Upon dissection it is found to be composed, like an onion, of very delicate laminae or coats, enclosing a liquid. The laminae approach each other at the lower end, and the embryo hangs from the root of the umbilicus almost like a fruit from the bough. The stone has now become changed, by metempsychosis, into a plant. Then the embryonic creature begins to shoot out its limbs from the inside outward, and develops its features. The eyes are visible as two black dots; the ears, nose, and mouth form depressions, like the points of a pineapple, before they begin to project. The embryo develops into an animal-like fetus—the shape of a tadpole—and like an amphibious reptile lives in water and develops from it. Its monad has not yet become either human or immortal, for the kabbalists tell us that comes only at the "fourth hour." One by one, the fetus assumes the characteristics of the human being; the first flutter of the immortal breath passes through his being; he moves; nature opens the way for him and ushers him into the world; and the divine essence settles in the infant frame, which it will inhabit until the moment of physical death, when man becomes a spirit.

This mysterious process of a nine-months formation, the kabbalists call the completion of the "individual cycle of evolution." As the fetus develops from the *liquor amnii* in the womb, so the earths germinate from the universal ether, or astral fluid, in the womb of the universe. These cosmic children, like their pigmy inhabitants, are first nuclei; then ovules; then gradually mature; and becoming mothers in their turn, develop mineral, vegetable, animal, and human forms. From center to circumference, from the imperceptible vesicle to the uttermost conceivable bounds of the cosmos, these glorious thinkers, the kabbalists, trace cycle merging into cycle, containing and contained in an endless series. The embryo evolving in its prenatal sphere, the individual in his family, the family in the state, the state in mankind, the earth in our system, that system in its central universe, the universe in the cosmos, and the cosmos in the First Cause—the Boundless and Endless. So runs their philosophy of evolution:

> All are but parts of one stupendous whole
> Whose body Nature is; and God the soul.[2]

> Worlds without number
> Lie in this bosom like children.

A case was reported in American newspapers of a boy who was killed by a stroke of lightning. Upon stripping the body, there was found imprinted upon his breast the faithful picture of a tree which grew near the window he was facing at the time of the catastrophe and which was also felled by the lightning. This electrical photography, which was accomplished by the blind forces of nature, furnishes an analogy by which we may understand how the mental images of the mother are transmitted to the unborn child. Her pores are opened; she exudes an odic emanation which is but another form of the *akasa*, the electricity or life principle, which, according to Reichenbach, produces mesmeric sleep and consequently is *magnetism*. Magnetic currents develop themselves into electricity upon their exit from the body. The image of an object making a violent impression on the mother's mind is instantly projected into the astral light, or the universal ether, which Jevons and Babbage, as well as the authors of *The Unseen Universe*, tell us is the repository of the *spiritual* images of all forms, and even human thoughts. Her magnetic emanations attract and unite themselves with the descending current which already bears the image upon it. It rebounds and, repercussing more or less violently, impresses itself upon the fetus, according to the very formula of physiology which shows how every maternal feeling reacts on the offspring.

Éliphas Lévi, who is certainly one of the best authorities on certain points among kabbalists, says: "Pregnant women are, more than others, under the influence of the astral light, which assists in the formation of their child, and constantly presents to them the reminiscences of forms with which it is filled. It is thus that very virtuous women deceive the malignity of observers by equivocal resemblances. They often impress upon the fruit of their marriage an image which has struck them in a dream, and thus are the same physiognomies perpetuated from age to age."[3]

If the soul of man is really an outcome of the essence of this universal soul, an infinitesimal fragment of this first creative principle, it must of necessity partake in degree of all the attributes of the demiurgic power. As the creator, breaking up the chaotic mass of dead, inactive matter, shaped it into form, so man, if he knew his powers, could to a degree do the same. As Phidias, gathering together the loose particles of clay and moistening them with water, could give plastic shape to the sublime idea evoked by his creative faculty, so the mother who knows her power can fashion the coming child into whatever form she likes. Ignorant of his powers, the sculptor produces only an inanimate though ravishing figure of inert matter; while the soul of the mother, violently affected by her imagination, blindly projects into the astral light an image of the object which impressed it and which, by repercussion, is stamped upon the fetus.

Science tells us that the law of gravitation assures us that any displacement which takes place in the very heart of the earth will be felt throughout the universe, "and we may even imagine that the same thing will hold true of those molecular motions which accompany thought."[4] Speaking of the transmission of energy throughout the universal ether or astral light, the same authority says: "Continual photographs of all occurrences are thus produced and retained. A large portion of the energy of the universe may thus be said to be invested in such pictures."

Such philosophers as Democritus, Aristotle, Euripides, Epicurus (or rather his biographer, Lucretius), Aeschylus, and other ancient writers, whom the materialists so willingly quote as authoritative opponents of the dreamy Platonists, were only theorists, not adepts. The latter, when they did write, either had their works burned by Christian mobs or they worded them in a way to be intelligible only to the initiated. Who of their modern detractors can warrant that he knows *all* about what they knew? Diocletian alone burned whole libraries of works upon the "secret arts"; not a manuscript treating the art of making gold and silver escaped the wrath of this unpolished tyrant.

What has become of all these books, and who knows the treasures of learning they may have contained? We know but one thing for a certainty, and that is that pagan and Christian vandals destroyed such literary treasures wherever they could find them. The emperor Alexander Severus went all over Egypt to collect the sacred books on mysticism and mythology, pillaging every temple; and the Ethiopians—old as the Egyptians were in arts and sciences—claimed a priority of antiquity as well as of learning over them, as well they might, for they were known in India at the earliest dawn of history.

We also know that Plato learned more secrets in Egypt than he was allowed to mention; and that, according to Champollion, all that is really good and scientific in Aristotle's works—so prized in our day by our modern inductionists—is due to his divine Master; and that, as a logical sequence, Plato having imparted the profound secrets he had learned from the priests of Egypt to his initiated disciples orally—who in their turn passed it from one generation to another of adepts—the latter know more of the occult powers of nature than our philosophers of the present day.

And here we may mention the works of Hermes Trismegistus as well. How many have had the opportunity to read them as they were in the Egyptian sanctuaries? In his *De mysteriis*, Iamblichus attributes to Hermes 1,100 books, and Seleucus reckons no less than 20,000 of his works before the period of Menes. Eusebius saw but forty-two of these "in his time," he says, and the last of the six books on medicine treated that art as practiced in the darkest ages; and Diodorus says that it was the oldest of the legislators, Mnevis, the third successor of Menes, who received them from Hermes.

Of such manuscripts as have descended to us, most are Latin retranslations of Greek translations, made principally by the Neoplatonists from the original books preserved by some adepts. Marsilio Ficino, who was the first to publish them in Venice, in 1488, has given us mere extracts, and the most important portions seemed to have been either overlooked or purposely omitted as too dangerous to publish in those days of *auto da fé*. And so it happens now that when a kabbalist, who has devoted his whole life to studying occultism and has conquered the great secret, ventures to remark that the Kabbala alone leads to the knowledge of the Absolute in the Infinite and the Indefinite in the Finite, he is laughed at by those who, because they know the impossibility of squaring the circle as a physical problem, deny the possibility of its being done in the metaphysical sense.

The unanimous testimony of mankind is said to be an irrefutable proof of truth. About what was testimony ever more unanimous than that for thousands of ages, among civilized people as among the most barbarous, there has existed a firm and unwavering belief in magic?

NOTES

1. J. Forbes, *Oriental Memoirs* (London, 1813), 1:44; 2:387.
2. [Pope, *Essay on Man* 1: 267.]
3. *Dogme et rituel de la haute magie* 1:113.
4. E. Fournié, *Physiologie du système nerveux cérébro-spinal* (Paris, 1872).

11

The "Impassable Chasm"

Esoteric philosophers held that everything in nature is but a materialization of spirit. The Eternal First Cause is latent spirit, they said,
and matter from the beginning. "In the beginning was the word . . .
and the word was God." While conceding the idea of such a God
to be an unthinkable abstraction to human reason, they claimed that
the unerring human instinct grasped it as a reminiscence of something
concrete to it though intangible to our physical senses. With the first
idea, which emanated from the double-sexed and hitherto inactive
Deity, the first motion was communicated to the whole universe, and
the electric thrill was instantaneously felt throughout the boundless
space. Spirit begat force, and force matter; and thus the latent deity
manifested itself as a creative energy.

When? At what point of the eternity, or how? The question must
always remain unanswered, for human reason is unable to grasp the
great mystery. But, though spirit-matter was from all eternity, it was in
the latent state; the evolution of our visible universe must have had a
beginning. To our feeble intellect, this beginning may seem so remote
as to appear to us eternity itself—a period inexpressible in figures or
language.

This mystery of first creation, which was ever the despair of science,
is unfathomable, unless we accept the doctrine of the Hermeticists.
Though matter is coeternal with spirit, that matter is certainly not
our visible, tangible, and divisible matter, but its extreme sublimation.
Pure spirit is but one remove higher. Unless we allow man to have
been evolved out of this primordial spirit-matter, how can we ever
come to any reasonable hypothesis as to the genesis of animate beings?
Darwin begins his evolution of species at the lowest point and traces

100

upward. His only mistake may be that he applies his system at the wrong end. Could he remove his quest from the visible universe into the invisible, he might find himself on the right path. But then he would be following in the footsteps of the Hermeticists.

We have shown elsewhere that the Secret Doctrine does not concede immortality to all men alike. If the human soul has neglected during its lifetime to receive its illumination from its Divine Spirit, our personal God, then it becomes difficult for the gross and sensual man to survive his physical death for a great length of time. No more than the misshapen monster can live long after its physical birth, can the soul, once it has become too material, exist after its birth into the spiritual world. The viability of the astral form is so feeble that the particles cannot cohere firmly once it is slipped out of the unyielding capsule of the external body. Its particles, gradually obeying the disorganizing attraction of universal space, finally fly asunder beyond the possibility of reaggregation. Upon the occurrence of such a catastrophe, the individual ceases to exist; his glorious augoeides has left him. During the intermediary period between his bodily death and the disintegration of the astral form, the latter, bound by magnetic attraction to its ghastly corpse, prowls about and sucks vitality from susceptible victims. The man, having shut out of himself every ray of the divine light, is lost in darkness and therefore clings to the earth and the earthy.

No astral soul, even that of a pure, good, and virtuous man, is immortal in the strictest sense; "from elements it was formed—to elements it must return." But while the soul of the wicked vanishes and is absorbed without redemption, that of every other person, even moderately pure, simply changes its ethereal particles for still more ethereal ones; and while there remains in it a spark of the Divine, the individual man, or rather his personal ego, cannot die. "After death," says Proclus, "the soul (the spirit) continueth to linger in the aerial body (astral form), till it is entirely purified from all angry and voluptuous passions . . . then doth it put off by a second dying the aerial body as it did the earthly one. Whereupon the ancients say that there is a celestial body always joined with the soul, which is immortal, luminous, and starlike."

But we will now turn from our digression to further consider the question of *reason* and *instinct*. The latter, according to the ancients, proceeded from the divine, the former from the purely human. One (the instinct) is the product of the senses, a sagaciousness shared by the lowest animals, even those who have no reason; the other is the product of the reflective faculties—*noêtikon*, denoting judiciousness and human intellectuality. Therefore, an animal devoid of reasoning powers has in its inherent instinct an unerring faculty which is but that spark of the divine which lurks in every particle of inorganic matter—itself materialized spirit. In the Jewish Kabbala, the second and third chapters of Genesis are explained thus: When the second Adam is created "out of the dust," matter has become so gross that it reigns supreme. Out of its lusts evolves woman, and Lilith has the best of spirit. The Lord God, "walking in the garden in the cool of the day" (the sunset of spirit, or divine light obscured by the shadows of matter), curses not only them who have committed the sin, but even the ground itself, and all living things—the tempting serpent-matter above all.

Who but the kabbalists are able to explain this seeming act of injustice? How are we to understand this cursing of all created things, innocent of any crime? The allegory is evident. The curse inheres in matter itself. Henceforth it is doomed to struggle against its own grossness for purification; the latent spark of divine spirit, though smothered, is still there; and its invincible attraction upward compels it to struggle in pain and labor to free itself.

Logic shows us that as all matter had a common origin, it must have attributes in common, and as the vital and divine spark is in man's material body, so it must lurk in every subordinate species. The latent mentality, which in the lower kingdoms is recognized as semiconsciousness, consciousness, and instinct, is largely subdued in man. Reason, the outgrowth of the physical brain, develops at the expense of instinct—the flickering reminiscence of a once divine omniscience: spirit. Reason, the badge of the sovereignty of physical man over all other physical organisms, is often put to shame by the instinct of an animal. As his brain is more perfect than that of any other creature, its emanations must naturally produce the highest results of mental action; but reason avails only for the consideration of material things; it is incapable of helping its possessor to a knowledge of spirit.

In losing instinct, man loses his intuitional powers, which are the crown and ultimatum of instinct. Reason is the clumsy weapon of the scientists, intuition the unerring guide of the seer. Instinct teaches plant and animal their seasons for the procreation of their species, and guides the dumb brute to find his appropriate remedy in the hour of sickness. Reason—the pride of man—fails to check the propensities of his matter and brooks no restraint upon the unlimited gratification of his senses. Far from leading him to be his own physician, its subtle sophistries lead him too often to his own destruction.

Prayer opens the spiritual sight of man, for prayer is desire, and desire develops will; the magnetic emanations proceeding from the body at every effort—whether mental or physical—produce self-magnetization and ecstasy. Plotinus recommended solitude for prayer as the most efficient means of obtaining what is asked; and Plato advised those who prayed to "remain silent in the presence of the divine ones, till they remove the cloud from thy eyes, and enable thee to see by the light which issues from themselves." Apollonius always isolated himself from men during the "conversation" he held with God, and whenever he felt the necessity for divine contemplation and prayer, he wrapped himself, head and all, in the drapery of his white woolen mantle. "When thou prayest enter into thy closet and when thou hast shut thy door, pray to thy Father in secret," says the Nazarene, the pupil of the Essenes.

Every human being is born with the rudiment of the inner sense called *intuition*, which may be developed into what the Scotch know as "second sight." All the great philosophers, who like Plotinus, Porphyry, and Iamblichus employed this faculty, taught the doctrine.

Were there no inner sight or intuition, the Jews would never have had their Bible, nor the Christians Jesus. What both Moses and Jesus gave to the world was the fruit of their intuition or illumination. What their subsequent elders and teachers allowed the world to understand was dogmatic misrepresentations, too often blasphemy.

For over fifteen centuries, thanks to the blindly brutal persecutions of those great vandals of early Christian history, Constantine and Justinian, ancient wisdom slowly degenerated until it gradually sank into the deepest mire of monkish superstition and ignorance. The Pythagorean "knowledge of things that are"; the profound erudition of the Gnostics; the world and time-honored teachings of the great philosophers—all were rejected as doctrines of Antichrist and paganism and committed to the flames. With the last seven wise men

103

of the Orient, the remnant group of the Neoplatonists—Hermeias, Priscianus, Diogenes, Eulamius, Damascius, Simplicius, and Isidorus, who fled from the fanatical persecutions of Justinian to Persia—the reign of wisdom closed. The books of Thoth (or Hermes Trismegistus), which contain within their sacred pages the spiritual and physical history of the creation and progress of our world, were left to mold in oblivion and contempt for ages.

That which is now termed the superstitious verbiage and gibberish of mere heathens and savages, composed many thousands of years ago, may be found to contain the master key to all religious systems. The cautious sentence of St. Augustine, which says that "there is no false religion which does not contain some elements of truth," may yet be triumphantly proved correct; the more so as, far from being original with the Bishop of Hippo, it was borrowed by him from the works of Ammonius Saccas, the great Alexandrian teacher.

It was Ammonius who first taught that every religion was based on one and the same truth, which is the wisdom found in the books of Thoth (Hermes Trismegistus), from which books Pythagoras and Plato had learned all their philosophy. And the doctrines of the former he affirmed to have been identical with the earliest teachings of the Brahmans—now embodied in the oldest Vedas. "The name Thoth," says Professor Wilder, "means a college or assembly," and "it is not improbable that the books were so named as being the collected oracles and doctrines of the sacerdotal fraternity of Memphis."[1]

But one thing is certainly known, and that is that before the word philosopher was first pronounced by Pythagoras at the court of the king of the Phliasians, the Secret Doctrine or wisdom was identical in every country. Therefore it is in the oldest texts—those least polluted by subsequent forgeries—that we have to look for the truth.

There is a phenomenon in nature that is unknown and therefore rejected by physiology and psychology in our age of unbelief. This phenomenon is a state of *half-death*. The body is virtually dead; and if left alone, in cases of persons in whom matter does not predominate over spirit and wickedness is not so great as to destroy spirituality, their astral soul will disengage itself by gradual efforts, and when the last link is broken it finds itself separated forever from its earthly body. Equal magnetic polarity will violently repulse the ethereal man from the decaying organic mass. The whole difficulty lies in that (1) the ultimate moment of separation between the two is believed to be when the body is declared dead by science, and (2) the same science has a prevailing unbelief in the existence of either soul or spirit in man.

If we are forced to believe in vampirism, it is on the strength of two irrefragable propositions of occult psychological science: (1) the astral soul is a separable distinct entity of our ego and can roam far away from the body without breaking the thread of life, and (2) the corpse is not *utterly* dead, and while it can yet be reentered by its tenant, the latter can gather sufficient material emanations from it to enable itself to appear in a quasi-terrestrial shape.

Therefore the Devil, in his various transformations, can be but a fallacy. When we imagine that we see, hear, and feel him, it is but too often the reflection of our own wicked, depraved, and polluted soul that we see, hear, and feel. Like attracts like, they say; thus, according to the mood in which our astral form oozes out during the hours of sleep, according to our thoughts, pursuits, and daily occupations, all of which are fairly impressed upon the plastic capsule called the *human soul*, the latter attracts around itself spiritual beings congenial to itself. Hence some dreams and visions are pure and beautiful, others fiendish and beastly. The person awakes and either hastens to the confessional or laughs in callous indifference at the thought.

Let the student of occult sciences make his own nature as pure and his thoughts as elevated as those of Indian seers, and he may sleep unmolested by vampire, incubus, or succubus. Around the insensible form of such a sleeper the immortal spirit sheds a power divine that protects it from evil approaches, as though it were a crystal wall.

NOTE

1. *New Platonism and Alchemy* (Albany, NY, 1869), 6.

12

———

Realities and Illusion

The unexplained mysteries of nature are many, and of those presumably explained hardly one may be said to have become absolutely intelligible. There is not a plant or mineral which has disclosed the last of its properties to the scientists. What do the naturalists know of the intimate nature of the vegetable and mineral kingdoms? How can they feel confident that for every one of the discovered properties there may not be many powers concealed in the *inner* nature of the plant or stone, which are only waiting to be brought in relation with some other plant, mineral, or force of nature to manifest themselves in what is termed a "supernatural manner"?

Men of science have speculated from time immemorial what this vital force or life principle is. To our mind, the Secret Doctrine alone is able to furnish the clue. Exact science recognizes only five powers in nature—one molar, and four molecular; the kabbalists recognize seven, and in these two additional ones is enwrapped the whole mystery of life. One of these is immortal spirit, whose reflection is connected by invisible links even with inorganic matter; the other we leave to every one to discover for himself.

Science regards man as an aggregation of atoms temporarily united by a mysterious force called the life principle. To the materialist, the only difference between a living and a dead body is that in the one case that force is active, in the other latent. When it is extinct or entirely latent the molecules obey a superior attraction, which draws them asunder and scatters them through space.

This dispersion must be death, if it is possible to conceive such a thing as death where the very molecules of the dead body manifest an intense vital energy. If death is but the stoppage of a digesting, locomotive, and thought-grinding machine, how can death be actual and not relative, before that machine is thoroughly broken up and its particles dispersed? So long as any of them cling together, the centripetal vital force may overmatch the dispersive centrifugal action. Says Éliphas Lévi: "Change attests movement, and movement only reveals life. The corpse would not decompose if it were dead; all the molecules which compose it are living and struggle to separate. And would you think that the spirit frees itself first of all to exist no more? That thought and love can die when the grossest forms of matter do not die? If the change should be called death, we die and are born again every day, for every day our forms undergo change."[1]

The kabbalists say that a man is not dead when his body is entombed. Death is never sudden; for, according to Hermes, nothing goes in nature by violent transitions. Everything is gradual, and as it required a long and gradual development to produce the living human being, so time is required to completely withdraw vitality from the carcass. "Death can no more be an absolute end than birth a real beginning. Birth proves the preexistence of the being, as death proves immortality," says the same French kabbalist.

The kabbalists say that death occurs at the instant when both the astral body, or life principle, and the spirit part forever with the corporeal body. The scientific physician who denies both astral body and spirit, and admits the existence of nothing more than the life principle, judges death to occur when life is apparently extinct. When the beating of the heart and the action of the lungs cease and rigor mortis is manifested, and especially when decomposition begins, they pronounce the patient dead. But the annals of medicine teem with examples of "suspended animation" as the result of asphyxia by drowning, the inhalation of gases, and other causes; life being restored in the case of drowning persons even after they had been apparently dead for twelve hours.

But in the case of what physiologists would call "real death," but which is not actually so, the astral body has withdrawn; perhaps local decomposition has set in. How shall the man be brought to life again? The answer is that the interior body must be forced back into the exterior one, and vitality reawakened in the latter. The clock has run down, and it must be wound. If death is absolute, if the organs have not only ceased to act but have lost the susceptibility of renewed action, then the whole universe would have to be thrown into chaos to resuscitate the corpse—a miracle would be demanded.

But as we said before, the man is not dead when he is cold, stiff, pulseless, breathless, and even showing signs of decomposition; he is not dead when buried, nor afterward, until a certain point is reached. That point is when the vital organs have become so decomposed that if reanimated, they could not perform their customary functions, when the mainspring and cogs of the machine, so to speak, are so eaten away by rust that they would snap upon the turning of the key. Until that point is reached, the astral body may be caused, without miracle, to reenter its former tabernacle, either by an effort of its own will or under the resistless impulse of the will of one who knows the potencies of nature and how to direct them. The spark is not extinguished, but only latent—latent as the fire in the flint, or the heat in the cold iron.

The kabbalists, as we find them interpreted by Éliphas Lévi in his *Science des esprits* [Pt. 2, ch. 2], say, "When a man falls into the last sleep, he is plunged at first into a sort of dream, before gaining consciousness in the other side of life. He sees, then, either in a beautiful vision or in a terrible nightmare, the paradise or hell in which he believed during his mortal existence. This is why it often happens that the affrighted soul breaks violently back into the terrestrial life it has just left and why some who were really dead, i.e., who if left alone and quiet would have peaceably passed away forever in a state of unconscious lethargy, when entombed too soon, reawake to life in the grave."

Lévi says that resuscitation is not impossible while the vital organism remains undestroyed and the astral spirit is yet within reach. "Nature," he says, "accomplishes nothing by sudden jerks, and eternal death is always preceded by a state which partakes somewhat of the nature of lethargy. It is a torpor which a great shock or the magnetism of a powerful will can overcome." He accounts in this manner for the resuscitation of the dead man thrown upon the bones of Elisha. He explains it by saying that the soul was hovering at that moment near the body; the burial party, according to tradition, were attacked by robbers; and their fright communicating itself sympathetically to it, the soul was seized with horror at the idea of its remains being desecrated and "reentered violently into its body to raise and save it." Those who believe in the survival of the soul can see in this incident nothing of a supernatural character—it is only a perfect manifestation of natural law. To narrate to the materialist such a case, however well attested, would be but idle talk; the theologian, always looking beyond nature for a special providence, regards it as a prodigy. Éliphas Lévi says: "They attributed the resuscitation to the contact with the bones of Elisha; and worship of relics dates logically from his epoch" [*La Science des esprits* Pt. 3, ch. 2].

Circumstances, independent of his own volition, either at birth or subsequently, may modify a person's aura so that strange manifestations, physical or mental, diabolical or angelic, may take place. Such mediumship, as well as mediatorship, has existed on earth since the first appearance here of living man. The former is the yielding of weak, mortal flesh to the control and suggestions of spirits and intelligences other than one's own immortal demon. It is literally obsession and possession; and mediums who pride themselves on being the faithful slaves of their "guides" and who repudiate with indignation the idea of "controlling" the manifestations, could not very well deny the fact without inconsistency. This mediumship is typified in the story of Eve succumbing to the reasonings of the serpent; of Pandora peeping in the forbidden casket and letting loose on the world sorrow and evil; and of Mary Magdalene, who from having been obsessed by "seven devils" was finally redeemed by the triumphant struggle of her immortal spirit, touched by the presence of a holy mediator, against the dweller. This mediumship, whether beneficent or maleficent, is always passive. Happy are the pure in heart, who by that very cleanness of their inner nature unconsciously repel the dark spirits of evil. For verily they have no other weapons of defense but that inborn goodness and purity. Mediumism, as practiced in our days, is a more undesirable gift than the robe of Nessus.

"The tree is known by its fruits." Side by side with passive mediums in the progress of the world's history appear active mediators. We designate them by this name for lack of a better one. The ancient witches and wizards, and those who had a "familiar spirit," generally made of their gifts a trade; and the Obeah woman of En-Dor—so well defined by Henry More—though she may have killed her calf for Saul, accepted hire from other visitors. In India, the jugglers, who by the way are less so than many a modern medium, and the *Essaoua* or sorcerers and serpent charmers of Asia and Africa all exercise their gifts for money.

Not so with the mediators, or hierophants. Buddha was a mendicant and refused his father's throne. The "Son of Man had not where to lay his head"; the chosen apostles provided "neither gold, nor silver, nor brass in their purses." Apollonius gave one half of his fortune to his relatives, the other half to the poor; Iamblichus and Plotinus were renowned for charity and self-denial; the fakirs or holy mendicants of India are fairly described by Jacolliot; the Pythagorean Essenes and Therapeutae believed their hands defiled by the contact of money. When the apostles were offered money to impart their spiritual powers, Peter, notwithstanding that the Bible shows him a coward and thrice a renegade, still indignantly spurned the offer, saying: "Thy money perish with thee, because thou hast thought that the gift of God may be purchased with money" [Acts 7.20]. These men were mediators, guided merely by their own personal spirit or divine soul, and availing themselves of the help of spirits but so far as these remained in the right path.

It is erroneous to speak of a medium having *powers* developed. A passive medium has no power. He has a certain moral and physical condition which induces emanations, or an aura in which his controlling intelligences can live and by which they manifest themselves. He is only the vehicle through which they display their power. This aura varies day by day and, as would appear from Mr. Crookes's experiments, even hour by hour. It is an external effect resulting from interior causes. The medium's moral state determines the kind of spirits that come, and the spirits that come reciprocally influence the medium intellectually, physically, and morally. The perfection of his mediumship is in ratio to his passivity, and the danger he incurs is in equal degree. When he is fully "developed"—perfectly passive—his own astral spirit may be benumbed and even crowded out of his body, which is then occupied by an elemental or, what is worse, by a human fiend of the eighth sphere, who proceeds to use it as his own. But too often the cause of the most celebrated crime is to be sought in such possessions.

Physical mediumship depending upon passivity, its antidote suggests itself naturally: let the medium cease being passive. Spirits never control persons of positive character who are determined to resist all extraneous influences.

The Hermetic axiom maintains that only the First Cause and its direct emanations, our spirits (scintillas from the eternal central sun which will be reabsorbed by it at the end of time), are incorrupt-ible and eternal. But in possession of a knowledge of occult natural forces yet undiscovered by the materialists, they asserted that both physical life and mechanical motion could be prolonged indefinitely. The philosopher's stone had more than one meaning attached to its mysterious origin.

Élie de Beaumont has recently reasserted the old doctrine of Hermes that there is a terrestrial circulation comparable to that of the blood of man.[2] Now, since it is a doctrine as old as time that nature is continually renewing her wasted energies by absorption from the source of energy, why should the child differ from the parent? Why may not man, by discovering the source and nature of this recuperative energy, extract from the earth herself the juice or quintessence with which to replenish his own forces? This may have been the great secret of the alchemists. Stop the circulation of the terrestrial fluids and we have stagnation, putrefaction, death; stop the circulation of the fluids in man, and stagnation, absorption, calcification from old age, and death ensue. If the alchemists had simply discovered some chemical compound capable of keeping the channels of our circulation unclogged, would not all the rest easily follow? And why, we ask, if the surface waters of certain mineral springs have such virtue in the cure of disease and the restoration of physical vigor, is it illogical to say that, if we could get the first runnings from the alembic of nature in the bowels of the earth, we might perhaps find that the fountain of youth was no myth after all.

"God geometrizes," said Plato.[3] "The laws of nature are the thoughts of God," exclaimed Oersted 2,000 years later. "His thoughts are im-mutable," repeated the solitary student of Hermetic lore, "therefore it is in the perfect harmony and equilibrium of all things that we must seek the truth." And thus, proceeding from the indivisible unity, he found emanating from it two contrary forces, each acting through the other and producing equilibrium, and the three were but one, the Pythagorean Eternal Monad. The primordial point is a circle; the circle squaring itself from the four cardinal points becomes a quaternary, the perfect square, having at each of its four angles a letter of the mirific name, the sacred Tetragram. It is the four Buddhas who came and have passed away; the Pythagorean *tetraktys*—absorbed and resolved by the one eternal No-Being.

111

Tradition declares that on the dead body of Hermes at Hebron an Ozarim (an initiate) found the tablet known as the *Smaragdine*. It contains, in a few sentences, the essence of the Hermetic wisdom. To those who read but with their bodily eyes, the precepts will suggest nothing new or extraordinary, for it merely begins by saying that it speaks not fictitious things, but that which is true and most certain.

What is below is like that which is above, and what is above is similar to that which is below to accomplish the wonders of one thing.

As all things were produced by the mediation of one being, so all things were produced from this one by adaptation.

Its father is the sun, its mother is the moon.

It is the cause of all perfection throughout the whole earth.

Its power is perfect if it is changed into earth.

Separate the earth from the fire, the subtle from the gross, acting prudently and with judgment.

Ascend with the greatest sagacity from the earth to heaven, and then descend again to earth, and unite together the power of things inferior and superior; thus you will possess the light of the whole world, and all obscurity will fly away from you.

This thing has more fortitude than fortitude itself, because it will overcome every subtle thing and penetrate every solid thing.

By it the world was formed.

This mysterious thing is the universal, magical agent, the astral light, which in the correlations of its forces furnishes the alkahest, the philosopher's stone, and the elixir of life. Hermetic philosophy names it Azoth, the soul of the world, the celestial virgin, the great Magnes, etc. Physical science knows it as "heat, light, electricity, and magnetism" but, by ignoring its spiritual properties and the occult potency contained in ether, rejects everything it ignores.

The philosophical cross, the two lines running in opposite directions, the horizontal and the perpendicular, the height and breadth, which the geometrizing Deity divides at the intersecting point and which forms the magical as well as the scientific quaternary when it is inscribed within the perfect square, is the basis of the occultist. Within its mystical precinct lies the master key which opens the door of every science, physical as well as spiritual. It symbolizes our human existence, for the circle of life circumscribes the four points of the cross, which represent in succession birth, life, death, and immortality. Everything in this world is a trinity completed by the quaternary,[4] and every element is divisible on this same principle. Physiology can divide man *ad infinitum*, as physical science has divided the four primal and principal elements in several dozens of others; she will not succeed in changing either. Birth, life, and death will ever be a trinity completed only at the cyclic end. Even were science to change the longed for immortality into annihilation, it will still ever be a quaternary, for God "geometrizes"!

The whole of the present work is a protest against such a loose way of judging the ancients. To be thoroughly competent to criticize their ideas and assure oneself whether their ideas were distinct and "appropriate to the facts," one must have sifted these ideas to the very bottom. It is idle to repeat that which we have frequently said and that which every scholar ought to know, namely that the quintessence of their knowledge was in the hands of the priests, who never wrote them, and in those of the "initiates" like Plato, who did not dare write them. Therefore, those few speculations on the material and spiritual universes which they did put in writing could not enable posterity to judge them rightly, even if the early Christian vandals, the later crusaders, and the fanatics of the Middle Ages had not destroyed three parts of that which remained of the Alexandrian library and its later schools.

Who then, of those who turn away from the Secret Doctrine as being "unphilosophical" and therefore unworthy of a scientific thought, has a right to say that he has studied the ancients, that he is aware of all that they knew and, knowing now far more, knows also that they knew little, if anything? This Secret Doctrine contains the alpha and the omega of universal science; therein lies the corner and the keystone of all ancient and modern knowledge; and alone in this "unphilosophical" doctrine remains buried the *absolute* in the philosophy of the dark problems of life and death.

NOTES

1. *La Science des esprits* (Paris, 1865).
2. [*Recherches* (Paris, 1829–30).]

3. See Plutarch, *Symposiacs* 8.2.1.

4. In ancient nations the Deity was a trine supplemented by a goddess—*Arba-il*, or fourfold God.

13

Egyptian Wisdom

How came Egypt by her knowledge? When broke the dawn of that civilization whose wondrous perfection is suggested by the bits and fragments supplied to us by the archaeologists? Alas! the lips of Memnon are silent, and no longer utter oracles; the Sphinx has become a greater riddle in her speechlessness than was the enigma propounded to Oedipus.

What Egypt taught to others she certainly did not acquire by the international exchange of ideas and discoveries with her Semitic neighbors, nor did she receive her stimulus from them. "The more we learn of the Egyptians," observes the writer of a recent article, "the more marvelous they seem!" From whom could she have learned her wondrous arts, the secrets of which died with her? She sent no agents throughout the world to learn what others knew, but the wise men of neighboring nations resorted to her for knowledge. Proudly secluding herself within her enchanted domain, the fair queen of the desert created wonders as if by the sway of a magic staff. "Nothing," remarks the same writer, "proves that civilization and knowledge then rise and progress with her as in the case of other peoples, but everything seems to be referable, in the same perfection, to the earliest dates. That no nation knew as much as herself is a fact demonstrated by history."

May we not assign as a reason for this remark the fact that until very recently nothing was known of Old India? That these two nations, India and Egypt, were akin? That they were the oldest in the group of nations; and that the Eastern Ethiopians—the mighty builders—had come from India as a matured people, bringing their civilization with them, and colonizing the perhaps unoccupied Egyptian territory?

As far back as we can glance into history—to the reign of Menes, the most ancient of the kings that we know anything about—we find proofs that the Egyptians were far better acquainted with hydrostatics and hydraulic engineering than ourselves. The gigantic work of turning the course of the Nile—or rather of its three principal branches—and bringing it to Memphis was accomplished during the reign of that monarch, who appears to us as distant in the abyss of time as a far-glimmering star in the heavenly vault. Wilkinson says Menes took accurately the measure of the power which he had to oppose, and he constructed a dyke "whose lofty mounds and enormous embankments turned the water eastward," and since that time the river is contained in its new bed.[1] Herodotus has left us a poetical but still accurate description of the lake Moeris, so called after the Pharaoh who caused this artificial sheet of water to be formed.

If we now turn to architecture, we find displayed before our eyes wonders which baffle all description. Referring to the temples of Philae, Abu Simbel, Dendera, Edfu, and Karnak, Professor Carpenter remarks that "these stupendous and beautiful erections . . . these gigantic pyramids and temples" have a "vastness and beauty" which are "still impressive after the lapse of thousands of years." He is amazed at "the admirable character of the workmanship, the stones in most cases being fitted together with astonishing nicety, so that a knife could hardly be thrust between the joints."[2]

According to [Baron Christian C. J. von] Bunsen, who is considered to have made the most exact calculations, the mass of masonry in the great Pyramid of Cheops measures 82,111,000 feet and would weigh 6,316,000 tons. The immense numbers of squared stones show us the unparalleled skill of the Egyptian quarrymen. Speaking of the great pyramid, Kenrick says: "The joints are scarcely perceptible, not wider than the thickness of silver paper, and the cement is so tenacious that fragments of the casing-stones still remain in their original position, notwithstanding the lapse of many centuries, and the violence by which they were detached."[3] Who of our modern architects and chemists will rediscover the indestructible cement of the oldest Egyptian buildings?

"The skill of the ancients in quarrying," says Bunsen, "is displayed the most in the extracting of the huge blocks, out of which obelisks and colossal statues were hewn—obelisks ninety feet high, and statues

116

forty feet high, made out of one stone!"[4] There are many such. They did not blast out the blocks for these monuments but adopted the following scientific method: "Instead of using huge iron wedges, which would have split the stone, they cut a small groove for the whole length of, perhaps, 100 feet, and inserted in it, close to each other, a great number of dry wooden wedges; after which they poured water into the groove, and the wedges swelling and bursting simultaneously, with a tremendous force, broke out the huge stone, as neatly as a diamond cuts a pane of glass."

Modern geographers and geologists have demonstrated that these monoliths were brought from a prodigious distance and have been at a loss to conjecture how the transport was effected. Old manuscripts say that it was done by the help of portable rails. These rested upon inflated bags of hide, rendered indestructible by the same process as that used for preserving the mummies. These ingenious air-cushions prevented the rails from sinking in the deep sand. Manetho mentions them, and remarks that they were so well prepared that they would endure wear and tear for centuries.

The date of the hundreds of pyramids in the Valley of the Nile is impossible to fix by any of the rules of modern science, but Herodotus informs us that each successive king erected one to commemorate his reign and serve as his sepulcher. But Herodotus did not tell all, although he knew that the real purpose of the pyramid was very different from that which he assigns to it. Were it not for his religious scruples, he might have added that externally it symbolized the creative principle of nature and illustrated also the principles of geometry, mathematics, astrology, and astronomy. Internally, it was a majestic fane in whose somber recesses were performed the Mysteries, and whose walls had often witnessed the initiation scenes of members of the royal family. The porphyry sarcophagus, which Professor Piazzi Smyth, Astronomer Royal of Scotland, degrades into a corn bin, was the baptismal font, upon emerging from which, the neophyte was "born again" and became an adept.

Before Greece came into existence, the arts of the Egyptians were ripe and old. Land measuring, an art resting on geometry, the Egyptians certainly knew well. And how could a people so skilled in natural philosophy as the Egyptians not be proportionately skilled in psychology and spiritual philosophy? The temple was the nursery of the highest civilization, and it alone possessed that higher knowledge of magic which was in itself the quintessence of natural philosophy. The occult powers of nature were taught in the greatest secrecy and the most wonderful cures were performed during the performing of the Mysteries. Herodotus (*History* 2.50) acknowledges that the Greeks learned all they knew, including the sacred services of the temple, from the Egyptians, and because of that their principal temples were consecrated to Egyptian divinities.

Wilkinson, corroborated later by others, says that the Egyptians divided time and knew the true length of the year and the precession of the equinoxes. By recording the rising and setting of the stars, they understood the particular influences which proceed from the positions and conjunctions of all heavenly bodies, and therefore their priests, prophesying meteorological changes as accurately as our modern astronomers, could in addition astrologize through astral motions. Though the sober and eloquent Cicero may be partially right in his indignation against the exaggerations of the Babylonian priests, who "assert that they have preserved upon monuments observations extending back during an interval of 470,000 years" (*De divinatione* 2.46), still the period at which astronomy had arrived at its perfection with the ancients is beyond the reach of modern calculation.

Egypt is the birthplace and the cradle of chemistry. The chemistry of colors seems to have been thoroughly well known in that country. Facts are facts. Where among our painters are we to search for the artist who can decorate our walls with imperishable colors? Ages after our pigmy buildings have crumbled into dust, and the cities enclosing them have themselves become shapeless heaps of brick and mortar with forgotten names—long after that will the halls of Karnak and Luxor (El-Uxor) still be standing; and the gorgeous mural paintings of the latter will doubtless be as bright and vivid 4,000 years hence as they were 4,000 years ago, and are today.

As to their knowledge in medicine, now that one of the lost *Books of Hermes* has been found and translated by Ebers [*Papyros Ebers* (Leipzig, 1875)], the Egyptians can speak for themselves. That they understood about the circulation of the blood appears certain from the healing manipulations of the priests, who knew how to draw blood downward, stop its circulation for a while, etc. A more careful study of their bas-reliefs representing scenes taking place in the healing hall of various temples will easily demonstrate it. They had their dentists and oculists, and no doctor was allowed to practice more than one specialty, which certainly warrants the belief that they lost fewer patients in those days than our physicians do now. It is also asserted by some authorities that the Egyptians were the first people in the world who introduced trial by jury, although we doubt this ourselves.

But the Egyptians were not the only people of remote epochs whose achievements place them in so commanding a position before the view of posterity. Besides others whose history is at present shut in behind the mists of antiquity—such as the prehistoric races of the two Americas, of Crete, of the Troad, of the Lacustrians, of the submerged continent of the fabled Atlantis, now classed with myths—the deeds of the Phoenicians stamp them with almost the character of demigods.

A writer in the *National Quarterly Review* (December 1875, 32:124) says that the Phoenicians were the earliest navigators of the world, founded most of the colonies of the Mediterranean, and voyaged to whatever other regions were inhabited. They visited the Arctic regions, whence they brought accounts of eternal days without a night, which Homer has preserved for us in the *Odyssey*. From the British Isles they imported tin into Africa, and Spain was a favorite site for their colonies. The description of Charybdis so completely answers to the maelstrom that, as this writer says: "It is difficult to imagine it to have had any other prototype." Their explorations, it seems, extended in every direction, their sails whitening the Indian Ocean, as well as the Norwegian fjords. Different writers have accorded to them the settlement of remote localities, while the entire southern coast of the Mediterranean was occupied by their cities. Some suppose these hardy navigators of Arctic and Antarctic waters to have been the progenitors of the races which built the temples and palaces of Palenque and Uxmal, of Copan and Arica.[5]

The perfect identity of the rites, ceremonies, traditions, and even the names of the deities, among the Mexicans and ancient Babylonians and Egyptians, are a sufficient proof of South America being peopled by a colony which mysteriously found its way across the Atlantic. When? At what period? History is silent on that point; but those who consider that there is no tradition, sanctified by ages, without a certain sediment of truth at the bottom of it, believe in the Atlantis legend.

There are, scattered throughout the world, a handful of thoughtful and solitary students, who pass their lives in obscurity, far from the rumors of the world, studying the great problems of the physical and spiritual universes. They have their secret records in which are preserved the fruits of the scholastic labors of the long line of recluses whose successors they are. The knowledge of their early ancestors, the sages of India, Babylonia, Nineveh, and the imperial Thebes; the legends and traditions commented upon by the masters of Solon, Pythagoras, and Plato in the marble halls of Heliopolis and Sais, traditions which, in their days, already seemed to hardly glimmer from behind the foggy curtain of the past—all this, and much more, is recorded on indestructible parchment, and passed with jealous care from one adept to another.

These men believe the story of Atlantis to be no fable but maintain that at different epochs of the past huge islands, and even continents, existed where now there is but a wild waste of waters. In those submerged temples and libraries the archaeologist would find, could he but explore them, the materials for filling all the gaps that now exist in what we imagine is history. They say that at a remote epoch a traveler could traverse what is now the Atlantic Ocean, almost the entire distance by land, crossing in boats from one island to another, where narrow straits then existed.

The Aztecs appeared in more than one way to have resembled the ancient Egyptians in civilization and refinement. Among both peoples, magic or the arcane natural philosophy was cultivated to the highest degree. Add to this that Greece, the "later cradle of the arts and sciences," and India, cradle of religions, were and are still devoted to its study and practice—and who shall venture to discredit its dignity as a study and its profundity as a science?

There never was nor can there be more than one universal religion, for there can be but one truth concerning God. Like an immense chain whose upper end, the alpha, remains invisibly emanating from a Deity—in *statu abscondito* with every primitive theology—it encircles our globe in every direction; it leaves not even the darkest corner unvisited, before the other end, the omega, turns back on its way to be again received where it first emanated. On this divine chain was strung the exoteric symbology of every people. Their variety of form is powerless to affect their substance, and under their diverse ideal types of the universe of matter, symbolizing its vivifying principles, the uncorrupted immaterial image of the spirit of being guiding them is the same.

Thus it is that all the religious monuments of old, in whatever land or climate, are the expression of the same identical thoughts, the key to which is in the esoteric doctrine. It would be vain, without studying the latter, to seek to unriddle the mysteries enshrouded for centuries in the temples and ruins of Egypt and Assyria or those of Central America, British Columbia, and the Nagkon-Wat of Cambodia. If each of these was built by a different nation, and no nation had had intercourse with the others for ages, it is also certain that all were planned and built under the direct supervision of the priests. And the clergy of every nation, though practicing rites and ceremonies which may have differed externally, had evidently been initiated into the same traditional mysteries which were taught all over the world.

In order to institute a better comparison between the specimens of prehistoric architecture to be found at the most opposite points of the globe, we have but to point to the grandiose Hindu ruins of Ellora in the Dekkan, the Mexican Chichén Itzá in Yucatan, and the still grander ruins of Copan in Guatemala. They present such features of resemblance that it seems impossible to escape the conviction that they were built by peoples moved by the same religious ideas, who had reached an equal level of highest civilization in arts and sciences.

What explanation can the archaeologists and philologists—in short, the chosen host of academicians—give us? None whatever. At best they have but hypotheses, every one of which is likely to be pulled down by its successor—a pseudotruth, perhaps, like the first. The keys to the biblical miracles of old and to the phenomena of modern days, and the problems of psychology, physiology, and the many "missing links" which have so perplexed scientists of late are all in the hands of secret fraternities. This mystery must be unveiled some day. But till then dark skepticism will constantly interpose its threatening, ugly shadow between God's truths and the spiritual vision of mankind; and many are those who, infected by the mortal epidemic of our century— hopeless materialism—will remain in doubt and mortal agony as to whether, when man dies, he will live again, although the question has been solved by long bygone generations of sages.

The answers are there. They may be found on the timeworn granite pages of cave temples, on sphinxes, propylons, and obelisks. They have stood there for untold ages, and neither the rude assault of time nor the still ruder assault of Christian hands have succeeded in obliterating their records. All are covered with the problems which were solved, perhaps by the archaic forefathers of their builders. The solution follows each question; and this the Christian could not appropriate, for no one except the initiates has understood the mystic writing. The key was in the keeping of those who knew how to commune with the invisible Presence and who had received, from the lips of mother Nature herself, her grand truths. And so stand these monuments like mute forgotten sentinels on the threshold of that unseen world, whose gates are thrown open but to a few elect.

Defying the hand of Time, the vain inquiry of profane science, and the insults of the revealed religions, they will disclose their riddles to none but the legatees of those by whom they were entrusted with the Mystery. The cold, stony lips of the once vocal Memnon and of these hardy sphinxes keep their secrets well. Who will unseal them? Who of our modern, materialistic dwarfs and unbelieving Sadducees will dare to lift the Veil of Isis?

Notes

1. [*Manners and Customs of the Ancient Egyptians* (London, 1837), 1:89.]
2. [W. B. Carpenter, *Ancient and Modern Egypt* (London, 1866).]
3. [J. Kenrick, *Ancient Egypt under the Pharaohs* (London, 1850), 1:124.]
4. [*Egypt's Place* 2:155.]
5. Such is not our opinion. They were probably built by the Atlanteans.

14

India: The Cradle of the Race

The Secret Doctrine has for many centuries been like the symbol-ical "man of sorrows" of the prophet Isaiah [53.1–3]. "Who hath believed our report?" its martyrs have repeated from one generation to another. The doctrine has grown up before its persecutors "as a tender plant and as a root out of a dry ground; it hath no form, nor comeliness . . . it is despised and rejected of men; and they hid their faces from it. . . . They esteemed him not."

There need be no controversy as to whether this doctrine agrees or not with the iconoclastic tendency of the skeptics of our times. It agrees with truth and that is enough. It would be idle to expect that it would be believed by its detractors and slanderers. But the tenacious vitality it exhibits all over the globe, wherever there are a group of men to quarrel over it, is the best proof that the seed planted by our fathers on "the other side of the flood" was that of a mighty oak, not the spore of a mushroom theology. No lightning of human ridicule can fell to the ground and no thunderbolts ever forged by the Vulcans of science are powerful enough to blast the trunk, or even scar the branches of this world tree of Knowledge.

Had the allegories contained in the first chapters of Genesis been better understood, even in their geographical and historical sense, which involve nothing at all esoteric, the claims of its true interpreters, the kabbalists, could hardly have been rejected for so long a time. Every student of the Bible must be aware that the first and second chapters of Genesis could not have proceeded from the same pen. They are evidently allegories and parables,[1] for the two narratives of the creation and peopling of our earth diametrically contradict each

123

other in nearly every particular of order, time, place, and methods employed in the so-called creation.

In accepting the narratives literally and as a whole, we lower the dignity of the unknown Deity. We drag him down to the level of humanity and endow him with the peculiar personality of man, who needs the "cool of the day" to refresh him, who rests from his labors, and who is capable of anger, revenge, and even of using precautions against man, "lest he put forth his hand and take also of the tree of life." (A tacit admission on the part of the Deity that man could do it, if not prevented by sheer force.) But in recognizing the allegorical coloring of the description of what may be termed historical facts, we find our feet instantly on firm ground.

To begin with—the garden of Eden as a locality is no myth at all; it belongs to those landmarks of history which occasionally disclose to the student that the Bible is not all mere allegory. "Eden, or the Hebrew *gan-eden*, meaning the park or the garden of Eden, is an archaic name of the country watered by the Euphrates and its many branches, from Asia and Armenia to the Erythraian Sea." In the Chaldean *Book of Numbers*, its location is designated in numerals, and in the Rosicrucian cipher manuscript left by Count Saint Germain it is fully described. In the Assyrian Tablets, it is rendered *gan-dunias*.[2]

"Behold," say the *Elohim* of Genesis, "the man is become as one of us." The Elohim may be accepted in one sense for gods or powers, and taken in another for the *Aleim*, or priests, the hierophants initiated into the good and the evil of this world; for there was a college of priests called the *Aleim*, while the head of their caste, or the chief of the hierophants, was known as *Yava Aleim*. Instead of becoming a neophyte and gradually obtaining his esoteric knowledge through a regular initiation, an *Adam*, or man, uses his intuitional faculties and prompted by the Serpent—*Woman* and matter—tastes of the Tree of Knowledge, the esoteric or Secret Doctrine, unlawfully.

Though containing the same substratum of esoteric truth as every early cosmogony, the Hebrew Scripture wears on its face the marks of its double origin. Its Genesis is purely a reminiscence of the Babylonian captivity. The names of places, men, and even objects can be traced from the original text to the Chaldeans and the Akkadians, the progenitors and Aryan instructors of the former. It is strongly contested that the Akkad tribes of Chaldea, Babylonia, and Assyria were in any way cognate with the Brahmans of Hindustan; but there are more proofs in favor of this opinion than otherwise. They were simply emigrants on their way to Asia Minor from India, the cradle of humanity, and their sacerdotal adepts tarried to civilize and initiate a barbarian people. Babylonian civilization was neither born nor developed in that country. It was imported from India, and the importers were Brahmanical Hindus.

No people in the world have ever attained to such a grandeur of thought in ideal conceptions of the Deity and its offspring, man, as the Sanskrit metaphysicians and theologians. "My complaint against many translators and Orientalists," says Jacolliot, "while admiring their profound knowledge, is that not having lived in India, they fail in exactness of expression and in comprehension of the symbolical sense of poetic chants, prayers, and ceremonies, and thus too often fall into material errors, whether of translation or appreciation."[3] Further, this author, who, after a long residence in India and the study of its literature, is better qualified to testify than those who have never been there, tells us that "the life of several generations would scarce suffice merely to read the works that ancient India has left us on history, ethics (*morale*), poetry, philosophy, religion, different sciences, and medicine."

It is to India, the country less explored and less known than any other, that all the other great nations of the world are indebted for their languages, arts, legislature, and civilization. Its progress was impeded for a few centuries before our era—for as Jacolliot shows, "India had already passed the period of her splendor" at the epoch of the great Macedonian conqueror [Alexander]—but was completely studied in the subsequent ages. The evidence of her past glories lies in her literature. What people in all the world can boast of such a literature, which, were the Sanskrit less difficult, would be more studied than now? Hitherto the general public has had to rely for information on a few scholars who, notwithstanding their great learning and trustworthiness, are unequal to the task of translating and commenting upon more than a few books out of the almost countless number that despite the vandalism of the missionaries are still left to swell the mighty volume of Sanskrit literature. And to do even so much is the labor of a European's lifetime. Hence people judge hastily, and often make the most ridiculous blunders.

We affirm that, if Egypt furnished Greece with her civilization and the latter bequeathed hers to Rome, Egypt herself had, in those unknown ages when Menes reigned,[4] received her laws, her social institutions, her arts, and her sciences, from pre-Vedic India.[5] Therefore it is in that old initiatrix of the priests—adepts of all the other countries—that we must seek for the key to the great mysteries of humanity.

And when we indiscriminately say "India," we do not mean the India of our modern days but that of the archaic period. In those ancient times countries which are now known to us by other names were all called India. There was an Upper, a Lower, and a Western India, the latter of which is now Persia (Iran). The countries now named Tibet, Mongolia, and Great Tartary were also considered by the ancient writers as India. We will now give a legend in relation to those places which science now fully concedes to have been the cradle of humanity.

Tradition says, and the records of the *Great Book* explain, that long before the days of Ad-am and his inquisitive wife, He-va, where now are found but salt lakes and desolate barren deserts, there was a vast inland sea, which extended over Middle Asia, north of the proud Himalayan range, and its western prolongation. An island, which for its unparalleled beauty had no rival in the world, was inhabited by the last remnant of the race which preceded ours. This race could live with equal ease in water, air, or fire, for it had an unlimited control over the elements. These were the "Sons of God"—not those who saw the daughters of men, but the real *Elohim*, though in the Oriental Kabbala they have another name. It was they who imparted Nature's most weird secrets to men, and revealed to them the ineffable and now lost "word."

This word, which is no word, has traveled once around the globe and still lingers as a far-off dying echo in the hearts of some privileged men. The hierophants of all the sacerdotal colleges were aware of the existence of this island, but the "word" was known only to the *Yava-Aleim*, or chief lord of every college, and was passed to his successor only at the moment of death. There were many such colleges and the old classic authors speak of them.

We have already seen that it is one of the universal traditions accepted by all the ancient peoples that there were many races of

126

men anterior to our present races. Each of these was distinct from the one which preceded it; and each disappeared as the following appeared. In *Manu*, six such races are plainly mentioned as having succeeded each other.

There was no communication with the fair island by sea, but subterranean passages known only to the chiefs communicated with it in all directions. Tradition points to many of the majestic ruins of India, Ellora, Elephanta, and the caverns of Ajanta (Chandor range), which belonged once to those colleges and with which were connected such subterranean ways. Who can tell but that the lost Atlantis—which is also mentioned in the *Secret Book*, but under another name, pronounced in the sacred language—did not still exist in those days? The great lost continent might have perhaps been situated south of Asia, extending from India to Tasmania. If the hypothesis now so much doubted, and positively denied by some learned authors who regard it as a joke of Plato's, is ever verified, then perhaps scientists will believe that the description of the god-inhabited continent was not altogether fable. And they may then perceive that Plato's guarded hints and the fact of his attributing the narrative to Solon and the Egyptian priests were but a prudent way of imparting the fact to the world and, by cleverly combining truth and fiction, of disconnecting himself from a story which the obligations imposed at initiation forbade him to divulge.

To continue the tradition, we have to add that the class of hierophants was divided into two distinct categories: those who were instructed by the "Sons of God" of the island and were initiated in the divine doctrine of pure revelation, and others who inhabited the lost Atlantis—if such must be its name—and who, being of another race, were born with a sight which embraced all hidden things and was independent of both distance and material obstacle. In short, they were the fourth race of men mentioned in the *Popol Vuh*, whose sight was unlimited and who knew all things at once. They were perhaps what we would now term "natural-born mediums," who neither struggled nor suffered to obtain their knowledge, nor did they acquire it at the price of any sacrifice.

Therefore, while the former walked in the path of their divine instructors and, acquiring their knowledge by degrees, learned at the same time to discern the evil from the good, the born adepts of Atlantis blindly followed the insinuations of the great and invisible "Dragon," the King *Thevetat* (the Serpent of Genesis?). Thevetat had neither learned nor acquired knowledge, but, to borrow an expression of Dr. Wilder in relation to the tempting Serpent, he was "a sort of Socrates who *knew* without being initiated." Thus, under the evil insinuations of their demon, Thevetat, the Atlantis race became a nation of wicked magicians. In consequence of this, war was declared, the story of which would be too long to narrate; its substance may be found in the disfigured allegories of the race of Cain, the giants, and that of Noah and his righteous family. The conflict came to an end by the submersion of Atlantis, which finds its imitation in the stories of the Babylonian and Mosaic flood: the giants and magicians "and all flesh died . . . and every man." All except Xisuthros and Noah, who are substantially identical with the great Father of the Thlinkithians in the *Popol Vuh*, the sacred book of the Guatemalans, which also tells of his escaping in a large boat, like the Hindu Noah—Vaivasvata.

If we believe the tradition at all, we have to credit the further story that from the intermarrying of the progeny of the hierophants of the island and the descendants of the Atlantean Noah there sprang up a mixed race of righteous and wicked. On the one hand, the world had its Enochs, Moseses, Gautama Buddhas, its numerous "Saviors," and great hierophants; and on the other hand, its "natural magicians" who, through lack of the restraining power of proper spiritual enlightenment and because of weakness of physical and mental organizations, unintentionally perverted their gifts to evil purposes. Moses had no word of rebuke for those adepts in prophecy and other powers who had been instructed in the colleges of esoteric wisdom[6] mentioned in the Bible. His denunciations were reserved for such as either wittingly or otherwise debased the powers inherited from their Atlantean ancestors to the service of evil spirits and to the injury of humanity. His wrath was kindled against the spirit of *Ob*, not that of *Od*.

The ruins which cover both Americas and are found on many West Indian islands are all attributed to the submerged Atlanteans. As well as the hierophants of the old world (which in the days of Atlantis was almost connected with the new one by land), the magicians of the now submerged country had a network of subterranean passages running in all directions.

Around no other locality, not even Peru, hang so many traditions as around the Gobi Desert. In independent Tartary this howling waste of shifting sand was once, if report speaks correctly, the seat of one of the richest empires the world ever saw. Beneath the surface are said to lie such wealth in gold, jewels, statuary, arms, utensils, and all that indicates civilization, luxury, and fine arts as no existing capital of Christendom can show today. The Gobi sand moves regularly from east to west before terrific gales that blow continually. Occasionally some of the hidden treasures are uncovered, but not a native dare touch them, for the whole district is under the ban of a mighty spell. Death would be the penalty. Bahti—hideous but faithful gnomes—guard the hidden treasures of this prehistoric people, awaiting the day when the revolution of cyclic periods shall again cause their story to be known for the instruction of mankind.

According to local tradition, the tomb of Ghengis Khan still exists near Lake Tabasun Nor. Within lies the Mongolian Alexander as though asleep. After three more centuries he will awake and lead his people to new victories and another harvest of glory. Though this prophetic tradition be received with ever so many grains of salt, we can affirm as a fact that the tomb itself is no fiction, nor has its amazing richness been exaggerated.

The district of the Gobi wilderness and, in fact, the whole area of independent Tartary and Tibet is jealously guarded against foreign intrusion. Those who are permitted to traverse it are under the particular care and pilotage of certain agents of the chief authority and are in duty bound to convey no intelligence respecting places and persons to the outside world. Except for this restriction, we might contribute to these pages accounts of exploration, adventure, and discovery that would be read with interest. The time will come, sooner or later, when the dreadful sand of the desert will yield up its long buried secrets, and then there will indeed be unlooked-for mortifications for our modern vanity.

For a belief to have become universal, it must have been founded on an immense accumulation of facts, tending to strengthen it from one generation to another. At the head of all such beliefs stands magic, or, if one would prefer, occult psychology. Who, of those who appreciate its tremendous powers even from its feeble, half-paralyzed effects in our civilized countries, would dare disbelieve in our days the assertions of Porphyry and Proclus that even inanimate objects, such as statues of gods, could be made to move and exhibit a factitious life for a few moments?

Be this as it may, the religion of the ancients is the religion of the future. A few centuries more, and there will linger no sectarian beliefs in any of the great religions of humanity. Brahmanism and Buddhism, Christianity and Islam will all disappear before the mighty rush of facts. "I will pour out my spirit upon all flesh," writes the prophet Joel [2.28]. "Verily I say unto you . . . greater works than these shall you do," promises Jesus [John 14.12]. But this can only come to pass when the world returns to the grand religion of the past, to the knowledge of those majestic systems which by far preceded Brahmanism and even the primitive monotheism of the ancient Chaldeans. Meanwhile, we must remember the direct effects of the revealed mystery. The only means by which the wise priests of old could impress upon the grosser senses of the multitudes the idea of the omnipotency of the creative will or First Cause was the divine animation of inert matter—the soul infused into it by the potential will of man, the microcosmic image of the great Architect—and the transportation of ponderous objects through space and material obstacles.

We know that from the remotest ages there has existed a mysterious, awful science under the name of *theopoiia*. This science taught the art of endowing the various symbols of gods with temporary life and intelligence. Statues and blocks of inert matter became animated under the potential will of the hierophant. The fire stolen by Prometheus had in the struggle fallen down to earth; it embraced the lower regions of the sky and settled in the waves of the universal ether as the potential *akasa* of the Hindu rites. We breathe and imbibe it into our organic system with every mouthful of fresh air. Our organism is full of it from the instant of our birth. But it becomes potential only under the influx of will and spirit.

Left to itself, this life principle will blindly follow the laws of nature and, according to conditions, will produce health and an exuberance of life or cause death and dissolution. But guided by the will of the adept, it becomes obedient; its currents restore the equilibrium in organic bodies and produce physical and psychological miracles well known to mesmerizers. Infused in inorganic and inert matter, they create an appearance of life, hence motion. If to that life an individual intelligence, a personality, is wanting, then the operator must either send his *scin-lac*, his own astral spirit, to animate it, or use his power over the region of nature spirits to force one of them to infuse his entity into the marble, wood, or metal, or else be helped by human spirits. But the latter—except the vicious, earthbound class[7]—will *not* infuse their essence into these inanimate objects. They leave the lower kinds to produce the similitude of life and animation, and only send their influence through the intervening spheres like a ray of divine light, when the so-called "miracle" is required for a good purpose. The condition—and this is a law in spiritual nature—is purity of motive, purity of the surrounding magnetic atmosphere, and personal purity of the operator. Thus it is that a pagan "miracle" may be by far holier than a Christian one.

Thus, gradually but surely, will the whole of antiquity be vindicated. Truth will be carefully sifted from exaggeration; much that is now considered fiction may yet be proved fact, and the "facts and laws" of modern science found to belong to the limbo of exploded myths.

The few elevated minds who interrogate nature instead of prescribing laws for her guidance, who do not limit her possibilities by the imperfections of their own powers, and who only disbelieve because they do not know, we would remind of that apothegm of Narada, the ancient Hindu philosopher:

> Never utter these words: "I do not know this—therefore it is false."

> One must study to know, know to understand, understand to judge.

NOTES

1. See Paul to the Galatians 4.24 and Matthew 13.10–15.
2. A. Wilder says that "Gan-dunias" is a name of Babylonia.
3. *La Bible dans l'Inde* (Paris, 1869, trans. London, 1870), 16.
4. Bunsen gives the first year of Menes as 3645 B.C. and of Manetho as 3892 B.C., *Egypt's Place* 5:33–34.
5. Louis Jacolliot, in *La Bible dans l'Inde* [Pt. 1, ch. 6], affirms the same.
6. 2 Kings 22.14; 2 Chronicles 34.22.

7. These, after their bodily death, unable to soar higher and attached to terrestrial regions, delight in the society of the kind of elementals which by their affinity with vice attract them the most. They identify themselves with these to such a degree that they very soon lose sight of their own identity and become a part of the elementals, the help of which they need to communicate with mortals. But as the nature spirits are not immortal, so the human elementaries who have lost their divine guide—spirit—can last no longer than the essence of the elements composing their astral bodies holds together.

Part Two

RELIGION

15

The Church: Where Is It?

The God of the Unitarians is a bachelor. The Deity of the Presbyterians, Methodists, Congregationalists, and the other orthodox Protestant sects is a spouseless Father with one Son, who is identical with Himself. In the attempt to outvie each other in the erection of their sixty-two thousand and odd churches, prayer houses, and meeting halls in which to teach these conflicting theological doctrines, $354,485,581 has been spent. The value of the Protestant parsonages alone, in which are sheltered the disputants and their families, is roughly calculated to approximate $54,115,297. Moreover, $16,179,887 is contributed every year for current expenses of the Protestant denominations only. One Presbyterian church in New York cost a round million; a Catholic altar alone, one-fourth as much![1]

We will not mention the multitude of smaller sects, communities, and extravagantly original little heresies in this country which spring up one year to die out the next, like so many spores of fungi after a rainy day. We will not even stop to consider the alleged millions of Spiritualists, for the majority lack the courage to break away from their respective religious denominations. These are the backdoor Nicodemuses.

And now, with Pilate, let us inquire, What is truth? Where is it to be searched for amid this multitude of warring sects? Each claims to be based upon divine revelation, and each to have the keys of the celestial gates. Are any in possession of this rare truth? Or must we exclaim with the Buddhist philosopher, "There is but one truth on earth, and it is unchangeable—and this is that there is no truth on it!"

Though we have no disposition whatever to trench upon the ground that has been so exhaustively gleaned by those learned scholars who

135

have shown that every Christian dogma has its origin in a heathen rite, still the facts which they have exhumed since the enfranchisement of science will lose nothing by repetition. Besides, we propose to examine these facts from a different and perhaps rather novel point of view: that of the old philosophies as esoterically understood. These we have barely glanced at in our first part. We will use them as the standard by which to compare Christian dogmas and miracles with the doctrines and phenomena of ancient magic. Since the materialists deny the phenomena without investigation, and since the theologians in admitting them offer us the poor choice of two palpable absurdities—the Devil and miracles—we can lose little by applying to the theurgists, and they may actually help us to throw a great light upon a very dark subject.

The only characteristic difference between modern Christianity and the old heathen faiths is the belief of the former in a personal devil and in hell. "The Aryan nations had no devil," says Max Müller. "Pluto, though of a somber character, was a very respectable personage; and Loki (the Scandinavian), though a mischievous person, was not a fiend."[2]

The same may be said of hell. Hades was quite a different place from our region of eternal damnation and might be termed rather an intermediate state of purification. Neither does the Scandinavian *Hel* or *Hela* imply either a state or a place of punishment; for when Frigga, the griefstricken mother of Balder, the white god, who died and found himself in the dark abodes of the shadows (Hades), sent Hermod (a son of Thor) in quest of her beloved child, the messenger found him in the inexorable region—alas! but still comfortably seated on a rock, and reading a book.[3] The Norse kingdom of the dead is moreover situated in the higher latitudes of the Polar regions; it is a cold and cheerless abode, and neither the gelid halls of Hela nor the occupation of Balder presents the least similitude to the blazing hell of eternal fire and the miserable "damned" sinners with which the Church so generously peoples it. Neither does the Egyptian Amenti, the region of judgment and purification, nor the Andhera—the abyss of darkness of the Hindus; for even the fallen angels hurled into it by Siva are allowed by Parabrahman to consider it as an intermediate state, in which an opportunity is afforded them to prepare for higher degrees of purification and redemption from their wretched condition.

136

The Gehenna of the New Testament was a locality outside the walls of Jerusalem, and in mentioning it Jesus used but an ordinary metaphor. Whence then came the dreary dogma of hell, that Archimedean lever of Christian theology, with which they have succeeded to hold in subjection the numberless millions of Christians for nineteen centuries? Assuredly not from the Jewish scriptures, and we appeal for corroboration to any well-informed Hebrew scholar. The only designation of something approaching hell in the Bible is Gehenna or Hinnom, a valley near Jerusalem, where Tophet was situated, a place where a fire was perpetually kept for sanitary purposes.

There are strange traditions current in various parts of the East—on Mount Athos and in the Desert of Nitria, for instance—among certain monks and with learned Rabbis in Palestine, who pass their lives in commenting upon the Talmud. They say that not all the rolls and manuscripts, reported in history to have been burned by Caesar, by the Christian mob in 389, and by the Arab General Amru, perished as it is commonly believed. The story they tell is the following.

In 51 B.C., at the time of the contest for the throne between Cleopatra and her brother Dionysius Ptolemy, the Bruchion, which contained over seven hundred thousand rolls, all bound in wood and fireproof parchment, was undergoing repairs; and a great portion of the original manuscripts, considered among the most precious and not duplicated, were stored away in the house of one of the librarians. As the fire which consumed the rest was but the result of accident, no precautions had been taken at the time. But they add that several hours passed between the burning of the fleet, set on fire by Caesar's order, and the moment when the first buildings situated near the harbor caught fire in their turn and that all the librarians, aided by several hundred slaves attached to the museum, succeeded in saving the most precious of the rolls. So perfect and solid was the fabric of the parchment that while in some rolls the inner pages and the wood binding were reduced to ashes, of others the parchment binding remained unscorched.

These particulars were all written out in Greek, Latin, and the Chaldeo-Syriac dialect by a learned youth named Theodas, one of the scribes employed in the museum. One of these manuscripts is alleged to be preserved till now in a Greek convent; the person who narrated the tradition to us had seen it himself. He said that many more will see it and learn where to look for important documents when a certain prophecy is fulfilled, adding that most of these works could be found in Tartary and India.[4]

The monk showed us a copy of the original which, of course, we could read only poorly, as we claim but little erudition in the matter of dead languages. But we were so particularly struck by the vivid and picturesque translation of the holy father that we perfectly remember some curious paragraphs, which run, as far as we can recall them, as follows: "When the Queen of the Sun (Cleopatra) was brought back to the half-ruined city, after the fire had devoured the Glory of the World; and when she saw the mountains of books—or rolls—covering the half-consumed steps of the *estrada*; and when she perceived that the inside was gone and the indestructible covers alone remained, she wept in rage and fury, and cursed the meanness of her fathers who had grudged the cost of the real Pergamos for the inside as well as the outside of the precious rolls." Further, our author, Theodas, indulges in a joke at the expense of the queen for believing that nearly all the library was burned, when in fact hundreds and thousands of the choicest books were safely stored in his own house and those of other scribes, librarians, students, and philosophers.

No more do sundry very learned Copts, scattered all over the East in Asia Minor, Egypt, and Palestine, believe in the total destruction of the subsequent libraries. For instance, they say that out of the library of Attalus III of Pergamum, presented by Antony to Cleopatra, not a volume was destroyed. At that time, according to their assertions, from the moment that the Christians began to gain power in Alexandria—about the end of the fourth century—and Anatolius, Bishop of Laodicea, began to insult the national gods, the pagan philosophers and learned theurgists adopted effective measures to preserve the repositories of their sacred learning. But history is far from being complete in the miserable remnants of books, which, crossing so many ages, have reached our own learned century; it fails to give the facts relating to the first five centuries of Christianity which are preserved in the numerous traditions current in the East. Unauthenticated as these may appear, there is unquestionably in the heap of chaff much good grain.

That these traditions are not oftener communicated to Europeans is not strange, when we consider how apt our travelers are to render themselves antagonistic to the natives by their skeptical bearing and, occasionally, dogmatic intolerance. When exceptional men, like some archaeologists who knew how to win the confidence and even friendship of certain Arabs, are favored with precious documents, it is declared simply a "coincidence." And yet there are widespread traditions of the existence of certain subterranean and immense galleries in the neighborhood of Ishmonia—the "petrified city"—in which are stored numberless manuscripts and rolls. For no amount of money would the Arabs go near it. At night, they say, from the crevices of the desolate ruins sunk deep in the unwatered sands of the desert, stream the rays from lights carried to and fro in the galleries by no human hands. The Afrits study the literature of the antediluvian ages, according to their belief, and the Jinn learns from the magic rolls the lesson of the following day.

It certainly does seem as if the events of the first centuries of Christianity were but the reflection of the images thrown upon the mirror of the future at the time of the Exodus. During the stormy days of Irenaeus, the Platonic philosophy, with its mystical submersion into Deity, was not so obnoxious after all to the new doctrine as to prevent the Christians from helping themselves to its abstruse metaphysics in every way and manner. Allying themselves with the ascetical therapeutae—forefathers and models of the Christian monks and hermits—it was in Alexandria, let it be remembered, that they laid the first foundations of the purely Platonic trinitarian doctrine. It later became the Plato-Philonean doctrine as we know it now.

Plato considered the divine nature under a threefold modification of the First Cause, the reason or Logos, and the soul or spirit of the universe. "The three archical or original principles," says Gibbon, "were represented in the Platonic system as three gods, united with each other by a mysterious and ineffable generation."[5] Blending this transcendental idea with the more hypostatic figure of the Logos of Philo—whose doctrine was that of the oldest Kabbala and who viewed the King Messiah as the Metatron, or "the angel of the Lord," the *Legatus* descended in flesh, but not the Ancient of Days Himself— the Christians clothed Jesus, the son of Mary, with this mythical representation of the Mediator for the fallen race of Adam. Under this unexpected garb his personality was all but lost. In the modern Jesus of the Christian Church we find the ideal of the imaginative

Irenaeus, not the adept of the Essenes, the obscure reformer from Galilee. We see him under the disfigured Plato-Philonean mask, not as the disciples heard him on the mount.

So far then the heathen philosophy had helped them in the building of the principal dogma. But when the theurgists of the third Neo-platonic school, deprived of their ancient Mysteries, strove to blend the doctrines of Plato with those of Aristotle and by combining the two philosophies added to their theosophy the primeval doctrines of the Oriental Kabbala, then the Christians instead of rivals became persecutors. Once the metaphysical allegories of Plato were being prepared to be discussed in public in the form of Grecian dialectics, all the elaborate system of the Christian trinity would be unraveled and the divine prestige completely upset. The eclectic school, revers-ing the order, had adopted the inductive method; and this method became its death knell. Of all things on earth, logic and reasonable explanations were the most hateful to the new religion of mystery; for they threatened to unveil the whole groundwork of the trinitarian conception and to apprise the multitude of the doctrine of emanations, and thus destroy the unity of the whole. It could not be permitted, and it was not. History records the "Christlike" means that were resorted to.

The universal doctrine of emanations, adopted from time immemo-rial by the greatest schools which taught the kabbalistic, Alexandrian, and Oriental philosophers, gives the key to that panic among the Christian fathers.

But if the Gnostics were destroyed, the Gnosis, based on the secret science of sciences, still lives. It is the earth which helps the woman and which is destined to open her mouth to swallow up medieval Christianity, the usurper and assassin of the great master's doctrine. The ancient Kabbala, the Gnosis or traditional secret knowledge, was never without its representatives in any age or country. The trinities of initiates, whether passed into history or concealed under the im-penetrable veil of mystery, are preserved and impressed throughout the ages.

And this very trinitarian idea, as well as the so bitterly denounced doctrine of emanations—whence is their remotest origin? The answer is easy, and every proof is now at hand: in the sublime and profoundest of all philosophies, that of the universal "Wisdom Religion," the first traces of which historical research now finds in the old pre-Vedic religion of India.

Truly the fate of many a future generation hung on a gossamer thread in the days of the third and fourth centuries. Had not the Emperor sent to Alexandria in 389 a rescript—which was forced from him by the Christians—for the destruction of every idol, our own century would never have had a Christian mythological pantheon of its own. Never did the Neoplatonic school reach such a height of philosophy as when nearest its end. Uniting the mystic theosophy of old Egypt with the refined philosophy of the Greeks, nearer to the ancient Mysteries of Thebes and Memphis than they had been for centuries; versed in the science of soothsaying and divination, as in the art of the Therapeutists; and friendly with the acutest men of the Jewish nation, who were deeply imbued with the Zoroastrian ideas—the Neoplatonists tended to amalgamate the old wisdom of the Oriental Kabbala with the more refined conceptions of the Occidental theosophists. Notwithstanding the treason of the Christians, who saw fit for political reasons after the days of Constantine to repudiate their tutors, the influence of the new Platonic philosophy is conspicuous in the subsequent adoption of dogmas, the origin of which can be traced but too easily to that remarkable school. Though mutilated and disfigured, they still preserve a strong family likeness which nothing can obliterate.

But if the knowledge of the occult powers of nature opens the spiritual sight of man, enlarges his intellectual faculties, and leads him unerringly to a profounder veneration for the Creator, on the other hand ignorance, dogmatic narrow-mindedness, and a childish fear of looking to the bottom of things invariably lead to fetish worship and superstition.

If we now stop to consider another of the fundamental dogmas of Christianity, the doctrine of atonement, we may trace it as easily back to heathendom. This cornerstone of a Church which had believed herself built on a firm rock for long centuries is now excavated by science and proved to come from the Gnostics. The New Testament never appeared in its complete form, such as we find it now, till 300 years after the period of apostles, and the *Zohar* and other kabbalistic books are found to belong to the first century before our era, if not to be far older still.

The Gnostics entertained many of the Essenean ideas, and the Essenes had their "greater" and "minor" Mysteries at least two centuries before our era. They were the *Ozarim* or Initiates, the descendants of the Egyptian hierophants, in whose country they had been settled for several centuries before they were converted to Buddhistic monasticism by the missionaries of King Asoka and later amalgamated with the earliest Christians; and they existed, probably, before the old Egyptian temples were desecrated and ruined in the incessant invasions of Persians, Greeks, and other conquering hordes. The hierophants had their atonement enacted in the Mystery of Initiation ages before the Gnostics, or even the Essenes, had appeared. It was known among hierophants as the Baptism of Blood, and was considered not as an atonement for the "fall of man" in Eden, but simply as an expiation for the past, present, and future sins of ignorant but nevertheless polluted mankind. The hierophant had the option of offering, as a sacrifice for his race to the gods whom he hoped to rejoin, either his own pure and sinless life or an animal victim. The former depended entirely on their own will. At the last moment of the solemn "new birth," the initiator passed "the word" to the initiated, and immediately after that the latter had a weapon placed in his right hand and was ordered to strike. This is the true origin of the Christian dogma of atonement.

Verily the "Christs" of the pre-Christian ages were many. But they died unknown to the world and disappeared as silently and as mysteriously from the sight of man as Moses from the top of Pisgah, the mountain of Nebo (oracular wisdom), after he had laid his hands upon Joshua, who thus became "full of the spirit of wisdom" (i.e., initiated).

In the foregoing lies the foundation of the fierce hatred of the Christians toward the "pagans" and the theurgists. Too much had been borrowed; they had taken enough from the ancient religions and the Neoplatonists to perplex the world for several thousand years. Had not the ancient creeds been speedily obliterated, it would have been found impossible to preach the Christian religion as a new dispensation or as a direct revelation from God the Father, through God the Son, and under the influence of God the Holy Ghost. As a political exigence the Fathers had even—to gratify the wishes of their rich converts—instituted the festivals of Pan. They went so far as to accept the ceremonies hitherto celebrated by the pagan world in honor of the

God of the gardens, in all their primitive sincerity. It was time to sever the connection. Either the pagan worship and the Neoplatonic theurgy, with all ceremonial of magic, must be crushed out forever, or the Christians become Neoplatonists.

The fierce polemics and single-handed battles between Irenaeus and the Gnostics are too well known to need repetition. They were carried on for over two centuries after the unscrupulous Bishop of Lyons had uttered his last religious paradox. Celsus, a Neoplatonist and a disciple of the school of Ammonius Saccas, had thrown the Christians into perturbation and had even arrested for a time the progress of proselytism by successfully proving that the original and purer forms of the most important dogmas of Christianity were to be found only in the teachings of Plato. Celsus accused them of accepting the worst superstitions of paganism and of interpolating passages from the books of the Sybils without rightly understanding their meaning. The accusations were so plausible, and the facts so patent, that for a long time no Christian writer had ventured to answer the challenge.

Origen, at the fervent request of his friend Ambrosius, was the first to take the defense in hand, for, having belonged to the same Platonic school of Ammonius, he was considered the most competent man to refute the well-founded charges. But his eloquence failed, and the only remedy that could be found was to destroy the writings of Celsus.[6] This could not be achieved until the fifth century, after copies had been made of this work, and many were those who had read and studied them. If no copy of it has descended to our present generation of scientists, it is not because there is none extant at present, but for the simple reason that the monks of a certain Oriental church on Mount Athos will neither show nor confess they have one in their possession. Perhaps they do not even know themselves the value of the contents of their manuscripts, on account of their great ignorance.

The dispersion of the Eclectic school had become the fondest hope of the Christians. It had been looked for and contemplated with intense anxiety. It was finally achieved. The members were scattered by the hand of the monsters Theophilus, Bishop of Alexandria, and his nephew Cyril, the murderer of the young, the learned, and the innocent Hypatia.

With the death of the martyred daughter of Theon, the mathematician, there remained no possibility for the Neoplatonists to continue their school at Alexandria. During the lifetime of the youthful Hypatia, her friendship and influence with Orestes, the governor of the city, had assured the philosophers security and protection against their murderous enemies. With her death they had lost their strongest friend.

NOTES

1. [These figures are for 1877.—ED.]
2. [*Chips from a German Workshop* (London, 1867), 2:235.]
3. P. H. Mallet, *Northern Antiquities* (London, 1859), 448.
4. The greater part of the literature included in the 700,000 volumes of the Alexandrian Library was due to India and her closest neighbors.
5. *Decline and Fall of the Roman Empire* ch. 21.
6. The above mentioned Celsus, who lived between the second and third centuries, is not Celsus the Epicurean. The latter wrote several works against magic and lived earlier, during the reign of Hadrian.

16

Christian Crimes and Heathen Virtues

For such men as Plotinus, Porphyry, Iamblichus, Apollonius, and even Simon Magus to be accused of having formed a pact with the Devil, whether the latter personage exists or not, is so absurd as to need but little refutation. If Simon Magus—the most problematical of all in a historical sense—ever existed otherwise than in the overheated fancy of Peter and the other apostles, he was evidently no worse than any of his adversaries. A difference in religious views, however great, is insufficient *per se* to send one person to heaven and the other to hell.

The erudite author of *Supernatural Religion*[1] assiduously endeavors to prove that by Simon Magus we must understand the apostle Paul, whose Epistles were secretly as well as openly calumniated by Peter and charged with containing "*dysnoëtic* learning." The Apostle of the Gentiles was brave, outspoken, sincere, and very learned; the Apostle of Circumcision, cowardly, cautious, insincere, and very ignorant. That Paul had been, at least partially if not completely, initiated into the theurgic mysteries admits of little doubt. His language— the phraseology so peculiar to the Greek philosophers—and certain expressions used only by the initiates are so many sure earmarks to that supposition.

Our suspicion has been strengthened by an able article in one of the New York periodicals entitled "Paul and Plato,"[2] in which the author puts forward one remarkable and, for us, very precious observation. He shows Paul in his Epistles to the Corinthians abounding with "expressions suggested by the initiations of Sabazius and Eleusis and the lectures of the (Greek) philosophers. He (Paul) designates himself an *idiôtês*—a person unskillful in the Word, but not in the *gnosis*

145

or philosophical learning. 'We speak wisdom among the perfect or initiated,' he writes; 'not the wisdom of this world, nor of the archons of this world, but divine wisdom in a mystery, which none of the archons of this world knew'" [1 Corinthians 2.6–8].

What else can the apostle mean by these unequivocal words but that he himself, as belonging to the *mystae* (initiated), spoke of things shown and explained only in the Mysteries? The "divine wisdom in a mystery which none of the archons of this world knew," evidently has some direct reference to the basileus of the Eleusinian initiation who *did* know. The basileus belonged to the staff of the great hierophant and was an archon of Athens, and as such was one of the chief mystae, belonging to the interior Mysteries, to which a very select and small number obtained an entrance.[3] The magistrates supervising the Eleusinians were called archons.

Another proof that Paul belonged to the circle of the "Initiates" lies in the following fact. The apostle had his head shorn at Cenchrea (where Lucius Apuleius was initiated) because "he had a vow." The *nazars* (ones who are set apart), as we see in the Jewish scriptures, had to cut their hair, which they wore long and which "no razor touched" at any other time, and sacrifice it on the altar of initiation. And the nazars were a class of Chaldean theurgists. We will show further that Jesus belonged to this class.

Paul declares that: "According to the grace of God which is given unto me, as a wise *master builder*, I have laid the foundation" (1 Corinthians 3.10). This expression, master builder, used only once in the whole Bible and by Paul, may be considered as a whole revelation. In the Mysteries, the third part of the sacred rites was called *Epopteia*, or revelation, reception into the secrets. In substance it means that stage of divine clairvoyance when everything pertaining to this earth disappears, earthly sight is paralyzed, and the soul is united free and pure with its Spirit, or God. But the real significance of the word is "overseeing." The word *epopteia* is a compound one—from *epi* (upon), and *eptomai* (to look)—for an overseer, an inspector, and also for a master builder. The title of Master Mason in Freemasonry is derived from this, in the sense used in the Mysteries. Therefore, when Paul entitles himself a "master builder," he is using a word preeminently kabbalistic, theurgic, and masonic, and one which no other apostle uses. He thus declares himself an adept, having the right to initiate others.

146

As for Peter, biblical criticism has shown before now that he had probably no more to do with the foundation of the Latin Church at Rome than to furnish the pretext so readily seized upon by the cunning Irenaeus: to benefit this Church with the new name of the apostle— *Petros* or *Kêphas*, a name which allowed so readily, by an easy play upon words, to connect it with *Petroma*, the double set of stone tablets used by the hierophant at the initiations during the final Mystery.

And so above, below, outside, and inside the Christian Church, with its priestly garments and religious rites, we recognize the stamp of exoteric heathenism. On no subject within the wide range of human knowledge has the world been more blinded or deceived with such persistent misrepresentation as on that of antiquity. Its hoary past and its religious faiths have been misrepresented and trampled under the feet of its successors; its hierophants and prophets, mystai and epoptai of the once sacred *adyta* of the temple, shown as demoniacs and devil-worshippers. Donned in the despoiled garments of the victim, the Christian priest now anathematizes the latter with rites and ceremonies which he has learned from the theurgists themselves. The mosaic Bible is used as a weapon against the people who furnished it.

The Mysteries are as old as the world, and one well versed in the esoteric mythologies of various nations can trace them back to the days of the pre-Vedic period in India. A condition of the strictest virtue and purity is required from the *vatu* (candidate) in India before he can become an initiate, whether he aims to be a simple fakir, a *purohita* (public priest), or a *sannyasi*, a saint of the second degree of initiation, the most holy and the most revered of them all. Having conquered, in the terrible trials preliminary to admittance to the inner temple in the subterranean crypts of his pagoda, the sannyasi passes the rest of his life in the temple, practicing the eighty-four rules and ten virtues prescribed to the Yogis.

"No one who has not practiced, during his whole life, the ten virtues which the divine Manu makes incumbent as a duty can be initiated into the Mysteries of the council," say the Hindu books of initiation. These virtues are: "Resignation; the act of rendering good for evil; temperance; probity; purity; chastity; repression of the physical senses; the knowledge of the Holy Scriptures; that of the Superior soul (spirit); worship of truth; abstinence from anger" [Manu 6.92]. These virtues alone must direct the life of a true Yogi. "No unworthy adept ought to defile the ranks of the holy initiates with his presence for twenty-four hours." The adept becomes guilty after having once broken any one of these vows. Surely the exercise of such virtues is inconsistent with the idea one has of devil-worship and lasciviousness of purpose!

And now we will try to give a clear insight into one of the chief objects of this work. What we desire to prove is that underlying every ancient popular religion was the same ancient wisdom doctrine, one and identical, professed and practiced by the initiates of every country, who alone were aware of its existence and importance. To ascertain its origin and the precise age in which it was matured is now beyond human possibility. A single glance, however, is enough to assure one that it could not have attained the marvelous perfection in which we find it pictured to us in the relics of the various esoteric systems except after a succession of ages. A philosophy so profound, a moral code so ennobling, and practical results so conclusive and so uniformly demonstrable are not the growth of a generation or even a single epoch. Fact must have been piled upon fact, deduction upon deduction, science must have begotten science, and myriads of the brightest human intellects reflected upon the laws of nature before this ancient doctrine had taken concrete shape.

The proofs of this identity of fundamental doctrine in the old religions are found in the prevalence of a system of initiation, in the secret sacerdotal castes who had the guardianship of mystical words of power, and in the public display of a phenomenal control over natural forces, indicating association with preterhuman beings. Every approach to the Mysteries of all these nations was guarded with the same jealous care, and in all the penalty of death was inflicted upon initiates of any degree who divulged the secrets entrusted to them. We have seen that such was the case in the Eleusinian and Bacchic Mysteries and among the Chaldean Magi and the Egyptian hierophants; while with the Hindus, from whom they were all derived, the same rule has prevailed from time immemorial.

Naturally enough, this same extreme penalty was prescribed in all the multifarious sects and brotherhoods which at different periods have sprung from the ancient stock. We find it with the early Essenes, Gnostics, theurgic Neoplatonists, and medieval philosophers; and in our day, even the Masons perpetuate the memory of the old obligations in the penalties of throat-cutting, dismemberment, and disemboweling, with which the candidate is threatened. As the Masonic "master's word" is communicated only at "low breath," so the selfsame precaution is prescribed in the Chaldean *Book of Numbers* and the Jewish *Merkabah*. When initiated, the neophyte was led by an ancient to a secluded spot, and there the latter whispered in his ear the great secret.[4]

As we proceed, we will point out the evidences of this identity of vows, formulas, rites, and doctrines between the ancient faiths. We will also show not only that their memory is still preserved in India, but also that the Secret Association is still alive and as active as ever; that, after reading what we have to say, it may be inferred that the chief pontiff and hierophant, the *Brahmatma*, is still accessible to those "who know," though perhaps recognized by another name; and that the ramifications of his influence extend throughout the world. But we will now return again to the early Christian period.

The gradation of the Mysteries is given us by Proclus in the fourth book of his *Theology of Plato*. "The perfective rite (*teletê*) precedes in order the initiation (*muêsis*), and the initiation, the final apocalypse (revelation)."[5] In *Mathematica*, Theon of Smyrna also divides the mystic rites into five parts, "the first of which is the previous purification; for neither are the Mysteries communicated to all who are willing to receive them . . . there are certain persons who are prevented by the voice of the crier . . . since it is necessary that such as are not expelled from the Mysteries should first be refined by certain purifications [which] the reception of the sacred rites follows. The third part is denominated *epopteia* or reception. And the fourth, which is the end and design of the revelation, is the binding of the head and fixing of the crowns[6] . . . whether after this he (the initiated person) becomes . . . an hierophant or sustains some other part of the sacerdotal office. But the fifth, which is produced from all these, is friendship and interior communion with God."[7] And this was the last and most awful of all the Mysteries.

If during the *Aporrheta* or preliminary arcanes, there were some practices which might have shocked the modesty of a Christian convert—though we doubt the sincerity of such statements—their mystical symbolism was sufficient to relieve the performance of any charge of licentiousness. Even the episode of the Matron Baubo— whose rather eccentric method of consolation was immortalized in the minor Mysteries—is explained by impartial mystagogues quite naturally. Ceres-Demeter and her earthly wanderings in search of her daughter are the euhemerized descriptions of one of the most metaphysico-psychological subjects ever treated of by human mind. It is a mask for the transcendent narrative of the initiated seers: the celestial vision of the freed soul of the initiate of the last hour, describing the process by which the soul that has not yet been incarnated descends for the first time into matter. Taylor shows, on the authority of more than one initiate, that the "dramatic performances of the Lesser Mysteries were designed by . . . their founders, to signify *occultly* the condition of the unpurified soul invested with an earthly body and enveloped in a material and physical nature . . . That the soul, indeed, till purified by philosophy, suffers death through its union with the body."[8]

The body is the sepulcher, the prison of the soul, and many Christian Fathers held with Plato that the soul is punished through its union with the body. Such is the fundamental doctrine of the Buddhists and of many Brahmans too. When Plotinus remarks that "when the soul has descended into generation (from its half-divine condition), she partakes of evil and is carried a great way into a state the opposite of her first purity and integrity" (*Enneads* 1.8), he only repeats the teachings of Gautama Buddha. If we believe the ancient initiates at all, we must accept their interpretation of the symbols. And if, moreover, we find them perfectly coinciding with the teachings of the greatest philosophers and that which we know symbolizes the same meaning in the modern Mysteries in the East, we must believe them to be right.

Whether in the "inner temple," through the private study of theurgy, or by the sole exertion of a whole life of spiritual labor, they all obtained the practical proof of such divine possibilities for man fighting his battle with life on earth to win a life in eternity. What the last epopteia was is alluded to by Plato in *Phaedrus* (250B, C): "being initiated in those Mysteries, which it is lawful to call the most blessed of all mysteries . . . we were freed from the molestations of evils which otherwise await us in a future period of time. Likewise, in consequence of this divine initiation, we became spectators of entire, simple, immovable, and blessed visions, resident in a pure light." This sentence shows that they saw visions, gods, spirits. As Taylor correctly observes, from all such passages in the works of the initiates it may be inferred "that the most sublime part of the epopteia . . . consisted in beholding the gods themselves invested with a resplendent light,"[9] or highest planetary spirits.

The second statement of Plato confirms our belief that the Mysteries of the ancients were identical with the Initiations as practiced now among the Buddhists and the Hindu adepts. The highest visions, the most truthful, are produced, not through natural ecstatics or "mediums," as it is sometimes erroneously asserted, but through a regular discipline of gradual initiations and development of psychical powers. The mystai were brought into close union with those whom Proclus calls "mystical natures" and "resplendent gods," because, as Plato says, "we were ourselves pure and immaculate, being liberated from this surrounding vestment, which we denominate body, and to which we are now bound like an oyster to its shell" (*Phaedrus* 250C).

Subjective communication with the human, godlike spirits of those who have preceded us to the silent land of bliss is in India divided into three categories. Under the spiritual training of a guru or sannyasi, the vatu (disciple or neophyte) begins to feel them. Were he not under the immediate guidance of an adept he would be controlled by the invisibles and utterly at their mercy, for among these subjective influences he is unable to discern the good from the bad. Happy the sensitive who is sure of the purity of his spiritual atmosphere!

This subjective consciousness is the first degree; after a time, that of clairaudience is added. This is the second degree or stage of development. The sensitive—when not naturally made so by psychological training—now audibly hears, but is still unable to discern and is incapable of verifying his impressions; and the tricky powers of the air but too often delude with semblances of voices and speech one who is unprotected. But the guru's influence is there; it is the most powerful shield against the intrusion of the *bhuta* into the atmosphere of the vatu, consecrated to the pure, human, and celestial Pitris.

The third degree is that in which the fakir or any other candidate feels, hears, and sees—when he can at will produce the reflections of the Pitris on the mirror of astral light. All depends upon his psychological and mesmeric powers, which are always proportionate to the intensity of his will. But the fakir will never control the Akasa, the spiritual life principle and omnipotent agent of every phenomenon, in the same degree as an adept of the third and highest initiation. And the phenomena produced by the will of the latter do not generally serve as marketplaces for the satisfaction of openmouthed investigators.

The unity of God, the immortality of the spirit, belief in salvation only through our works, merit and demerit: such are the principal articles of faith of the Wisdom Religion, and the groundwork of Vedaism, Buddhism, and Parsiism. Such we even find to have been the basis of the ancient Osirism, when we, after abandoning the popular sun god to the materialism of the rabble, confine our attention to the Books of Hermes, the thrice-great.

The reason why in every age so little has been generally known of the mysteries of initiation is twofold. The first has already been explained by more than one author and lies in the terrible penalty following the least indiscretion. The second is the superhuman difficulties and even dangers which the daring candidate of old had to encounter, and either conquer or die in the attempt, when—what is still worse—he did not lose his reason. There was no real danger to him whose mind had become thoroughly spiritualized, and so prepared for every terrific sight. He who fully recognized the power of his immortal spirit and never doubted for one moment its omnipotent protection had naught to fear. But woe to the candidate in whom the slightest physical fear—sickly child of matter—made him lose sight and faith in his own invulnerability. He who was not wholly confident of his moral fitness to accept the burden of these tremendous secrets was doomed.

We have no quarrel with Christians whose faith is sincere and whose practice coincides with their profession. But with an arrogant, dogmatic, and dishonest clergy, we have nothing to do except to see the ancient philosophy defended and righted so far as we are able, so that its grandeur and sufficiency may be thoroughly displayed. It is not alone for the esoteric philosophy that we fight, nor for any modern system of moral philosophy, but for the inalienable right of private judgment, and especially for the ennobling idea of a future life of activity and accountability.

We eagerly applaud such commentators as Godfrey Higgins, Thomas Inman, Richard Payne Knight, C. W. King, S. F. Dunlap, and Dr. Newton, however much they disagree with our own mystical views, for their diligence is constantly being rewarded by fresh discoveries of the pagan paternity of Christian symbols. But otherwise all these learned works are useless. Their researches only cover half the ground.

Lacking the true key of interpretation, they see the symbols only in a physical aspect. They have no password to cause the gates of mystery to swing open; ancient spiritual philosophy is to them a closed book.

True philosophy and divine truth are convertible terms. A religion which dreads the light cannot be a religion based on either truth or philosophy—hence it must be false. The ancient Mysteries were mysteries to the profane only, whom the hierophant never sought nor would accept as proselytes; to the initiates the Mysteries became explained as soon as the final veil was withdrawn. No mind like that of Pythagoras or Plato would have contented itself with an unfathomable and incomprehensible mystery, like that of the Christian dogma. There can be but one truth, for two small truths on the same subject can but constitute one great error.

Among thousands of exoteric or popular conflicting religions which have been propagated since the days when the first men were enabled to interchange their ideas, there has not been a nation, a people, or the most abject tribe that has not, after their own fashion, believed in an Unseen God, the First Cause of unerring and immutable laws, and in the immortality of our spirit. No creed, no false philosophy, no religious exaggerations could ever destroy that feeling. It must, therefore, be based upon an absolute truth. On the other hand, every one of the numberless religions and religious sects views the Deity after its own fashion; and, fathering on the unknown their own speculations, they enforce these purely human outgrowths of overheated imagination on the ignorant masses and call them "revelation." As the dogmas of every religion and sect often differ radically, they cannot be true. And if untrue, what are they?

NOTES

1. [W. R. Cassels (London, 1875), 2: pt. 2, ch. 5.]
2. Alexander Wilder.
3. See Thomas Taylor, *The Eleusinian and Bacchic Mysteries*, ed. A. Wilder (New York, 1875), 8.
4. A. Franck, *La Kabbale* (Paris, 1843), ch. 1.
5. [*On the Theology of Plato*, trans. Thomas Taylor (London, 1816), 220.]

6. This expression must not be understood literally, for as in the initiation of certain Brotherhoods it has a secret meaning, hinted at by Pythagoras when he describes his feelings after the initiation and tells that he was crowned by the gods in whose presence he had drunk "the waters of life."
7. [Taylor, *Eleus.* 46–47.]
8. [Taylor, *Eleus.* 4–5.]
9. [Taylor, *Eleus.* 65.]

17

Divisions among the Early Christians

Clement describes Basilides, the Gnostic, as "a philosopher devoted to the contemplation of divine things." This very appropriate expression may be applied to many of the founders of the more important sects which later were all engulfed in one—that stupendous compound of unintelligible dogmas enforced by Irenaeus, Tertullian, and others, which is now termed Christianity. If these must be called heresies, then early Christianity itself must be included in the number. Neither divine right nor truth brought about the triumph of their Christianity; fate alone was propitious. We can assert, with entire plausibility, that there is not one of all these sects—Kabbalism, Judaism, and our present Christianity included—that did not spring from the two main branches of that one mother-trunk, the once universal religion, which antedated the Vedic ages—we speak of that prehistoric Buddhism which merged later into Brahmanism.

The religion which the primitive teaching of the few early apostles most resembled—a religion preached by Jesus himself—is the elder of these two, Buddhism. The latter, as taught in its primitive purity and carried to perfection by the last of the Buddhas, Gautama, based its moral ethics on three fundamental principles. It alleged that (1) everything existing exists from natural causes, (2) that virtue brings its own reward, and vice and sin their own punishment, and (3) that the state of man in this world is probationary. We might add that on these three principles rested the universal foundation of every religious creed: God and individual immortality for every man—if he could but win it. However puzzling the subsequent theological tenets and however seemingly incomprehensible the metaphysical abstractions which have convulsed the theology of every one of the great religions

155

of mankind as soon as it was placed on a sure footing, the above is found to be the essence of every religious philosophy, with the exception of later Christianity. It was that of Zoroaster, of Pythagoras, of Plato, of Jesus, and even of Moses, albeit the teachings of the Jewish lawgiver have been so piously tampered with.

We will devote the present chapter mainly to a brief survey of the numerous sects which have recognized themselves as Christians—that is to say, that have believed in a *Christos*, or an ANOINTED ONE. We will also endeavor to explain the latter appellation from the kabbalistic standpoint and show it reappearing in every religious system.

History finds the first Christian sects to have been either Nazarenes like John the Baptist; Ebionites, among whom were many of the relatives of Jesus; or Essenes (Iessaens), the Therapeutae healers, of which the Nazaria were a branch. All these sects, which only in the days of Irenaeus began to be considered heretical, were more or less kabbalistic. They believed in the expulsion of demons by magical incantations and practiced this method; Jervis terms the Nabathaeans and other such sects "wandering Jewish exorcists,"[1] the Arabic word *nabae* meaning "to wander," and the Hebrew *naba*, "to prophesy." The Talmud indiscriminately calls all the Christians *Nozari*.

The real meaning of the word *nazar* signifies to vow or consecrate one's self to the service of God. As a noun it is a "diadem" or emblem of such consecration, or a head so consecrated. The nazars or prophets, as well as the Nazarenes, in common with all the initiated prophets, held to the spirit of the symbolical religions and offered a strong opposition to the idolatrous and exoteric practices of the dead letter. Hence the frequent stoning of the prophets by the populace and under the leadership of those priests who made a profitable living out of the popular superstitions.

The Nazireate sect existed long before the laws of Moses and originated among people most inimical to the "chosen" ones of Israel, viz., the people of Galilee, the ancient *olla-podrida* of idolatrous nations, where was built Nasera, the present Nazareth. It is in Nasera that the ancient Nazaria or Nazireates held their "Mysteries of Life" or "assemblies," as the word now stands in the translation, which were but the secret mysteries of initiation, utterly distinct in their practical form from the popular Mysteries which were held at Byblus in honor of Adonis.

The oldest Nazarenes, whose last prominent leader was John the Baptist, although never very orthodox in the sight of the scribes and Pharisees of Jerusalem were, nevertheless, respected and left unmolested. Even Herod "feared the multitude" because they regarded John as a prophet (Matthew 14.5). But the followers of Jesus evidently adhered to a sect which became a still more exasperating thorn in their side. It appeared as a heresy within another heresy; for while the nazars of the olden times, the "Sons of the Prophets," were Chaldean kabbalists, the adepts of the new dissenting sect showed themselves reformers and innovators from the first.

The great similitude traced by some critics between the rites and observances of the earliest Christians and those of the Essenes may be accounted for without the slightest difficulty. The Essenes were the converts of Buddhist missionaries who had overrun Egypt, Greece, and even Judea at one time, since the reign of Asoka the zealous propagandist; and while it is evidently to the Essenes that belongs the honor of having had the Nazarene reformer, Jesus, as a pupil, still the latter is found disagreeing with his early teachers on several questions of formal observance. He cannot strictly be called an Essene, for reasons which we will indicate further on, neither was he a nazar, or Nazaria of the older sect. What Jesus was may be found in the Codex Nazaraeus, in the unjust accusations of the Bardesanian Gnostics.

The Nazarene reformer had undoubtedly belonged to one of these sects, though perhaps it would be next to impossible to decide absolutely which. But what is self-evident is that he preached the philosophy of Buddha Sakyamuni. The motive of Jesus was evidently like that of Gautama Buddha: to benefit humanity at large by producing a religious reform which should give it a religion of pure ethics, the true knowledge of God and nature having remained until then solely in the hands of the esoteric sects and their adepts. As Jesus used oil and the Essenes never used aught but pure water,[2] he cannot be called a strict Essene. On the other hand, the Essenes were also "set apart"; they were healers (*asaya*) and dwelt in the desert as all ascetics did.

Our Nazarene sect is known to have existed some 150 years B.C., and to have lived on the banks of the Jordan and on the eastern shore of the Dead Sea, according to Pliny and Josephus.[3] But in King's *Gnostics* we find quoted another statement by Josephus, which says that the Essenes had been established on the shores of the Dead Sea "for thousands of ages" before Pliny's time.[4]

The secret doctrines of the Magi, of the pre-Vedic Buddhists, of the hierophants of the Egyptian Thoth or Hermes, and of the adepts of whatever age and nationality, including the Chaldean kabbalists and the Jewish nazars, were identical from the beginning. When we use the term *Buddhists*, we do not mean to imply by it either the exoteric Buddhism instituted by the followers of Gautama Buddha or the modern Buddhistic religion, but the secret philosophy of Sakyamuni, which in its essence is certainly identical with the ancient wisdom religion of the sanctuary, the pre-Vedic Brahmanism.

Already at some time before our era, the adepts had ceased to congregate in large communities, except in India; but whether among the Essenes, the Neoplatonists, or again among the innumerable struggling sects born but to die, the same doctrines—identical in substance and spirit, if not always in form—are encountered. By *Buddhism*, therefore, we mean that religion signifying literally the doctrine of wisdom, and which by many ages antedates the metaphysical philosophy of Siddhartha Sakyamuni.

In his discourses and sermons, Jesus always spoke in parables and used metaphors with his audience. This habit was again that of the Esseneans and the Nazarenes; the Galileans who dwelt in cities and villages were never known to use such allegorical language. Indeed, some of his disciples who were Galileans like himself were surprised to find him using with the people such a form of expression. "Why speakest thou unto them in parables?" they often inquired. "Because it is given unto you to know the Mysteries of the kingdom of heaven, but to them it is not given," was the reply, which was that of an initiate. "Therefore I speak unto them in parables; because seeing, they see not, and hearing, they hear not, neither do they understand" (Matthew 13.10–13). Moreover, we find Jesus expressing his thoughts still clearer—and in sentences which are purely Pythagorean—when, during the Sermon on the Mount, he says:

> Give ye not that which is sacred to the dogs,
> Neither cast ye your pearls before swine;
> For the swine will tread them under their feet
> And the dogs will turn and rend you.

Professor A. Wilder, the editor of Taylor's *Eleusinian Mysteries* (15fn.), observes "a like disposition on the part of Jesus and Paul to classify their doctrines as esoteric and exoteric, the Mysteries of the Kingdom of God 'for the apostles,' and 'parables' for the multitude. 'We speak wisdom,' says Paul, 'among them that are perfect' (or initiated)."

In the Eleusinian and other Mysteries the participants were always divided into two classes, the *neophytes* and the *perfect*. The former were sometimes admitted to the preliminary initiation: the dramatic performance of Ceres, or the soul, descending to Hades.[5] But it was given only to the "perfect" to enjoy and learn the Mysteries of the divine Elysium, the celestial abode of the blessed, this Elysium being unquestionably the same as the "Kingdom of Heaven." To contradict or reject the above would be merely to shut one's eyes to the truth.

Thus, in common with Pythagoras and other hierophant reformers, Jesus divided his teachings into exoteric and esoteric. Following faithfully the Pythagorean Essenean ways, he never sat at a meal without saying "grace." "The priest prays before his meal," says Josephus, describing the Essenes [*Jewish Wars* 2.8.5]. Jesus also divided his followers into "neophytes," "brethren," and the "perfect," if we may judge by the difference he made between them. But his career, at least as a public Rabbi, was of too short duration to allow him to establish a regular school of his own; and perhaps with the exception of John, it does not seem that he had initiated any other apostle.

All this points undeniably to the fact that, except for a handful of self-styled Christians who subsequently won the day, all the civilized portion of the pagans who knew of Jesus honored him as a philosopher, an adept whom they placed on the same level with Pythagoras and Apollonius. Whence such a veneration on their part for a man, were he simply, as represented by the Synoptics, a poor, unknown Jewish carpenter from Nazareth? As an incarnated God there is no single record of him on this earth capable of withstanding the critical examination of science; but as one of the greatest reformers, an inveterate enemy of every theological dogmatism, a persecutor of bigotry, and a teacher of one of the most sublime codes of ethics, Jesus is one of the grandest and most clearly defined figures in the panorama of human history. His age may, with every day, be receding farther and farther back into the gloomy and hazy mists of the past; and his theology—based on human fancy and supported by untenable dogmas—may, nay, must with every day lose more of its unmerited prestige; alone the grand figure of the philosopher and moral reformer, instead of growing paler, will become with every century more pronounced and more clearly defined. It will reign supreme and universal only on that day when the whole of humanity recognizes but one father—the Unknown One above—and one brother—the whole of mankind below.

In the very first remark made by Jesus about John the Baptist, we find him stating that he is "Elias, which was for to come." This assertion, if it is not a later interpolation for the sake of having a prophecy fulfilled, means again that Jesus was a kabbalist, unless indeed we have to adopt the doctrine of the French spiritists and suspect him of believing in reincarnation. Except for the kabbalistic sects of the Essenes, the Nazarenes, the disciples of Shimon ben-Yohai, and Hillel, neither the orthodox Jews nor the Galileans believed or knew anything about the doctrine of permutation. And the Sadducees rejected even that of the resurrection.

But this doctrine of permutation, or *revolutio*, must not be understood as a belief in reincarnation. That Moses was considered the transmigration of Abel and Seth does not imply that the kabbalists— those who were initiated at least—believed that the identical spirit of either of Adam's sons reappeared under the corporeal form of Moses. It only shows the mode of expression they used when hinting at one of the profoundest mysteries of the Oriental Gnosis, one of the most majestic articles of faith of the Secret Wisdom. It was purposely veiled so as to half conceal and half reveal the truth. It implied that Moses, like certain other godlike men, was believed to have reached the highest of all states on earth—the rarest of all psychological phenomena— the perfect union of the immortal spirit with the terrestrial *duad* had occurred. The trinity was complete. A god was incarnate. But how rare such incarnations!

That expression, "Ye are gods," which to our biblical students is a mere abstraction, has for the kabbalists a vital significance. Each immortal spirit that sheds its radiance upon a human being is a god—the Microcosmos of the Macrocosmos, part and parcel of the Unknown God, the First Cause of which it is a direct emanation. It is possessed of all the attributes of its parent source. Among these attributes are omniscience and omnipotence. Endowed with these, yet unable to fully manifest them while in the body, during which time they are obscured, veiled, and limited by the capabilities of physical nature, the thus divinely inhabited man may tower far above his kind, evince a godlike wisdom, and display deific powers; for while the rest of mortals around him are but overshadowed by their divine SELF, with every chance given to them to become immortal hereafter, but no other security than their personal efforts to win the kingdom of heaven, the so chosen man has already become an immortal while yet on earth. His prize is secured. Henceforth he will live forever in eternal life. Not only may he have "dominion" (Psalms 8.6) over all the works of creation by employing the "excellence" of the NAME (the ineffable one), but he will also be higher in this life, not, as Paul is made to say, "a little lower than the angels."

The ancients never entertained the sacrilegious thought that such perfected entities were incarnations of the one supreme and forever invisible God. No such profanation of the awful Majesty entered into their conceptions. Moses and his antitypes and types were to them but complete men, gods on earth, for their gods (divine spirits) had entered unto their hallowed tabernacles, the purified physical bodies. The disembodied spirits of the heroes and sages were termed gods by the ancients—hence the accusation of polytheism and idolatry on the part of those who were the first to anthropomorphize the holiest and purest abstractions of their forefathers.

The real and hidden sense of this doctrine was known to all the initiates. The Tannaim imparted it to their elect ones, the Ozarim, in the solemn solitudes of crypts and deserted places. It was one of the most esoteric and jealously guarded [secrets], for human nature was the same then as it is now, and the sacerdotal caste as confident as now in the supremacy of its knowledge, and ambitious of ascendancy over the weaker masses, with the difference perhaps that its hierophants could prove the legitimacy of their claims and the plausibility of their doctrines, whereas now believers must be content with blind faith.

While the kabbalists called this mysterious and rare occurrence of the union of spirit with the mortal charge entrusted to its care the "descent of the Angel Gabriel" (the latter being a kind of generic name for it), the Messenger of Life, and the angel Metatron, and while the Nazarenes termed the same Hibil-Ziwa,[6] the *Legatus* sent by the Lord of Celsitude, it was universally known as the "Anointed Spirit."

Thus it is the acceptance of this doctrine which caused the Gnostics to maintain that Jesus was a man overshadowed by the Christos or Messenger of Life, and that his despairing cry from the cross, "Eli, Eli, lama shabachthani," was wrung from him at the instant when he felt that this inspiring Presence had finally abandoned him, for—as some affirmed—his faith had also abandoned him when on the cross.

The early Nazarenes, who must be numbered among the Gnostic sects, believing that Jesus was a prophet, nevertheless held in relation to him the same doctrine of the divine "overshadowing" of certain "men of God," sent for the salvation of nations and to recall them to the path of righteousness.

And now, in order to make such passages as the above more intelligible, we will endeavor to define as briefly as possible the dogmas in which, with very trifling differences, nearly all the Gnostic sects believed.

It is in Ephesus that flourished in those days the greatest college, wherein the abstruse Oriental speculations and the Platonic philosophy were taught in conjunction. It was a focus of the universal "secret" doctrines, the weird laboratory whence, fashioned in elegant Grecian phraseology, sprang the quintessence of Buddhist, Zoroastrian, and Chaldean philosophy. Artemis, the gigantic concrete symbol of theosophical-pantheistic abstractions and the great mother Multimamma, androgyne and patroness of the "Ephesian writings," was conquered by Paul; but although the zealous converts of the apostles pretended to burn all their books on "curious arts," enough of these remained for them to study when their first zeal had cooled off.

It is from Ephesus that nearly all the Gnosis spread, which clashed so fiercely with the Irenaean dogmas; and still it was Ephesus, with her numerous collateral branches of the great college of the Essenes, which proved to be the hotbed of all the kabbalistic speculations brought by the Tannaim from the captivity. "In Ephesus," says A. J. Matter, "the notions of the Jewish-Egyptian school and the semi-Persian speculations of the kabbalists had then recently come to swell the vast conflux of Grecian and Asiatic doctrines, so there is no wonder that teachers should have sprung up there who strove to combine the religion newly preached by the apostle with the ideas there so long established" [in King, Gnostics 3].

162

Now let us see what are the greatest heresies of the Gnostics. We will select Basilides as the standard for our comparisons, for all the founders of other Gnostic sects group round him like a cluster of stars borrowing light from their sun.

Basilides maintained that he had had all his doctrines from the Apostle Matthew and from Peter through Glaucus, the disciple of the latter (Clem. Alex., *Stromateis* 7.17). According to Eusebius (*Eccles. Hist.* 4.7) he published twenty-four volumes of *Interpretations upon the Gospels*,[7] all of which were burned, a fact which makes us suppose that they contained more truthful matter than the school of Irenaeus was prepared to deny. He asserted that the unknown, eternal, and uncreated Father having first brought forth *Nous*, or Mind, the latter emanated from itself the *Logos*. The Logos (the Word of John) emanated in its turn *Phronêsis*, or the Intelligences (Divine-human spirits). From Phronêsis sprang *Sophia*, or feminine wisdom, and *Dynamis*—strength. These were the personified attributes of the mysterious godhead, the Gnostic quinternion, typifying the five spiritual but intelligible substances, personal virtues or beings external to the unknown godhead. This is preeminently a kabbalistic idea. It is still more Buddhistic.

The earliest system of the Buddhist philosophy, which preceded Gautama Buddha by far, is based upon the uncreated substance of the "Unknown," the Adi Buddha.[8] This eternal, infinite Monad possesses, as proper to his own essence, five acts of wisdom. From these it, by five separate acts of Dhyana, emitted five Dhyani Buddhas; these, like Adi Buddha, are quiescent (passive) in their system. Neither Adi nor either of the five Dhyani Buddhas were ever incarnated, but seven of their emanations became Avatars, i.e., were incarnated on this earth.

Describing the Basilidean system, Irenaeus, quoting the Gnostics, declares as follows: "When the uncreated, unnamed Father saw the corruption of mankind, he sent his firstborn Nous into the world in the form of Christ, for the redemption of all who believe in him, out of the power of those who fabricated the world (the Demiurge and his six sons, the planetary genii). He appeared among men as the man Jesus and wrought miracles. This Christ did not die in person, but Simon the Cyrenian suffered in his stead, to whom he lent his bodily form; for the Divine Power, the Nous of the Eternal Father, is not corporeal and cannot die. Whoso, therefore, maintains that Christ has died is still the bondsman of ignorance; whoso denies the same, he is free, and hath understood the purpose of the Father" (Irenaeus, *Adv. Haer.* 1.24.4).

So far, taken in its abstract sense, we do not see anything blasphemous in this system. It may be a heresy against the theology of Irenaeus and Tertullian, but there is certainly nothing sacrilegious about the religious idea itself, and it will seem to every impartial thinker far more consistent with divine reverence than the anthropomorphism of actual Christianity. The Gnostics were called by the orthodox Christians *Docetae*, or Illusionists, for believing that Christ did not and could not actually suffer death—in physical body. The later Brahmanical books likewise contain much that is repugnant to the reverential feeling and idea of the Divinity; and like the Gnostics, the Brahmans explain such legends as may shock the divine dignity of the spiritual beings called gods by attributing them to *Maya*, or illusion.

The profoundest and most transcendental speculations of the ancient metaphysicians of India and other countries are all based on that great Buddhist and Brahmanical principle underlying the whole of their religious metaphysics—*illusion* of the senses. Everything that is finite is illusion, all that which is eternal and infinite is reality. Form, color, that which we hear and feel or see with our mortal eyes exists only so far as it can be conveyed to each of us through our senses. The universe for a man born blind does not exist in either form or color, but it exists in its privation (in the Aristotelian sense) and is a reality for the spiritual senses of the blind man. We all live under the powerful dominion of fantasy. Only the highest and invisible *originals* emanated from the thought of the Unknown are real and permanent beings, forms, and ideas; on earth we see but their reflections, more or less correct, and ever dependent on the physical and mental organization of the person who beholds them.

The objects of sense, being ever delusive and fluctuating, cannot be a reality. Spirit alone is unchangeable, hence alone is no illusion. This is pure Buddhist doctrine. The religion of the Gnosis, the most evident offshoot of Buddhism, was utterly based on this metaphysical tenet. Christos suffered spiritually for us, and far more acutely than did the illusionary Jesus while his body was being tortured on the cross.

In the ideas of the Christians, Christ is but another name for Jesus. The philosophy of the Gnostics, the initiates, and hierophants understood it otherwise. Christos, as a unity, is but an abstraction: a general idea representing the collective aggregation of the numberless spirit entities which are the direct emanations of the infinite, invisible, incomprehensible First Cause—the individual spirits of men, erroneously called souls. They are the divine sons of God, some of which only overshadow mortal men; some remain forever planetary spirits, and some—the smaller and rare minority—unite themselves during life with some men. Such godlike beings as Gautama Buddha, Jesus, Lao-Tzu, Krishna, and a few others had united themselves with their spirits permanently—hence they became gods on earth. Others, such as Moses, Pythagoras, Apollonius, Plotinus, Confucius, Plato, Iamblichus, and some Christian saints, having at intervals been so united, have taken rank in history as demigods and leaders of mankind. When unburdened of their terrestrial tabernacles, their freed souls, henceforth united forever with their spirits, rejoin the whole shining host, which is bound together in one spiritual solidarity of thought and deed and called "the anointed." Hence the meaning of the Gnostics, who by saying that "Christos" suffered spiritually for humanity implied that his Divine Spirit suffered most.

Such and far more elevating were the ideas of Marcion, the great "Heresiarch" of the second century, as he is termed by his opponents. He came to Rome at 139–142 A.D., according to Tertullian, Irenaeus, Clement, and most of his modern commentators. His influence must have been powerful, as we find Epiphanius writing more than two centuries later that in his time the followers of Marcion were to be found throughout the whole world.[9]

Marcion, who recognized no other Gospels than a few Epistles of Paul, rejected totally the anthropomorphism of the Old Testament, drew a distinct line of demarcation between the old Judaism and Christianity, and viewed Jesus neither as a King, Messiah of the Jews, nor as the son of David, who was in any way connected with the law or prophets, but as "a divine being sent to reveal to man a spiritual religion, wholly new, and a God of goodness and grace hitherto unknown." The "Lord God" of the Jews in his eyes, the Creator (Demiurge), was totally different and distinct from the Deity who sent Jesus to reveal the divine truth and preach the glad tidings, to bring reconciliation and salvation to all. The mission of Jesus— according to Marcion—was to abrogate the Jewish "Lord," who "was opposed to the God and Father of Jesus Christ as matter is to spirit, impurity to purity" [*Supernatural Religion* 2:104].

Was Marcion so far wrong? Was it blasphemy or was it intuition, divine inspiration in him, to express that which every honest heart yearning for truth more or less feels and acknowledges? If in his sincere desire to establish a purely spiritual religion, a universal faith based on unadulterated truth, he found it necessary to make of Christianity an entirely new and separate system from that of Judaism, did not Marcion have the very words of Christ for his authority? "No man putteth a piece of new cloth into an old garment . . . for the rent is made worse. . . . Neither do men put new wine into old bottles, else the bottles break, and the wine runneth out, and the bottles perish; but they put new wine into new bottles, and both are preserved" [Matthew 9.16–17]. In what particular does the jealous, wrathful, revengeful God resemble the unknown deity, the God of mercy preached by Jesus—*his* Father who is in Heaven, and the Father of all humanity? This Father alone is the God of spirit and purity, and to compare Him with the subordinate and capricious Sinaitic Deity is an error.

Did Jesus ever pronounce the name of Jehovah? Did he ever place his Father in contrast with this severe and cruel Judge, his God of mercy, love, and justice, with the genius of retaliation? Never! From that memorable day when he preached his Sermon on the Mount, an immeasurable void opened between his God and that other deity who fulminated his commands from that other mount—Sinai. The language of Jesus is unequivocal; it implies not only rebellion but defiance of the Mosaic "Lord God." "Ye have heard," he tells us, "that it hath been said, an eye for an eye, and a tooth for a tooth: but I say unto you, that ye resist not evil: but whosoever shall smite thee on thy right cheek, turn to him the other also. Ye have heard that it hath been said: Thou shalt love thy neighbor and hate thine enemy. But I say unto you: Love your enemies, bless them that curse you, do good to them that hate you, and pray for them which despitefully use you and persecute you" (Matthew 5.38–44).

"Good master, what shall I do that I may have eternal life?" asks a man of Jesus. "Keep the commandments." "Which?" "Thou shalt do no murder, thou shalt not commit adultery, thou shalt not steal, thou shalt not bear false witness," is the answer (Matthew 19.16–18).

166

"What shall I do to obtain possession of Bodhi (knowledge of eternal truth)?" asks a disciple of his Buddhist master. "What way is there to become an Upasaka?" "Keep the commandments." "What are they?" "Thou shalt abstain all thy life from murder, theft, adultery, and lying," answers the master (*Pitakattayan* bk. 3, Pali version).

Identical injunctions, are they not? Divine injunctions, living up to which would purify and exalt humanity. But are they more divine when uttered through one mouth than another? If it is godlike to return good for evil, does the enunciation of the precept by a Nazarene give it any greater force than its enunciation by an Indian or Tibetan philosopher? We see that the Golden Rule was not original with Jesus, that its birthplace was India. Do what we may, we cannot deny Sakyamuni Buddha a less remote antiquity than several centuries before the birth of Jesus. In seeking a model for his system of ethics, why should Jesus have gone to the foot of the Himalayas rather than to the foot of Sinai except for the fact that the doctrines of Manu and Gautama harmonized exactly with his own philosophy, while those of Jehovah were to him abhorrent and terrifying? The Hindus taught to return good for evil, but the Jehovistic command was: "An eye for an eye" and "a tooth for a tooth."

If the Mosaic "Lord God" was the only living God, and Jesus His only Son, how account for the rebellious language of the latter? Without hesitation or qualification he sweeps away the Jewish *lex talionis* and substitutes for it the law of charity and self-denial. If the Old Testament is a divine revelation, how can the New Testament be? Are we required to believe and worship a Deity who contradicts himself every few hundred years? Was Moses inspired, or was Jesus not the son of God? This is a dilemma from which the theologians are bound to rescue us. It is from this very dilemma that the Gnostics endeavored to snatch budding Christianity.

NOTES

1. J. Jervis-White Jervis, *Genesis Elucidated* (London, 1852), 324.
2. "The Essenes considered oil as a defilement," says Josephus (*The Jewish Wars* 2.8.3).

3. Pliny, *Nat. Hist.* 5.15.73; Josephus, *Antiq.* 13.5.9, 15.10.4–5, 18.1.5.

4. King thinks it is a great exaggeration and is inclined to believe that these Essenes, who were most undoubtedly Buddhist monks, were "merely a continuation of the associations known as 'Sons of the Prophets.'" *The Gnostics and Their Remains* (London, 1864), 22fn.

5. This descent to Hades signified the inevitable fate of each soul to be united for a time with a terrestrial body. This union, or dark prospect for the soul to find itself imprisoned within the dark tenement of a body, was considered by all the ancient philosophers and is even by the modern Buddhists as a punishment.

6. Codex Nazaraeus, trans. M. Norberg (London, 1815), 1:23.

7. The gospels interpreted by Basilides were not our present gospels, which, as it is proved by the greatest authorities, were not in existence in his day. See "Basilides," 2.6 in *Supernatural Religion.*

8. The five mystically make ten. They are androgynes. "Having divided his body in two parts, the Supreme Wisdom became male and female" (*Manu* bk. 1, sloka 32). There are many early Buddhistic ideas to be found in Brahmanism.

9. *Panarion* lib. 1, tom. 3; *Adv. Haer.* 42.1.

18

Oriental Cosmogonies and Bible Records

I f, leaving for the present the prominent founders of Christian sects, we now turn to that of the Ophites, which assumed a definite form about the time of Marcion and the Basilideans, we may find in it the reason for the heresies of all others. Like all other Gnostics, they rejected the Mosaic Bible entirely. Nevertheless, their philosophy, apart from some deductions original with several of the most important founders of the various branches of Gnosticism, was not new. Passing through the Chaldean kabbalistic tradition, it gathered its materials in the Hermetic books, and pursuing its flight still farther back for its metaphysical speculations, we find it floundering among the tenets of Manu and the earliest Hindu ante-sacerdotal genesis.

Many of our eminent antiquarians trace the Gnostic philosophies right back to Buddhism, which does not impair in the least either their or our arguments. We repeat again: Buddhism is but the primitive source of Brahmanism. It is not against the primitive Vedas that Gautama protests. It is against the sacerdotal and official state religion of his country; and the Brahmans, who in order to make room for and give authority to the castes at a later period crammed the ancient manuscripts with interpolated slokas, intended to prove that the castes were predetermined by the Creator by the very fact that each class of men was issued from a more or less noble limb of Brahma.

Gautama Buddha's philosophy was that taught from the beginning of time in the impenetrable secrecy of the inner sanctuaries of the pagodas. We need not be surprised, therefore, to find again in all the fundamental dogmas of the Gnostics the metaphysical tenets of both

Brahmanism and Buddhism. They held that the Old Testament was the revelation of an inferior being, a subordinate divinity, and did not contain a single sentence of their *Sophia*, the Divine Wisdom. As for the New Testament, it had lost its purity when the compilers became guilty of interpolations.

The Gnostic Ophites taught the doctrine of Emanations, so hateful to the defenders of the unity in the trinity and vice versa. The Unknown Deity with them had no name, but his first female emanation was called Bythos or Depth.[1] It answered to the Shekhînah of the kabbalists, the "Veil" which conceals the "Wisdom" in the cranium of the highest of the three heads. Like the Pythagorean Monad, this nameless Wisdom was the Source of Light, and *Ennoia* or Mind is Light itself. The latter was also called the "Primitive Man," like the Adam Kadmon, or ancient ADAM of the Kabbala.

Thus the "nameless and the unrevealed," Bythos (his female reflection), and Ennoia (the revealed Mind proceeding from both, or their Son) are the counterparts of the Chaldean first triad as well as those of the Brahmanic Trimurti. We will compare; in all the three systems we see:

THE GREAT FIRST CAUSE as the ONE, the primordial germ, the unrevealed and grand ALL, existing through itself. In these pantheons:

INDIAN	CHALDEAN	OPHITE
Brahman-Dyaus.	Ilu, Kabbalistic	The Nameless, or
	EN-SOF.	Secret Name.

Whenever the Eternal awakes from its slumber and desires to manifest itself, it divides itself into male and female. It then becomes in every system the Double-Sexed Deity, the universal Father and Mother:

INDIAN	CHALDEAN	OPHITE
Brahma.	Eikon or EN-SOF.	Nameless Spirit.
Nara (male),	Anu (male),	Abrasax (male),
Nari (female).	Anata (female).	Bythos (female).

From the union of the two emanates a third, or creative Principle— the Son, or the manifested Logos, the product of the Divine Mind:

INDIAN	CHALDEAN	OPHITE
Viraj, the Son.	Bel, the Son.	Ophis (another name for Ennoia), the Son.

Moreover, each of these systems has a triple male trinity, each proceeding separately through itself from one female Deity. So, for instance:

INDIAN	CHALDEAN	OPHITE
The trinity Brahma, Vishnu, Siva, are blended into ONE, who is Brahma (neuter gender), creating and being created through Nari (the mother of perpetual fecundity).	The trinity Anu, Bel, Hoa (or Sin, Samas, Bin) blend into ONE, who is Anu (double-sexed) through the Virgin Mylitta.	The trinity Sigê, Bythos, Ennoia become ONE, who is Abrasax, from the Virgin Sophia (or Pneuma), who herself is an emanation of Bythos and the Mystery God and through them emanates Christos.

Though he is termed the "Primitive Man," Ennoia is like the Egyptian Pimander, the "Power of the Thought Divine," the first intelligible manifestation of the Divine Spirit in material form; he is like the "Only Begotten" Son of the "Unknown Father" of all other nations. He is the emblem of the first appearance of the divine Presence in his own works of creation, tangible and visible, and therefore comprehensible.

The Mystery God, or the ever unrevealed Deity, fecundates through His will Bythos, the unfathomable and infinite depth that exists in silence (Sigê) and darkness (for our intellect); this represents the abstract idea of all nature, the ever producing Cosmos. As neither the male nor the female principle, blended into the idea of a double-sexed Deity in ancient conceptions, could be comprehended by an ordinary human intellect, the theology of every people had to create for its religion a Logos, or manifested word, in some shape or other. With the Ophites and other Gnostics who took their models directly from more ancient originals, the unrevealed Bythos and her male counterpart

171

produce Ennoia, and the three in their turn produce Sophia[2]—thus completing the Tetraktys, which will emanate Christos, the very essence of the Father Spirit.

Fecundated by the Divine Light of the Father and Son, the highest spirit and Ennoia, Sophia produces in her turn two other emanations —one perfect Christos, and the second imperfect Sophia-Akhamôth, who becomes the mediatrix between the intellectual and material worlds.

Christos was the mediator and guide between God (the Higher) and everything spiritual in man; Akhamôth—the younger Sophia—held the same duty between the "Primitive man," Ennoia, and matter.

There is a great distinction made in the Gnostic metaphysics between the first unrevealed Logos and the "anointed," who is Christos. Such an identification with the Unknown God, even of Christos (the Aeon who overshadowed him), let alone of the man Jesus, never entered the head of the Gnostics nor even of the direct apostles and of Paul, whatever later forgeries may have added.

And now we ask again the question: Who were the first Christians? Those who were readily converted by the eloquent simplicity of Paul, who promised them, with the name of Jesus, freedom from the narrow bonds of ecclesiasticism. They understood but one thing, that they were the "children of promise" (Galatians 4.28). The "allegory" of the Mosaic Bible was unveiled to them; the covenant "from the Mount Sinai which gendereth to bondage" was Agar (ibid., 24), the old Jewish synagogue, and she was "in bondage with her children" to Jerusalem, the new and the free, "the mother of us all." On the one hand the synagogue and the law which persecuted every one who dared to step across the narrow path of bigotry and dogmatism; on the other, paganism[3] with its grand philosophical truths concealed from sight, unveiling itself but to the few and leaving the masses hopelessly seeking to discover who was *the* god, among this overcrowded pantheon of deities and subdeities.

To others, the apostle of circumcision [Peter], supported by all his followers, was promising, if they obeyed the "law," a life hereafter and a resurrection of which they had no previous idea. At the same time he never lost an occasion to contradict Paul without naming him, but indicating him so clearly that it is next to impossible to doubt whom Peter meant. While he may have converted some men, who—

whether they had believed in the Mosaic resurrection promised by the Pharisees, or had fallen into the nihilistic doctrines of the Sadducees, or had belonged to the polytheistic heathenism of the pagan rabble—had no future after death, nothing but a mournful blank, we do not think that the work of contradiction, carried on so systematically by the two apostles, had much helped their work of proselytism. With the educated thinking classes they succeeded very little, as ecclesiastical history clearly shows. Where was the truth; where the inspired word of God?

"Who then *were* the first Christians?" may still be asked. Doubtless the Ebionites, and in this we follow the authority of the best critics. And who were the Ebionites? The pupils and followers of the early Nazarenes, the kabbalistic Gnostics.

It is a most suggestive fact that there is not a word in the so-called sacred scriptures to show that Jesus was actually regarded as a God by his disciples. Neither before nor after his death did they pay him divine honors. Their relation to him was only that of disciples and "master," by which name they addressed him, as the followers of Pythagoras and Plato addressed their respective masters before them. Whatever words may have been put into the mouths of Jesus, Peter, John, Paul, and others, there is not a single act of adoration recorded on their part, nor did Jesus himself ever declare his identity with his Father. He accused the Pharisees of stoning their prophets, not of deicide. He termed himself the son of God, but took care to assert repeatedly that they were all the children of God, who was the Heavenly Father of all. In preaching this, he but repeated a doctrine taught ages earlier by Hermes, Plato, and other philosophers. Strange contradiction!

There are traditions among the tribes living scattered about beyond the Jordan, as there are many such also among the descendants of the Samaritans at Damascus, Gaza, and at Naplus (the ancient Shechem). Many of these tribes have, notwithstanding the persecutions of eighteen centuries, retained the faith of their fathers in its primitive simplicity. It is there that we have to go for traditions based on historical truths, however disfigured by exaggeration and inaccuracy, and compare them with the religious legends of the Fathers, which they call revelation. Eusebius states that before the siege of Jerusalem, the small Christian community—comprising members of whom many, if not all, knew Jesus and his apostles personally—took refuge in the little town of Pella, on the opposite shore of the Jordan. Surely these simple people, separated for centuries from the rest of the world, ought to have preserved their traditions fresher than any other nation! It is in Palestine that we have to search for the clearest waters of Christianity, let alone its source.

After the death of Jesus, the first Christians all joined together for a time, whether they were Ebionites, Nazarenes, Gnostics, or others. They had no Christian dogmas in those days, and their Christianity consisted in believing Jesus to be a prophet, this belief varying from seeing in him simply a "just man," or a holy, inspired prophet, a vehicle used by Christos and Sophia to manifest themselves. These all united together in opposition to the synagogue and the tyrannical technicalities of the Pharisees, until the primitive group separated into two distinct branches—which we may correctly term the Christian kabbalists of the Jewish Tannaim school and the Christian kabbalists of the Platonic Gnosis.[4] The former were represented by the party composed of the followers of Peter and John, the author of the Apocalypse [or Revelation]; the latter ranged with the Pauline Christianity, blending itself, at the end of the second century, with the Platonic philosophy, and still later engulfing the Gnostic sects, whose symbols and misunderstood mysticism overflowed the Church of Rome.

When the metaphysical conceptions of the Gnostics, who saw in Jesus the Logos and the anointed, began to gain ground, the earliest Christians separated from the Nazarenes, who accused Jesus of perverting the doctrines of John and changing the baptism of the Jordan.[5] "Directly," says H. H. Milman, as "it (the Gospel) got beyond the borders of Palestine, and the name of 'Christ' had acquired sanctity and veneration in the Eastern cities, he became a kind of metaphysical impersonation, while the religion lost its purely moral cast and assumed the character of a speculative theogony."[6] The only half-original document that has reached us from the primitive apostolic days is the *Logia* of Matthew. The real, genuine doctrine has remained in the hands of the Nazarenes, in the Gospel of Matthew containing the Secret Doctrine, the "Sayings of Jesus" mentioned by Papias. These sayings were, no doubt, of the same nature as the small manuscripts placed in the hands of the neophytes, who were candidates for the Initiations into the Mysteries, and which contained the *Aporrheta,* the revelations of some important rites and symbols. For why should Matthew take such precautions to make them "secret" were it otherwise?

Primitive Christianity had its grip, passwords, and degrees of initiation. The innumerable Gnostic gems and amulets are weighty proofs of it. It is a whole symbolical science. The kabbalists were the first to embellish the universal Logos with such terms as "Light of Light" and "the Messenger of Life and Light," and we find these expressions adopted *in toto* by the Christians, with the addition of nearly all the Gnostic terms such as Pleroma (fullness), Archons, Aeons, etc. As to the First-Born, the First, and the Only-Begotten, these are as old as the world. The Acts and the fourth Gospel teem with Gnostic expressions.

The "Christ," then, and the "Logos" existed long before the days of Moses, and we have to seek for the origin of all these in the archaic periods of the primeval Asiatic philosophy.

NOTES

1. We give the systems according to an old diagram preserved among some Copts and the Druzes of Mount Lebanon.
2. Sophia is the highest prototype of woman—the first spiritual Eve. In the Bible the system is reversed and, the intervening emanation being omitted, Eve is degraded to simple humanity.
3. Professor Alexander Wilder, in his edition of R. Payne Knight's *Symbolical Language of Ancient Art and Mythology* (New York, 1876), 16fn., says: "The ancient worship, after it had been excluded from its former shrines and from the metropolitan towns, was maintained for a long time by the inhabitants of humble localities. To this fact it owes its later designation. From being kept up in the *pagi,* or rural districts, its votaries were denominated *pagans,* or provincials."
4. Porphyry makes a distinction between what he calls "the Antique or Oriental philosophy" and the properly Grecian system, that of the Neoplatonists. King says that all these religions and systems

are branches of one antique and common religion, the Asiatic or Buddhistic (*Gnostics and their Remains* 1).

5. Codex Nazaraeus 2:109.
6. *The History of Christianity* (London, 1840), 2:102–103.

19

Mysteries of the Kabbala

We will now give attention to some of the most important Mysteries of the Kabbala and trace their relations to the philosophical myths of various nations.

In the oldest Oriental Kabbala, the Deity is represented as three circles in one, shrouded in a certain smoke or chaotic exhalation. In the preface to the *Zohar*, the three primordial circles are transformed into three Heads; over these is described an exhalation or smoke, neither black nor white, but colorless, and circumscribed within a circle. This is the unknown Essence. The origin of the Jewish image may, perhaps, be traced to Hermes' *Pimander*, the Egyptian Logos, who appears within a cloud of a humid nature, with a smoke escaping from it. In the *Zohar* the highest God is, as we have shown in the preceding chapter and as in the case of the Hindu and Buddhist philosophies, a pure abstraction, whose objective existence is denied by the latter.

The "three Heads," superposed above each other, are evidently taken from the three mystic triangles of the Hindus, which also superpose each other. The highest head contains the Trinity in Chaos, out of which springs the manifested trinity. EN-SOF, the Unrevealed Forever, who is boundless and unconditioned, cannot create, and therefore it seems to us a great error to attribute to him a "creative thought," as is commonly done by the interpreters. In every cosmogony this supreme Essence is passive; if boundless, infinite, and unconditioned, it can have no thought or idea. It acts not as the result of volition, but in obedience to its own nature and according to the fatality of the law of which it is itself the embodiment. Thus with the Hebrew kabbalists, EN-SOF is non-existent, for it is incomprehensible to our

177

finite intellects and therefore cannot exist to our minds. Its first emanation was *Sephirah*, the crown, *Kether*.

When the time for an active period had come, a natural expansion of this Divine essence was produced from within outwardly, obedient to eternal and immutable law; and from this eternal and infinite light (which to us is darkness) was emitted a spiritual substance. This was the First Sephirah, containing in herself the other nine Sephiroth, or intelligences. In their totality and unity they represent the archetypal man, Adam Kadmon, the *protogonos*, who in his individuality or unity is yet dual, or bisexual, the Greek *Didymos*, for he is the prototype of all humanity.

Thus we obtain three trinities, each contained in a "head." In the first head, or face (the three-faced Hindu Trimurti), we find Sephirah [Kether], the first androgyne, at the apex of the upper triangle, emitting *Hokhmah*, or Wisdom, a masculine and active potency—also called Yâh—and *Binah*, or Intelligence, a female and passive potency, also represented by the name Jehovah. These three form the first trinity or "face" of the Sephiroth. This triad emanated *Hesed*, or Mercy, a mascu-line active potency, also called Eloah, from which emanated *Geburah*, or Justice, also called Pa'had, a feminine passive potency; from the union of these two was produced *Tiphereth*, or Beauty, Clemency, the Spiritual Sun, known by the divine name Elohim; and the sec-ond triad, "face," or "head" was formed. These emanated in their turn the masculine potency *Netzah*, Firmness, or Yehovah-Tsabaôth, who issued the feminine passive potency *Hod*, Splendor, or Elohim-Tsabaôth; the two produced *Yesod*, or Foundation, who is the mighty living one El Hay, thus yielding the third trinity or "head."

The tenth Sephirah is rather a duad, and is represented on the dia-grams as the lowest circle. It is *Malkhuth*, or Kingdom, and Shekhînah, also called Adonai, and Cherubim among the angelic hosts. The first "head" is called the intellectual world; the second "head" is the sensuous, or the world of perception; and the third is the material or physical world.

"Before he gave any shape to the universe," says the Kabbala, "before he produced any form, he was alone without any form and resemblance to anything else. Who, then, can comprehend him, how he was before the creation, since he was formless? Hence it is forbidden to represent him by any form, similitude, or even by his sacred name, by a single letter, or a single point. . . . The Aged of the Aged, the Unknown of the Unknown, has a form, and yet no form. He has a form whereby the universe is preserved, and yet has no form, because he cannot be comprehended. When he first assumed a form (in Sephirah, his first emanation), he caused nine splendid lights to emanate from it" (*Idrah Zutah* 1.41–45).

And now we will turn to the Hindu esoteric cosmogony and definition of "Him who is, and yet is not." "From him who is,[1] from this immortal Principle which exists in our minds but cannot be perceived by the senses, is born Purusha, the Divine male and female, who became *Narayana*, or the Divine Spirit moving on the water" (*Manu* 1.11).

Svayambhu, the unknown essence of the Brahmans, is identical with EN-SOF, the unknown essence of the kabbalists. As with the latter, the ineffable name could not be pronounced by the Hindus, under the penalty of death. In the ancient primitive trinity of India, that which certainly may be considered pre-Vedic, the germ which fecundates the mother-principle, the mundane egg, or the universal womb, is called *Nara*, the Spirit, or the Holy Ghost, which emanates from the primordial essence. It is like Sephirah, the oldest emanation, called the primordial point and the White Head, for it is the point of divine light appearing from within the fathomless and boundless darkness. In *Manu* it is "Nara or the Spirit of God, which moves on Ayana (Chaos, or place of motion) and is called NARAYANA, or moving on the waters" (1.10). In the literature of Hermes, the Egyptian, we read: "In the beginning of the time there was naught in the chaos." But when the "verbum," issuing from the void like a "colorless smoke," makes its appearance, then "this verbum moved on the humid principle" (*Corpus Hermeticum* 3.1). And in Genesis (1.2) we find: "And darkness was upon the face of the deep (chaos). And the Spirit of God moved upon the face of the waters."

The first beginning opens invariably with the unknown and passive deity, producing from himself a certain active power or virtue, "Rational," which is sometimes called WISDOM, sometimes the SON, very often God, Angel, Lord, and LOGOS. The last is sometimes applied to the very first emanation, but in several systems it proceeds from the first androgyne or double ray produced at the beginning by the unseen. Philo depicts this wisdom as male and female.

179

Strictly speaking, it is difficult to view the Book of Genesis otherwise than as a chip from the trunk of the mundane tree of universal
cosmogony, rendered in Oriental allegories. As cycle succeeded cycle,
and one nation after another came upon the world's stage to play
its brief part in the majestic drama of human life, each new people
evolved its own religion from ancestral traditions, giving it a local
color and stamping it with its individual characteristics. While each
of these religions had its distinguishing traits, by which, were there
no other archaic vestiges, the physical and psychological status of
its creators could be estimated, all preserved a common likeness to
one prototype. This parent cult was none other than the primitive
"Wisdom Religion."

The Jewish scriptures are no exception. Their national history, if
they can claim any autonomy before the return from Babylon and
were anything more than migratory septs of Hindu pariahs, cannot be
carried back a day beyond Moses; and if this ex-Egyptian priest must,
from theological necessity, be transformed into a Hebrew patriarch, we
must insist that the Jewish nation was lifted with that smiling infant
out of the bulrushes of Lake Moeris. Abraham, their alleged father,
belongs to the universal mythology. Most likely he is but one of the
numerous aliases of *Zeruan* (Saturn), the king of the golden age, who
is also called the old man (emblem of time).

The thread of glory emitted by EN-SOF from the highest of the three
kabbalistic heads, through which "all things shine with light," the
thread which makes its exit through Adam Primus, is the individual
spirit of every man. The immortal spirit delights in the sons of men,
who, without this spirit, are but dualities (physical body and astral
soul, or that life principle which animates even the lowest of the
animal kingdom). But we have seen that the doctrine teaches that
this spirit cannot unite itself with that man in whom matter and the
grossest propensities of his animal soul will ever be crowding it out.
Therefore Solomon, who is made to speak under the inspiration of his
own spirit that possesses him for the time being, utters the following
words of wisdom: "Hearken unto me, my son" (the dual man), "blessed
are they who keep my ways. . . . Blessed is the man that heareth me,
watching daily at my gates. . . . for whoso findeth me, findeth life,
and shall obtain favor of the Lord. . . . But he that sinneth against me
wrongeth his own soul . . . and loves death" (Proverbs 8.32–36).

180

These endless emanations of the one First Cause, all of which were gradually transformed by the popular fancy into distinct gods, spirits, angels, and demons, were so little considered immortal that all were assigned a limited existence. And this belief, common to all the peoples of antiquity, to the Chaldean Magi as well as to the Egyptians, and even in our day held by the Brahmans and Buddhists, most triumphantly evidences the monotheism of the ancient religious systems. This doctrine calls the life period of all the inferior divinities "one day of Brahma." After a cycle of four billion, three hundred and twenty million human years, the tradition says, the trinity itself, with all the lesser divinities, will be annihilated together with the universe and cease to exist. Then another universe will gradually emerge from the pralaya (dissolution), and men on earth will be enabled to comprehend Svayambhu as he is. Alone, this primal cause will exist forever, in all his glory, filling the infinite space. What better proof could be adduced of the deep reverential feeling with which the "heathen" regard the one supreme, eternal cause of all things visible and invisible.

If the Christians understood Genesis in their own way and if, accepting the texts literally, they enforced upon the uneducated masses the belief in a creation of our world out of nothing and moreover assigned to it a *beginning*, it is surely not the Tannaim, the sole expounders of the hidden meaning contained in the Bible, who are to be blamed. No more than any other philosophers had they ever believed in spontaneous, limited, or *ex nihilo* creations. The Kabbala has survived to show that their philosophy was precisely that of the modern Nepal Buddhists, the Svabhavikas. They believed in the eternity and the indestructibility of matter and hence in many prior creations and destructions of worlds before our own. "There were old worlds which perished" (*Idrah Zutah* 10.421).

Moreover, they believed, again like the Svabhavikas (now termed atheists), that everything proceeds (is created) from its own nature and that once the first impulse is given by that Creative Force inherent in the "Self-created substance," or Sephirah, everything evolves out of itself, following its pattern, the more spiritual prototype which precedes it in the scale of infinite creation. "The indivisible point, which has no limit and cannot be comprehended (for it is absolute), expanded from within and formed a brightness which served as a garment (a veil) to the indivisible points. It too expanded from within. . . . Thus, everything originated through a constant upheaving agitation, and thus finally the world originated" (*Zohar*).

This cosmogony, adopted with a change of names in the Rabbinical Kabbala, found its way later, with some additional speculations of Manes, the half-Magus and half-Platonist, into the great body of Gnosticism. The real doctrines of the Basilideans, Valentinians, and the Marcionites cannot be correctly ascertained in the prejudiced and calumnious writings of the Fathers of the Church, but rather in what remains of the works of the Bardesanians, known as the Nazarenes. It is next to impossible, now that all their manuscripts and books are destroyed, to assign to any of these sects its due part in dissenting views. But there are a few men still living who have preserved books and direct traditions about the Ophites, although they care little to impart them to the world. Among the unknown sects of Mount Lebanon and Palestine the truth has been concealed for more than a thousand years.

Having thus traced the similarity of views respecting the Logos, Metatron, and Mediator, as found in the Kabbala and the codex of the Christian Nazarenes and Gnostics, the reader is prepared to appreciate the audacity of the patristic scheme to reduce a purely metaphysical figure into concrete form and make it appear as if the finger of prophecy had from time immemorial been pointing down the vista of ages to Jesus as the coming Messiah. A theomythos intended to symbolize the coming day—near the close of the great cycle, when the "glad tidings" from heaven should proclaim the universal brotherhood and common faith of humanity, the day of regeneration—was violently distorted into an accomplished fact.

And thus, one by one, perished the Gnostics, the only heirs to whose share had fallen a few stray crumbs of the unadulterated truth of primitive Christianity. All was confusion and turmoil during these first centuries, till the moment when all these contradictory dogmas were finally forced upon the Christian world, and examination was forbidden. For long ages it was made a sacrilege, punishable with severe penalties, often death, to seek to comprehend that which the Church had so conveniently elevated to the rank of divine mystery. But since biblical critics have taken upon themselves to "set the house in order," the cases have become reversed. Pagan creditors now come from every part of the globe to claim their own, and Christian theology begins to be suspected of complete bankruptcy.

And so all our philosophers were swept away by the ignorant and superstitious masses. The Philaletheians, the lovers of truth, and their eclectic school perished. And there, where the young Hypatia had taught the highest philosophical doctrines and where Ammonius Saccas had explained that "the whole which Christ had in view was to reinstate and restore to its primitive integrity the wisdom of the ancients—to reduce within bounds the universally prevailing dominion of superstition . . . and to exterminate the various errors that had found their way into the different popular religions"[2] — there, we say, freely raved the hoi polloi of Christianity. No more precepts from the mouth of the "God-taught philosopher," but others expounded by the incarnation of a most cruel, fiendish superstition.

Notes

1. *Ego sum qui sum* (Exodus 3.14).
2. J. L. von Mosheim, *Historical Commentaries on the State of Christianity*, trans. R. S. Vidal (New York, 1868), 1:352.

20

Esoteric Doctrines of Buddhism
Parodied in Christianity

At the beginning of the fourth century crowds began gathering at the door of the academy where the learned and unfortunate Hypatia expounded the doctrines of the divine Plato and Plotinus, and thereby impeded the progress of Christian proselytism. She had too successfully dispelled the mist hanging over the religious "mysteries" invented by the Fathers not to be considered dangerous. This alone would have been sufficient to imperil both herself and her followers. It was precisely the teachings of this pagan philosopher, which had been so freely borrowed by the Christians to give a finishing touch to their otherwise incomprehensible scheme, that had seduced so many into joining the new religion; and now the Platonic light began shining so inconveniently bright upon the pious patchwork as to allow every one to see whence the "revealed" doctrines were derived. But there was a still greater peril. Hypatia had studied under Plutarch, the head of the Athenian school, and had learned all the secrets of theurgy. While she lived to instruct the multitude, no divine miracles could be produced before one who could divulge the natural causes by which they took place. Her doom was sealed by Cyril, whose eloquence she eclipsed and whose authority, built on degrading superstitions, had to yield before hers, which was erected on the rock of immutable natural law.

The hated and erudite pagan scholars and the no less learned Gnostics held in their doctrines alone the hitherto concealed wires of all these theological marionettes. Once the curtain was lifted, the connection between the old pagan and the new Christian religions would have been exposed. And then what would have become of the

184

Mysteries into which it is sin and blasphemy to pry? With such a coincidence between the astronomical allegories of various pagan myths and the dates adopted by Christianity for the nativity, crucifixion, and resurrection, and such an identity of rites and ceremonies, what would have been the fate of the new religion had not the Church, under the pretext of serving Christ, got rid of the too well-informed philosophers? To guess what, if the coup d'état had then failed, might have been the prevailing religion in our own century would indeed be a hard task. But in all probability, the state of things which made of the Middle Ages a period of intellectual darkness, degraded the nations of the Occident, and lowered the European of those days almost to the level of a Papuan savage could not have occurred.

The fears of the Christians were but too well founded, and their pious zeal and prophetic insight were rewarded from the very first. In the demolition of the Serapeion, after the bloody riot between the Christian mob and the pagan worshippers had ended with the interference of the emperor, a Latin cross, of a perfect Christian shape, was discovered hewn upon the granite slabs of the adytum. This was a lucky discovery, indeed; and the monks did not fail to claim that the cross had been hallowed by the pagans in a spirit of prophecy. But, archaeology and symbolism, those tireless and implacable enemies of clerical false pretenses, have found in the hieroglyphics of the legend running around the design at least a partial interpretation of its meaning.

According to C. W. King and other numismatists and archaeologists, the cross was placed there as the symbol of eternal life. Such a Tau, or Egyptian cross, was used in the Bacchic and Eleusinian Mysteries. Symbol of the dual generative power, it was laid upon the breast of the initiate after his "new birth" was accomplished and the Mystai had returned from their baptism in the sea. It was a mystic sign that his spiritual birth had regenerated and united his astral soul with his divine spirit and that he was ready to ascend in spirit to the blessed abodes of light and glory—the Eleusinia.

The Tau was both a magic talisman and a religious emblem. It was adopted by the Christians through the Gnostics and kabbalists, who used it widely, as their numerous gems testify, and who had the Tau (or handled cross) from the Egyptians and the Latin cross from the Buddhist missionaries, who brought it from India. The Assyrians,

Egyptians, ancient Americans, Hindus, and Romans had it in various but very slight modifications of shape. Till very late in the medieval ages, it was considered a potent spell against epilepsy and demoniacal possession; and the "signet of the living God," brought down in St. John's vision by the angel ascending from the east to "seal the servants of our God in their foreheads," was but the same mystic Tau—the Egyptian cross.

In its mystical sense, the Egyptian cross owes its origin as an emblem to the realization by the earliest philosophy of an androgynous dualism of every manifestation in nature, which proceeds from the abstract ideal of a likewise androgynous deity, while the Christian emblem is simply due to chance. Had the Mosaic law prevailed, Jesus would have been stoned. The crucifix was an instrument of torture, and as utterly common among Romans as it was unknown among Semitic nations. It was called the "Tree of Infamy." Later it was adopted as a Christian symbol, but during the first two decades the apostles looked upon it with horror. It is certainly not the Christian Cross that John had in mind when speaking of the "signet of the living God" but the *mystic* Tau—the Tetragrammaton, or mighty name, which on the most ancient kabbalistic talismans was represented by the four Hebrew letters composing the Holy Word.

It is well known that the earliest Christian emblems—before it was ever attempted to represent the bodily appearance of Jesus— were the Lamb, the Good Shepherd, and the Fish. The origin of the last emblem, which has so puzzled the archaeologists, thus becomes comprehensible: The whole secret lies in the easily ascertained fact that, while in the Kabbala the King Messiah is called "Interpreter" or Revealer of the mystery and is shown to be the fifth emanation, in the Talmud the Messiah is very often designated as "Dag," or the Fish. This is an inheritance from the Chaldeans and relates— as the very name indicates—to the Babylonian Dagon, the man-fish, who was the instructor and interpreter of the people to whom he appeared.

[Such mythological animal forms symbolize stages in the evolution of the world, the various cycles through which the Earth and its inhabitants pass.]

The grand cycle, as we have heretofore remarked, includes the progress of mankind from its germ in the primordial man of spiritual

form to the deepest depth of degradation he can reach—each successive step in the descent being accompanied by a greater strength and
grossness of the physical form than its precursor—and ends with the
Flood. But while the grand cycle or age is running its course, seven
minor cycles are passed, each marking the evolution of a new race out
of the preceding one in a new world. Each of these races or grand types
of humanity breaks up into subdivisions of families, and they again
into nations and tribes, as we see the earth's inhabitants subdivided
today into Mongols, Caucasians, Indians, etc.

The esoteric doctrine then teaches, like Buddhism and Brahmanism, and even the persecuted Kabbala, that the one infinite and unknown Essence exists from all eternity, and in regular and harmonious
successions is either passive or active. In the poetical phraseology
of Manu these conditions are called the "day" and the "night" of
Brahma. The latter is either "awake" or "asleep." The Svabhavikas,
or philosophers of the oldest school of Buddhism (which still exists in
Nepal), speculate only upon the active condition of this "Essence,"
which they call Svabhavat, and deem it foolish to theorize upon the
abstract and "unknowable" power in its passive condition.

The Buddhists maintain that there is no Creator but an infinitude
of creative powers, which collectively form the one eternal substance,
the essence of which is inscrutable—hence not a subject for speculation for any true philosopher. Upon inaugurating an active period, says
the Secret Doctrine, an expansion of this Divine essence occurs from
within outwardly, in obedience to eternal and immutable law, and the
phenomenal or visible universe is the ultimate result of the long chain
of cosmic forces thus progressively set in motion. In like manner, when
the passive condition is resumed, a contraction of the Divine essence
takes place, and the previous work of creation is gradually and progressively undone. The visible universe becomes disintegrated, its material
dispersed; and "darkness," solitary and alone, broods once more over
the face of the "deep." To use a metaphor which will convey the idea
still more clearly, an outbreathing of the "unknown essence" produces
the world; and an inhalation causes it to disappear. The process has
been going on from all eternity, and our present universe is but one
of an infinite series which had no beginning and will have no end.

Thus we are enabled to build our theories solely on the visible
manifestations of the Deity, on its objective natural phenomena. To

187

apply to these creative principles the term God is puerile and absurd. One might as well call the fire which fuses the metal or the air that cools it when it is run in the mold by the name of Benvenuto Cellini. If the inner and ever-concealed spiritual, and to our minds abstract, Essence within these forces can ever be connected with the creation of the physical universe, it is but in the sense given to it by Plato. At best it may be termed the framer of the abstract universe which developed gradually in the Divine Thought, within which it had lain dormant.

When the cycle of creation is run down, the energy of the manifested word is weakening. He alone, the Unconceivable, is unchangeable (ever latent), but the Creative Force, though also eternal, as it has been in the former from "no beginning," yet must be subject to periodical cycles of activity and rest; as it had a beginning in one of its aspects when it first emanated, it must therefore also have an end. Thus the evening succeeds the day, and the night of the deity approaches. Brahma is gradually falling asleep. In one of the books of *Zohar*, we read the following:

> As Moses was keeping a vigil on Mount Sinai in company with the Deity, who was concealed from his sight by a cloud, he felt a great fear overcome him and suddenly asked: "Lord, where art Thou . . . sleepest thou O Lord?" And the Spirit answered him: "I never sleep; were I to fall asleep for a moment before my time, all the Creation would crumble into dissolution in one instant."

And Vamadeva-Modaliyar describes the "Night of Brahma," or the second period of the Divine Unknown existence, thus:

> Strange noises are heard, proceeding from every point. . . . These are the precursors of the Night of Brahma; dusk rises at the horizon and the Sun passes away behind the thirtieth degree of Makara (sign of the zodiac), and will reach no more the sign of the *Mina* (zodiacal Pisces, or fish). The gurus of the pagodas appointed to watch the rasi-chakra (zodiac) may now break their circle and instruments, for they are henceforth useless.
>
> Gradually light pales, heat diminishes, uninhabitable spots multiply on the earth, the air becomes more and more rarefied; the springs of waters dry up, the great rivers see their waves exhausted, the ocean shows its sandy bottom, and plants die. Men and animals decrease in size daily. Life and motion lose their force, planets can

188

hardly gravitate in space; they are extinguished one by one, like a lamp which the hand of the chokra (servant) neglects to replenish. Surya (the Sun) flickers and goes out, matter falls into dissolution (pralaya), and Brahma merges back into Dyaus, the Unrevealed God, and his task being accomplished, he falls asleep. Another day is passed, night sets in and continues until the future dawn.

And now again reenter into the golden egg of His Thought, the germs of all that exist, as the divine Manu tells us. During His peaceful rest, the animated beings endowed with the principles of action cease their functions, and all feeling (manas) becomes dormant. When they are all absorbed in the Supreme Soul, this Soul of all the beings sleeps in complete repose, till the day when it resumes its form, and awakes again from its primitive darkness.[1]

If we now examine the ten mythical avatars of Vishnu, we find them recorded in the following progression:

1. Matsya-Avatar: as a fish. It will also be his tenth and last avatar, at the end of the Kali-yuga.

2. Kurma-Avatar: as a tortoise.

3. Varaha: as a boar.

4. Nara-Sinha: as a man-lion, the last animal stage.

5. Vamana: as a dwarf, the first step toward the human form.

6. Parasu-Rama: as a hero, but yet an imperfect man.

7. Rama-Chandra: as the hero of the *Ramayana*. Physically a perfect man; his next of kin, friend, and ally is Hanuman, the monkey god, the monkey endowed with speech.[2]

8. Krishna-Avatar: the Son of the Virgin Devanaguy (or Devaki), one formed by God, or rather by the manifested Deity Vishnu, who is identical with Adam Kadmon. Krishna is also called Kaneya, the Son of the Virgin.

9. Gautama Buddha, Siddhartha, or Sakyamuni. (The Buddhists reject this doctrine of their Buddha being an incarnation of Vishnu.)

10. This avatar has not yet occurred. It is expected in the future, like the Christian Advent, an idea undoubtedly copied from the Hindu. When Vishnu appears for the last time he will come as a "Savior." According to the opinion of some Brahmans he will appear himself in the form of the horse Kalki. Others maintain that he will be mounting it. This horse is the envelope of the spirit of evil, and Vishnu will

mount it, invisible to all, till he has conquered it for the last time. The "Kalki-Avatar," or the last incarnation, divides Brahmanism into two sects. That of the Vaishnava refuses to recognize the incarnations of their god Vishnu in animal forms literally. They claim that these must be understood as allegorical.

In this diagram of avatars we see traced the gradual evolution and transformation of all species out of the pre-Silurian mud of Darwin and the *ilus* of Sanchoniathon and Berosus. Beginning with the Azoic time, corresponding to the ilus in which Brahma implants the creative germ, we pass through the Paleozoic and Mesozoic times, covered by the first and second incarnations as the fish and tortoise; then the Cenozoic, which is embraced by the incarnations in the animal and semihuman forms of the boar and man-lion; and then we come to the fifth and crowning geological period, designated as the "era of mind, or age of man," whose symbol in the Hindu mythology is the dwarf—the first attempt of nature at the creation of man. In this diagram we should follow the main idea, not judge the degree of knowledge of the ancient philosophers by the literal acceptance of the popular form in which it is presented to us in the grand epical poem of the Mahabharata and its chapter the Bhagavad Gita.

Even the four ages of the Hindu chronology contain a far more philosophical idea than appears on the surface. It defines them according to both the psychological or mental and the physical states of man during their period. Krita-yuga, the golden age, the "age of joy," or spiritual innocence of man; Treta-yuga, the age of silver, or that of fire—the period of supremacy of man and of giants and of the sons of God; Dvapara-yuga, the age of bronze—a mixture already of purity and impurity (spirit and matter), the age of doubt; and at last our own, the Kali-yuga, or age of iron, of darkness, misery, and sorrow. In this age, Vishnu had to incarnate himself in Krishna, in order to save humanity from the goddess Kali, consort of Siva, the all-annihilating—the goddess of death, destruction, and human misery. Kali is the best emblem to represent the "fall of man," the falling of spirit into the degradation of matter with all its terrific results. We have to rid ourselves of Kali before we can ever reach "Moksha," or Nirvana, the abode of blessed Peace and Spirit.

With the Buddhists the last incarnation is the fifth. When Maitreya-Buddha comes, then our present world will be destroyed, and a new and a better one will replace it. The four arms of every Hindu Deity are the emblems of the four preceding manifestations of our earth from its invisible state, while its head typifies the fifth and last Kalki-Avatar, when this world will be destroyed, and the power of Budh—Wisdom (of Brahma, among the Hindus)—will be again called into requisition to manifest itself as a Logos to create the future world.

In this succession of avatars we see just as clearly the truly philosophical idea of a simultaneous spiritual and physical evolution of creatures and man. From a fish the progress of this dual transformation carries on the physical form through the shape of a tortoise, a boar, and a man-lion; and then, appearing in the dwarf of humanity, it shows Parasu-Rama, a physically perfect but spiritually undeveloped entity, until it carries mankind, personified by one godlike man, to the apex of physical and spiritual perfection—a god on earth.

But this does not relate to our degenerated mankind; it is only occasionally that men are born who are the types of what man should be but is not yet. The first races of men were spiritual, and their protoplastic bodies were not composed of the gross and material substances which we now see. The first men were created with all the faculties of the Deity and powers far transcending those of the angelic host; for they were the direct emanations of Adam Kadmon, the primitive man, the Macrocosm, while the present humanity is several degrees removed even from the earthly Adam, who was the Microcosm, or "the little world."

Hence man was intended from the first to be of both a progressive and a retrogressive nature. Beginning at the apex of the divine cycle, he gradually began receding from the center of Light, acquiring at every new and lower sphere of being (worlds each inhabited by a different race of human beings) a more solid physical form and losing a portion of his divine faculties.

In the "fall of Adam" we must see, not the personal transgression of man, but simply the law of the dual evolution. Adam, or "Man," begins his career of existences by dwelling in the garden of Eden, "dressed in the celestial garment, which is a garment of heavenly light" (*Zohar* 2.229b); but when expelled he is "clothed" by God, or the eternal law of Evolution or necessarianism, with coats of skin. But even on this earth of material degradation—in which the divine spark (Soul, a corruscation of the Spirit) was to begin its physical progression in a series of imprisonments from a stone up to a man's body—if he but exercises his will and calls his deity to his help, man can transcend the powers of the angel. "Know ye not that we shall judge angels?" asks Paul (1 Corinthians 6.3). The real man is the Soul (Spirit), teaches the *Zohar*.

In the writings of Paul, the entity of man is divided into a trine—flesh, psychical existence or soul, and the overshadowing and at the same time interior entity or Spirit. His phraseology is very definite when he teaches the *anastasis*, or the continuation of life of those who have died. He maintains that there is a psychical body which is sown in the corruptible, and a spiritual body that is raised in incorruptible substance. "The first man is of the earth earthy, the second man from heaven." Even James (3.15) identifies the soul by saying that its "wisdom descendeth not from above but is terrestrial, psychical, demoniacal" (see Greek text). Plato, speaking of the Soul (*psyche*), observes that "when she allies herself to the *nous* (divine substance, a god, as psyche is a goddess), she does everything aright and felicitously; but the case is otherwise when she attaches herself to *anoia*."

What Plato calls *nous*, Paul terms the Spirit; and Jesus makes the heart what Paul calls the flesh. The natural condition of mankind was called in Greek *apostasia*; the new condition *anastasis*. In Adam came the former (death), in Christ the latter (resurrection), for it is he who first publicly taught mankind the "Noble Path" to eternal life, as Gautama pointed the same Path to Nirvana. To accomplish both ends there was but one way, according to the teachings of both: "Poverty, chastity, contemplation or inner prayer, contempt for wealth and the illusive joys of this world."

NOTES

1. L. Jacolliot, *Les Fils de Dieu* (Paris, 1875), 229–30.
2. May it not be that Hanuman is the representative of that link of beings half-man and half-monkey, which according to the theories of Hovelacque and Schleicher were arrested in their development, and fell, so to say, into a retrogressive evolution?

21

Early Christian Heresies and Secret Societies

In the next two chapters we shall notice the most important of the Christian secret sects—the so-called "heresies" which sprang into existence between the first and fourth centuries of our era.

Glancing rapidly at the Ophites and Nazareans, we shall pass to their scions which yet exist in Syria and Palestine under the name of the Druzes of Mount Lebanon and near Basra or Bassorah, in Persia, under that of the Mandaeans, or Disciples of St. John. All these sects have an immediate connection with our subject, for they are of kabbalistic parentage and have once held to the secret "Wisdom Religion," recognizing as the One Supreme the Mystery God of the Ineffable Name. Noticing these numerous secret societies of the past, we will bring them into direct comparison with several of the modern ones. We will conclude with a brief survey of the Jesuits, and of that venerable nightmare of the Roman Catholic Church, modern Freemasonry. All of these modern as well as ancient fraternities—present Freemasonry excepted—were and are more or less connected with magic, practically as well as theoretically; and every one of them— Freemasonry *not* excepted—was and still is accused of demonolatry, blasphemy, and licentiousness.

Our object is not to write the history of any of them, but only to compare these sorely abused communities with the Christian sects, past and present, and then, taking historical facts for our guidance, to defend the secret science, as well as the men who are its students and champions, against any unjust imputation.

193

One by one the tide of time engulfed the sects of the early centuries, until of the whole number only one survived in its primitive integrity. That one still exists, still teaches the doctrine of its founder, still exemplifies its faith in works of power. The quicksands which swallowed up every other outgrowth of the religious agitation of the time of Jesus, with its records, relics, and traditions, proved firm ground for this. Driven from their native land, its members found refuge in Persia, and today the anxious traveler may converse with the direct descendants of the "Disciples of John," who listened on the Jordan's shore to the "man sent from God" and were baptized and believed. This curious people, numbering 30,000 or more, are miscalled "Christians of St. John," but in fact should be known by their old name of Nazareans, or their new one of Mandaeans.

To term them Christians is wholly unwarranted. They neither believe in Jesus as Christ, nor accept his atonement, nor adhere to his Church, nor revere its "Holy Scriptures." Neither do they worship the Jehovah God of the Jews and Christians, a circumstance which of course proves that their founder, John the Baptist, did not worship him either. And if not, what right has he to a place in the Bible, or in the portrait gallery of Christian saints?

But we must proceed in our work of showing the various origins of Christianity, and also the sources from which Jesus derived his own ideas of God and humanity.

The Koinobioi lived in Egypt, where Jesus passed his early youth. They were usually confused with the Therapeutae, who were a branch of this widespread society. After the downfall of the principal sanctuaries, which had already begun in the days of Plato, the many different sects, such as the Gymnosophists and the Magi, the Pythagoreans, the Sufis, and the Rishis of Kashmir, instituted a kind of international and universal freemasonry among their esoteric societies.

The mysterious Druzes of Mount Lebanon are the descendants of all these. Solitary Copts, earnest students scattered hither and thither throughout the sandy solitudes of Egypt, Arabia Petraea, Palestine, and the impenetrable forests of Abyssinia, though rarely met with, may sometimes be seen. Many and various are the nationalities of the disciples of that mysterious school, and many the sideshoots of that one primitive stock. The secrecy preserved by these sublodges, as well as by the one and supreme great lodge, has ever been proportionate to the activity of religious persecutions; and now, in the face of growing materialism, their very existence is becoming a mystery.

Whoever desires to assure himself that there now exists a religion which for centuries has baffled the impudent inquisitiveness of missionaries and the persevering inquiry of science, let him violate, if he can, the seclusion of the Syrian Druzes.

That their religion exhibits traces of Magianism and Gnosticism is natural, as the whole of the Ophite esoteric philosophy is at the bottom of it. But the characteristic dogma of the Druzes is the absolute unity of God. He is the essence of life and, although incomprehensible and invisible, is to be known through occasional manifestations in human form.[1] Like the Hindus they hold that he was incarnated more than once on earth. H'amza was the precursor of the last manifestation to be (the tenth avatar),[2] not the inheritor of Hakim, who is yet to come. H'amza was the personification of the "Universal Wisdom." Their ideas on transmigration are Pythagorean and kabbalistic. The spirit, or al-Tamîmî (the divine soul), was in Elijah and John the Baptist; and the soul of Jesus was that of H'amza, that is to say, of the same degree of purity and sanctity. Until their resurrection, by which they understand the day when the spiritual bodies of men will be absorbed into God's own essence and being (the Nirvana of the Hindus), the souls of men will keep their astral forms, except the few chosen ones who, from the moment of their separation from their bodies, begin to exist as pure spirits. They divide the life of man into soul, body, and intelligence or mind. It is the last which imparts and communicates to the soul the divine spark from its H'amza (Christos).

"Chastity, honesty, meekness, and mercy" are thus the four theological virtues of all Druzes, besides several others demanded from the initiates; "murder, theft, cruelty, covetousness, slander" are the five sins, to which several other sins are added in the sacred tablets, but which we must abstain from giving. The morality of the Druzes is strict and uncompromising. Nothing can tempt one of these Lebanon Unitarians to go astray from what he is taught to consider his duty. Their ritual being unknown to outsiders, their would-be historians have hitherto denied them one. Their "Thursday meetings" are open to all, but no interloper has ever participated in the rites of initiation which take place occasionally on Fridays in the greatest secrecy. Women are admitted to the rites as well as men, and they play a part of great importance at the initiation of men. The probation, unless some extraordinary exception is made, is long and severe.

Once in a certain period of time, a solemn ceremony takes place, during which all the elders and the initiates of the highest two degrees start out for a pilgrimage of several days to a certain place in the mountains. They meet within the safe precincts of a monastery said to have been erected during the earliest times of the Christian era. Outwardly one sees but old ruins of a once grand edifice, used (says the legend) by some Gnostic sects as a place of worship during the religious persecutions. The ruins above ground, however, are but a convenient mask, the subterranean chapel, halls, and cells covering an area of ground far greater than the upper building, while the richness of ornamentation, the beauty of the ancient sculptures, and the gold and silver vessels in this sacred resort appear like "a dream of glory," according to the expression of an initiate.

As the lamaseries of Mongolia and Tibet are visited upon grand occasions by the holy shadow of "Lord Buddha," so here, during the ceremonial, appears the resplendent ethereal form of H'amza, the Blessed, which instructs the faithful. The most extraordinary feats of what would be termed magic take place during the several nights that the convocation lasts; and one of the greatest mysteries—faithful copy of the past—is accomplished within the discreet bosom of our mother earth. Not an echo, nor the faintest sound, not a glimmer of light betrays to the outside world the grand secret of the initiates.

H'amza, like Jesus, was a mortal man, and yet "H'amza" and "Christos" are synonymous terms as to their inner and hidden meaning. Both are symbols of the Nous, the divine and higher soul of man—his spirit. The doctrine taught by the Druzes on that particular question of the duality of spiritual man, consisting of one soul mortal and another immortal, is identical with that of the Gnostics, the older Greek philosophers, and other initiates.

Before we close the subject we may add that if a stranger asks for admission to a "Thursday" meeting he will never be refused. Only, if he is a Christian, the 'Uqqâl will open a Bible and read from it; and if a Mohammedan, he will hear a few chapters of the Koran, and the ceremony will end with this. They will wait until he is gone, and then, shutting well the doors of their convent, take to their own rites and books, passing for this purpose into their subterranean sanctuaries.

And yet the Druzes may be said to belong to one of the least esoteric of secret societies. There are others far more powerful and learned, the existence of which is not even suspected in Europe. There are many branches belonging to the great "Mother Lodge" which, mixed up with certain communities, may be termed secret sects within other sects.

From the very day when the first mystic found the means of communication between this world and the worlds of the invisible host, between the sphere of matter and that of pure spirit, he concluded that to abandon this mysterious science to the profanation of the rabble was to lose it. An abuse of it might lead mankind to speedy destruction; it was like surrounding a group of children with explosive batteries and furnishing them with matches. The first self-made adept initiated but a select few and kept silence with the multitudes. He recognized his God and felt the great Being within himself. The "Atman," the Self, the mighty Lord and Protector—once man knew him as the "I am," the "*Ego Sum*," the "*Asmi*"—showed his full power to him who could recognize the "still small voice."

From the days of the primitive man described by the first Vedic poet down to our modern age, there has not been a philosopher worthy of that name who did not carry in the silent sanctuary of his heart the grand and mysterious truth. If initiated, he learned it as a sacred science; if otherwise, then, like Socrates repeating to himself, as well as to his fellowmen, the noble injunction, "O man, know thyself," he succeeded in recognizing his God within himself. "Ye are gods," the king-psalmist tells us, and we find Jesus reminding the scribes that the expression "Ye are gods" was addressed to other mortal men, claiming for himself the same privilege without any blasphemy (John 10.34–35). And as a faithful echo, Paul, while asserting that we are all "the temple of the living God" (2 Corinthians 6.16), cautiously adds that, after all, these things are only for the "wise," and it is "unlawful" to speak of them.

Therefore we must accept the reminder and simply remark that even in the tortured and barbarous phraseology of the Codex Nazaraeus we detect throughout the same idea. Like an undercurrent, rapid and clear, it runs without mixing its crystalline purity with the muddy and heavy waves of dogmatism. We find it in the Codex as well as in the Vedas, in the Avesta as in the Abhidharma, and in Kapila's

Sankhya Sutras not less than in the Fourth Gospel. We cannot attain the "Kingdom of Heaven" unless we unite ourselves indissolubly with our *Rex Lucis*, the Lord of Splendor and of Light, our Immortal God. We must first conquer immortality and "take the Kingdom of Heaven by violence," offered to our material selves. "The first man is of the earth earthy; the second man is from heaven. . . . Behold, I show you a mystery," says Paul (1 Corinthians 15.47, 51).

In the religion of Sakyamuni, which learned commentators have delighted so much of late to set down as purely nihilistic, the doctrine of immortality is very clearly defined, notwithstanding the European or rather Christian ideas about Nirvana. As Jesus is alleged to have appeared to his disciples after death, so to the present day Gautama is believed to descend from Nirvana. And if he has an existence there, then this state cannot be a synonym for annihilation.

Gautama, like all other great reformers, had a doctrine for his "elect" and another for the outside masses, though the main object of his reform consisted in initiating all, without distinction of castes or wealth, to the great truths hitherto kept so secret by the selfish Brahmanical class so far as it was permissible and prudent to do so. Gautama Buddha was the first we see in the world's history, moved by that generous feeling which locks the whole humanity within one embrace, inviting the "poor," the "lame," and the "blind" to the King's festival table, from which he excluded those who had hitherto sat alone in haughty seclusion. It was he, who with a bold hand first opened the door of the sanctuary to the pariah, the fallen one, and all those "afflicted by men" clothed in gold and purple, often far less worthy than the outcast to whom their finger was scornfully pointing. All this Siddhartha did six centuries before another reformer as noble and as loving, though less favored by opportunity, in another land.

If both, aware of the great danger of furnishing an uncultivated populace with the double-edged weapon of knowledge which gives power, left the innermost corner of the sanctuary in the profoundest shade, who acquainted with human nature can blame them for it? But while one was actuated by prudence, the other was forced into such a course. Gautama left the esoteric and most dangerous portion of the "secret knowledge" untouched, and lived to the ripe old age of eighty with the certainty of having taught the essential truths and having converted to them one-third of the world; Jesus promised his disciples the knowledge which confers upon man the power of producing far greater miracles than he ever did himself, and he died, leaving but a few faithful men, only half way to knowledge, to struggle with the world to which they could impart only what they half-knew themselves. Later, their followers disfigured truth still more than they themselves had done.

It is not true that Gautama never taught anything concerning a future life, or that he denied the immortality of the soul. Nirvana means the certitude of personal immortality in Spirit, not in Soul, which, as a finite emanation, must certainly disintegrate its particles—a compound of human sensations, passions, and yearning for some objective kind of existence—before the immortal spirit of the Ego is quite freed and henceforth secure against further transmigration in any form. And how can man ever reach this state so long as the *Upadana*, that state of longing for life, more life, does not disappear from the sentient being, from the *Ahankara* clothed in a sublimated body? It is the "Upadana" or the intense desire which produces will, and it is will which develops force, and force generates matter, or an object having form.

Thus the disembodied Ego, through this sole undying desire in him, unconsciously furnishes the conditions of his successive self-procreations in various forms, which depend on his mental state and *karma*, the good or bad deeds of his preceding existence, commonly called "merit and demerit." This is why the "Master" recommended to his mendicants the cultivation of the four degrees of Dhyana, the noble "Path of the Four Truths," i.e., that gradual acquirement of stoical indifference for either life or death; that state of spiritual self-contemplation during which man utterly loses sight of his physical and dual individuality, composed of soul and body; and uniting himself with his third and higher immortal self, the real and heavenly man merges, so to say, into the divine Essence, whence his own spirit proceeded like a spark from the common hearth. Thus the Arhat, the holy mendicant, can reach Nirvana while yet on earth; and his spirit, totally freed from the trammels of the "psychical, terrestrial, devilish wisdom," as James calls it, and being in its own nature omniscient and omnipotent, can on earth, through the sole power of his thought, produce the greatest of phenomena.

It is clear that Gautama Buddha, the son of the King of Kapilavastu and the descendant of the first Sakya through his father, who was of the Kshatriya, or warrior caste, did not invent his philosophy. Philanthropist by nature, his ideas were developed and matured while under the tuition of Tirthankara, the famous guru of the Jaina sect. The latter claim present Buddhism as a diverging branch of their own philosophy, and themselves as the only followers of the first Buddha who were allowed to remain in India after the expulsion of all other Buddhists, probably because they had made a compromise and admitted some of the Brahmanic notions. It is curious, to say the least, that three dissenting and inimical religions like Brahmanism, Buddhism, and Jainism should agree so perfectly in their traditions and chronology. If the birth of Gautama may, with some show of reason, be placed at about 600 B.C., then the preceding Buddhas ought to have some place allowed them in chronology. The Buddhas are not gods, but simply individuals overshadowed by the spirit of Buddha—the divine ray.

While the mythical birth and life of Jesus are a faithful copy of those of the Brahmanical Krishna, his historical character of a religious reformer in Palestine is the true type of Buddha in India. In more than one respect their great resemblance in philanthropic and spiritual aspirations, as well as external circumstances, is truly striking. Though the son of a king, while Jesus was but a carpenter, Buddha was not of the high Brahmanical caste by birth. Like Jesus, he felt dissatisfied with the dogmatic spirit of the religion of his country, the intolerance and hypocrisy of the priesthood, their outward show of devotion, and their useless ceremonials and prayers.

As Buddha broke violently through the traditional laws and rules of the Brahmans, so did Jesus declare war against the Pharisees and the proud Sadducees. What the Nazarene did as a consequence of his humble birth and position, Buddha did as a voluntary penance. He traveled about as a beggar, and later in life—again like Jesus— he sought by preference the companionship of publicans and sinners. Each aimed at a social as well as at a religious reform; and giving a deathblow to the religions of his countries, each became the founder of a new one.

NOTES

1. This is the doctrine of the Gnostics who held Christos to be the personal immortal Spirit of man.
2. The ten Messiahs or avatars remind us again of the five Buddhistic and ten Brahmanical avatars.

22

Jesuitry and Masonry

T he Masonic commandment "Mouth to ear, and the word at low breath" is an inheritance from the Tannaim and the old pagan Mysteries. Its modern use must certainly be due to the indiscretion of some renegade kabbalist, though the "word" itself is but a "substitute" for the "lost word" and is a comparatively modern invention, as we will further show. The real sentence has remained forever in the sole possession of the adepts of various countries of the Eastern and Western hemispheres. Only a limited number among the chiefs of the Templars and some Rosicrucians of the seventeenth century, always in close relations with Arabian alchemists and initiates, could really boast of its possession. From the seventh to the fifteenth centuries there was no one who could claim it in Europe; and although there had been alchemists before the days of Paracelsus, he was the first who had passed through the true initiation.

Who was, in fact, the first operative Mason of any consequence? Elias Ashmole, the last of the Rosicrucians and alchemists. Admitted to the freedom of the Operative Masons' Company in London in 1646, he died in 1692. At that time Masonry was not what it became later; it was neither a political nor a Christian institution, but a true secret organization which admitted into the ties of fellowship all men anxious to obtain the priceless boon of liberty of conscience and avoid clerical persecution. Not until about thirty years after his death did what is now termed modern Freemasonry see the light. It was born on the 24th day of June, 1717, in the Apple Tree Tavern, Charles Street, Covent Garden, London. And it was then, as we are told in Anderson's *Constitutions*, that the only four lodges in the south of England elected Anthony Sayer first Grand Master of Masons. Notwithstanding its great youth, this grand lodge has ever claimed the acknowledgment of its supremacy by the whole body of the fraternity throughout the whole world, as the Latin inscription on the plate put beneath the cornerstone of Freemasons' Hall, London, in 1775 would tell to those who could see it.

We owe a place to the Jesuits in this chapter on secret societies, for more than any other they are a secret body and have a far closer connection with actual Masonry—in France and Germany at least—than people are generally aware of. The cry of an outraged public morality was raised against this order from its very birth in 1540. Barely fifteen years had elapsed after the bull approving its constitution was promulgated, when its members began to be driven away from one place to the other. Portugal and the Low Countries got rid of them in 1578; France in 1594; Venice in 1606; Naples in 1622. They were expelled from St. Petersburg in 1815, and from all Russia in 1820.

This noble fraternity, which many preachers have of late so vehemently denied to have ever been a secret one, has been sufficiently proved as such. Their constitutions were translated into Latin by the Jesuit Polancus and printed in the college of the Society at Rome in 1558. "They were jealously kept secret, the greater part of the Jesuits themselves knowing only extracts from them. They were never produced to the light until 1761, when they were published by order of the French Parliament (in 1761 and 1762), in the famous process of Father La Valette."[1] The degrees of the Order are (1) Novices, (2) Lay Brothers, or Temporal Coadjutors, (3) Scholastics, (4) Spiritual Coadjutors, (5) Professed of Three Vows, and (6) Professed of Five Vows. "There is also a secret class, known only to the General and a few faithful Jesuits, which, perhaps more than any other, contributed to the dreaded and mysterious power of the Order," says Nicolini.

All that the Jews learned they had from older nations than themselves. The Chaldean Magi were their masters in the Secret Doctrine, and it was during the Babylonian captivity that they learned its metaphysical as well as practical tenets. Pliny mentions three schools of Magi: one that he shows to have been founded at an unknown antiquity; the second established by Osthanes and Zoroaster; the third by Moses and Jannes [Pliny, *Nat. Hist.* 30.2]. And all the knowledge possessed by these different schools, whether Magian, Egyptian, or Jewish, was derived from India, or rather from both sides of the

Himalayas. Many a lost secret lies buried under wastes of sand in the Gobi desert of Eastern Turkestan, and the wise men of Khotan have preserved strange traditions and knowledge of alchemy.

The doctrine of the immortality of the soul dates from the time when the soul was an objective being, hence when it could hardly be denied by itself; when humanity was a spiritual race and death existed not. Toward the decline of the cycle of life, the ethereal man-spirit then fell into the sweet slumber of temporary unconsciousness in one sphere, only to find himself awakening in the still brighter light of a higher one. But while the spiritual man is ever striving to ascend higher and higher toward its source of being, passing through the cycles and spheres of individual life, physical man had to descend with the great cycle of universal creation until it found itself clothed with the terrestrial garments. Thenceforth the soul was too deeply buried under physical clothing to reassert its existence, except in the cases of those more spiritual natures, which with every cycle became more rare. And yet none of the prehistorical nations ever thought of denying either the existence or the immortality of the inner man, the real "self." But we must bear in mind the teachings of the old philosophies: the spirit alone is immortal—the soul, per se, is neither eternal nor divine. When linked too closely with the physical brain of its terrestrial casket, it gradually becomes a finite mind, a simple animal and sentient life principle, the *nephesh* of the Hebrew Bible.

The doctrine of man's triune nature is as clearly defined in the Hermetic books as it is in Plato's system, or again in that of the Buddhist and Brahmanical philosophies. And this is one of the most important as well as least understood of the doctrines of Hermetic science. The Egyptian Mysteries, so imperfectly known by the world and only through the few brief allusions to them in the *Metamorphoses* of Apuleius, taught the greatest virtues. They unveiled to the aspirant in the "higher" mysteries of initiation that which many of our modern Hermetic students vainly search for in the kabbalistic books.

In the Egyptian notions, as in those of all other faiths founded on philosophy, man was not merely, as with the Christians, a union of soul and body; he was a trinity when spirit was added to it. Moreover, that doctrine made him consist of *khat*—body; *khaibit*—astral form, or shadow; *ka*—animal soul or life principle; *ba*—the higher soul; and *akh*—terrestrial intelligence. They had also a sixth principle named *sahu*—or mummy; but the functions of this one commenced only after the death of the body. After due purification, during which the soul, separated from its body, continued to revisit the latter in its mummified condition, this astral soul "became a God," for it was finally absorbed into "the Soul of the world." It became transformed into one of the creative deities, "the god of Ptah," the Demiurge, a generic name for the creators of the world, rendered in the Bible as the Elohim.

In the Ritual [of the Book of the Dead] the good or purified soul, in conjunction with its higher or uncreated spirit, is more or less the victim of the dark influence of the dragon Apophis. If it has attained the final knowledge of the heavenly and the infernal mysteries—the gnosis, i.e., complete reunion with the spirit—it will triumph over its enemies; if not, the soul could not escape its second death. It is "the lake that burneth with fire and brimstone" (elements), into which those that are cast undergo a "second death" (Revelation 21.8). This death is the gradual dissolution of the astral form into its primal elements, alluded to several times already in the course of this work. But this awful fate can be avoided by the knowledge of the "Mysterious Name," the "Word," say the kabbalists.

The Temple was the last European secret organization which, as a body, had in its possession some of the mysteries of the East. True, there were in the past century (and perhaps still are) isolated "Brothers" faithfully and secretly working under the direction of Eastern Brotherhoods. But these, when they did belong to European societies, invariably joined them for objects unknown to the Fraternity, though at the same time for the benefit of the latter. It is through them that modern Masons have all they know of importance; and the similarity now found between the speculative rites of antiquity, the mysteries of the Essenes, Gnostics, and the Hindus, and the highest and oldest of the Masonic degrees well proves the fact. If these mysterious brothers became possessed of the secrets of the societies, they could never reciprocate the confidence, though in their hands these secrets were safer, perhaps, than in the keeping of European Masons. When certain of the latter were found worthy of becoming affiliates of the Orient, they were secretly instructed and initiated, but the others were none the wiser for that.

No one could ever lay hands on the Rosicrucians; and notwithstanding the alleged discoveries of "secret chambers," vellums called

"T," and fossil knights with ever-burning lamps, this ancient association and its true aims are to this day a mystery. Pretended Templars and sham Rose Croix, with a few genuine kabbalists, were occasionally burned, and some unlucky theosophists and alchemists sought and put to the torture; delusive confessions were even wrung from them by the most ferocious means, yet the true Society remains today as it has ever been, unknown to all and especially to its cruelest enemy—the Church.

Connecting the modern with the ancient Templars, we can at best allow them an adoption of certain rites and ceremonies of purely ecclesiastical character after they had been cunningly inoculated into that grand and antique Order by the clergy. Since this desecration, it gradually lost its primitive and simple character and went fast to its final ruin. Founded in 1118 by the Knights Hugues des Payens and Geoffroy de Saint-Adhémar, nominally for the protection of pilgrims, its true aim was the restoration of the primitive secret worship.

The true version of the history of Jesus and early Christianity was imparted to Hugues des Payens by the Grand Pontiff of the Order of the Temple (of the Nazarene or Johannite sect), named Theocletes, after which it was learned by some Knights in Palestine from the higher and more intellectual members of the St. John sect, who were initiated into its mysteries. Freedom of intellectual thought and the restoration of one universal religion was their secret object. Sworn to the vow of obedience, poverty, and chastity, they were at first the true Knights of John the Baptist, crying in the wilderness and living on wild honey and locusts. Such is the tradition and the true kabbalistic version.

It is a mistake to state that the Order only later became anti-Catholic. It was so from the beginning, and the red cross on the white mantle, the vestment of the Order, had the same significance as with the initiates in every other country. It pointed to the four quarters of the compass, and was the emblem of the universe. When later the Brotherhood was transformed into a Lodge, the Templars, in order to avoid persecution, had to perform their own ceremonies in the greatest secrecy, generally in the hall of the chapter, more frequently in isolated caves or country houses built amidst woods, while the ecclesiastical form of worship was carried on publicly in the chapels belonging to the Order.

Though many of the accusations brought against them by order of Philip IV were infamously false, the main charges were certainly correct, from the standpoint of what the Church considers heresy. The present-day Templars, adhering strictly as they do to the Bible, can hardly claim descent from those who did not believe in Christ as God-man or as the Savior of the world; who rejected the miracle of his birth, and those miracles performed by himself; who did not believe in transubstantiation, the saints, holy relics, purgatory, etc. The Christ Jesus was, in their opinion, a false prophet, but the man Jesus a Brother. They regarded John the Baptist as their patron but never viewed him in the light in which he is presented in the Bible. They reverenced the doctrines of alchemy, astrology, magic, and kabbalistic talismans, and adhered to the secret teachings of their chiefs in the East.

The building of the Temple of Solomon is the symbolical representation of the gradual acquirement of the secret wisdom, or magic; the erection and development of the spiritual from the earthly; the manifestation of the power and splendor of the spirit in the physical world, through the wisdom and genius of the builder. The builder, when he has become an adept, is a mightier king than Solomon himself, the emblem of the sun or Light itself—the light of the real subjective world, shining in the darkness of the objective universe. This is the Temple which can be reared without the sound of the hammer, or any tool of iron being heard in the house while it is "in building."

In the East, this science is called in some places the "seven-storied," in others the "nine-storied" Temple; every story answers allegorically to a degree of knowledge acquired. Throughout the countries of the Orient, wherever magic and the Wisdom Religion are studied, its practitioners and students are known among their craft as Builders—for they build the temple of knowledge, of secret science. Those of the adepts who are active are styled practical or operative Builders, while the students or neophytes are classed as speculative or theoretical. The former exemplify in works their control over the forces of inanimate as well as animate nature; the latter are but perfecting themselves in the rudiments of the sacred science. These terms were evidently borrowed at the beginning by the unknown founders of the first Masonic guilds. In the now popular jargon,

"Operative Masons" are understood to be the bricklayers and the handicraftsmen who composed the Craft down to Sir Christopher Wren's time, and "Speculative Masons" all members of the Order as it now is.

The initiated became a builder himself, for he was made acquainted with the *dodecahedron*, or the geometrical figure on which the universe was built. To what he had learned in previous initiations of the use of the rule and of architectural principles, was added a cross, the perpendicular and horizontal lines of which were supposed to form the foundation of the spiritual temple by placing them across the junction, or central primordial point, the element of all existences, representing the first concrete idea of deity. Henceforth he could, as a Master builder (1 Corinthians 3.10), erect a temple of wisdom on that rock of Petra for himself, and having laid a sure foundation, let "another build thereon."

The wisdom of the archaic ages or the Secret Doctrine embodied in the Oriental Kabbala, of which, as we have said, the Rabbinical is but an abridgment, did not die out with the Philaletheans of the last Eclectic school. The Gnosis lingers still on earth, and its votaries are many, albeit unknown. Such secret brotherhoods have been mentioned by more than one great author. If they have been regarded as mere fictions of the novelist, that fact has only helped the brother adepts to keep their incognito the more easily. We have personally known several of them who, to their great merriment, had had the story of their lodges, the communities in which they lived, and the wondrous powers which they had exercised for many long years laughed at and denied by unsuspecting skeptics to their very faces.

Some of these brothers belong to the small groups of "travelers." Until the close of the happy Louis-Philippian reign, they were pompously termed by the Parisian garçon and trader the *nobles étrangers*, and as innocently believed to be "Boyards," Walachian "'Gospodars," Indian "Nabobs," and Hungarian "Margraves," who had gathered at the capital of the civilized world to admire its monuments and partake of its dissipations. There are, however, some insane enough to connect the presence of certain of these mysterious guests in Paris with the great political events that subsequently took place. Such recall at least as very remarkable coincidences the breaking out of the Revolution of 1793 and the earlier explosion of the South Sea Bubble soon after the appearance of the "noble foreigners," who had convulsed all Paris for more or less longer periods with their mystical doctrines or "supernatural gifts." The Saint-Germains and Cagliostros of this century, having learned bitter lessons from the vilifications and persecutions of the past, pursue different tactics nowadays.

But there are numbers of these mystic brotherhoods which have naught to do with "civilized" countries; and it is in their unknown communities that are concealed the skeletons of the past. These "adepts" could, if they chose, lay claim to strange ancestry and exhibit verifiable documents that would explain many a mysterious page in both sacred and profane history. Had the keys to the hieratic writings and the secret of Egyptian and Hindu symbolism been known to the Christian Fathers, they would not have allowed a single monument of old to stand unmutilated. And yet, if we are well informed—and we think we are—there was not one such in all Egypt, but the secret records of its hieroglyphics were carefully registered by the sacerdotal caste. These records still exist, though "not extant" for the general public, though perhaps the monuments may have passed away forever out of human sight.

"The kingdom of Heaven suffereth violence, and the violent take it by force" [Matthew 11.12]. Many are the candidates at the doors of those who are supposed to know the path that leads to the secret brotherhoods. The great majority are refused admittance, and these turn away interpreting the refusal as an evidence of the nonexistence of any such secret society. Of the minority accepted, more than two-thirds fail upon trial. The seventh rule of the ancient Rosicrucian brotherhoods, which is universal among all true secret societies, "The Rosy Crux becomes and is not made," is more than the generality of men can bear to have applied to them. But let no one suppose that of the candidates who fail, any will divulge to the world even the trifle they may have learned, as some Masons do. None know better than themselves how unlikely it is that a neophyte should ever talk of what was imparted to him. Thus these societies will go on and hear themselves denied without uttering a word until the day shall come for them to throw off their reserve and show how completely they are masters of the situation.

209

NOTE

1. G. B. Nicolini, *History of the Jesuits* (London, 1873), 30fn.

23

The Vedas and the Bible

Our task will have been ill performed if the preceding chapters have not demonstrated that Judaism, earlier and later Gnosticism, Christianity, and even Christian Masonry have all been erected upon identical cosmic myths, symbols, and allegories, whose full comprehension is possible only to those who have inherited the key from their inventors.

In the following pages we will endeavor to show how much these have been misinterpreted by the widely different, yet intimately related systems enumerated above, in fitting them to their individual needs. Thus not only will a benefit be conferred upon the student, but a long deferred and now much needed act of justice will be done to those earlier generations whose genius has laid the whole human race under obligation. Let us begin by once more comparing the myths of the Bible with those of the sacred books of other nations, to see which is the original and which copies.

There are but two methods which, correctly explained, can help us to this result. They are the Vedas—Brahmanical literature—and the Jewish Kabbala. The former has, in a most philosophical spirit, conceived these grandiose myths; the latter, borrowing them from the Chaldeans and Persians, shaped them into a history of the Jewish nation, in which their spirit of philosophy was buried beyond the recognition of all but the elect, and under a far more absurd form than the Aryans had given them. The Bible of the Christian Church is the latest receptacle of this scheme of disfigured allegories which have been erected into an edifice of superstition, such as never entered into the conceptions of those from whom the Church obtained her knowledge. The abstract fictions of antiquity, which for ages had filled the popular fancy with but flickering shadows and uncertain images, have in Christianity assumed the shapes of real personages and become accomplished facts. Allegory, metamorphosed, becomes sacred history, and pagan myth is taught to the people as a revealed narrative of God's intercourse with His chosen people.

The myths, says Horace in his *Ars Poetica*, have been invented by wise men to strengthen the laws and teach moral truths. While Horace endeavored to make clear the very spirit and essence of the ancient myths, Euhemerus pretended, on the contrary, that "myths were the legendary history of kings and heroes, transformed into gods by the admiration of the nations."

We will try to systematize our subject as much as the ever recurring necessity to draw parallels between the conflicting opinions that have been based on the same myths will permit. We will begin with the book of Genesis, and seek its hidden meaning in the Brahmanical traditions and the Chaldeo-Judaic Kabbala.

The first scripture lesson taught us in our infancy is that God created the world in six days and rested on the seventh. Hence a peculiar solemnity is supposed to attach to the seventh day, and the Christians, adopting the rigid observances of the Jewish Sabbath, have enforced it upon us with the substitution of the first instead of the seventh day of the week.

All systems of religious mysticism are based on numerals. With Pythagoras, the Monas or unity, emanating the duad, and thus forming the trinity, and the quaternary or Arba-il (the mystic four), compose the number seven. The sacredness of numbers begins with the great First, the ONE, and ends only with zero—symbol of the infinite and boundless circle which represents the universe. All the intervening figures, in whatever combination, or however multiplied, represent philosophical ideas, from vague outlines down to a definitely established scientific axiom, relating either to a moral or a physical fact in nature. They are a key to the ancient views on cosmogony in its broad sense, including man and beings, and the evolution of the human race, spiritually as well as physically.

The number seven is the most sacred of all and is undoubtedly of Hindu origin. Everything of importance was calculated by and fitted into this number by the early Indic philosophers—ideas as well as localities.

This number reappears likewise on almost every page of Genesis and throughout the Mosaic books, and we find it conspicuous (see following chapter) in the Book of Job and the Oriental Kabbala. If the Hebrew Semitics adopted it so readily, we must infer that it was not blindly, but with a thorough knowledge of its secret meaning, and hence that they adopted the doctrines of their "heathen" neighbors as well. It is but natural, therefore, that we should seek in heathen philosophy for the interpretation of this number, which again reappeared in Christianity with its seven sacraments, seven churches in Asia Minor, seven capital sins, seven virtues (four cardinal and three theological), etc.

Have the seven prismatic colors of the rainbow seen by Noah no other meaning than that of a covenant between God and man to refresh the memory of the former? To the kabbalist, at least, they have a significance inseparable from the seven labors of magic, the seven upper spheres, the seven notes of the musical scale, the seven numerals of Pythagoras, the seven wonders of the world, the seven ages, and even the seven steps of the Masons, which lead to the Holy of Holies after passing the flights of three and five.

Whence the identity then of these enigmatical, ever recurring numerals that are found in every page of the Jewish scriptures, as in every ola and sloka of Buddhist and Brahmanical books? Whence these numerals that are the soul of Pythagorean and Platonic thought, and that no unilluminated Orientalist or biblical student has ever been able to fathom? And yet they have a key ready in their hand, if they but knew how to use it. Nowhere is the mystical value of human language and its effects on human action so perfectly understood as in India, nor any better explained than by the authors of the oldest Brahmanas. Ancient as their epoch is now found to be, they only try to express, in a more concrete form, the abstract metaphysical speculations of their own ancestors.

Such is the respect of the Brahmans for the sacrificial mysteries, that they hold that the world itself sprang into creation as a consequence of a "sacrificial word" pronounced by the First Cause. This word is the "Ineffable Name" of the kabbalists, discussed in the last chapter.

The secret of the Vedas, "Sacred Knowledge" though they may be, is impenetrable without the help of the Brahmanas. Properly speaking, the Vedas (which are written in verse and comprise four books) constitute that portion called the Mantra, or magical prayer, and the Brahmanas (which are in prose) contain their key. While the Mantra part alone is holy, the Brahmana portion contains all the theological exegesis and the speculations and explanations of the sacerdotal.

There are words which have a destructive quality in their very syllables, as though objective things; for every sound awakens a corresponding one in the invisible world of spirit, and the repercussion produces either a good or bad effect. Harmonious rhythm, a melody vibrating softly in the atmosphere, creates a beneficent and sweet influence and acts most powerfully on the psychological as well as physical natures of every living thing on earth; it reacts even on inanimate objects, for matter is still spirit in its essence, invisible as it may seem to our grosser senses.

So it is with numerals. Turn wherever we will, from the Prophets to the Apocalypse, and we will see the biblical writers constantly using the numbers three, four, seven, and twelve.

Meanwhile, unmindful of any alleged authorities, let us try to sift for ourselves a few of these myths of old. We will search for an explanation within the popular interpretation and feel our way with the help of the magic lamp of Trismegistus—the mysterious number seven. There must have been some reason why this figure was universally accepted as a mystic calculation. With every ancient people the Creator, or Demiurge, was placed over the seventh heaven.

One must consult the Pythagoreans and kabbalists to learn the potentiality of this number. Esoterically the seven rays of the solar spectrum are represented concretely in the seven-rayed god Heptaktys. These seven rays, epitomized into three primary rays (red, blue, and yellow), form the solar trinity and typify respectively spirit-matter and spirit-essence.

The Pythagoreans called the number seven the vehicle of life, as it contains body and soul. They explained it by saying that the human body consists of four principal elements and that the soul is triple, comprising reason, passion, and desire.

The Heptaktys is not the Supreme Cause, but simply an emanation from Him—the first visible manifestation of the Unrevealed Power. This is the emanation of the Highest, the Demiurge, a multiplicity in a unity, the Elohim, whom we see creating our world, or rather fashioning it, in six days and resting on the seventh. And who are these Elohim but the euhemerized powers of nature, the faithful manifested servants, the laws of Him who is immutable law and harmony Himself?

They remain over the seventh heaven (or spiritual world), for it is they who, according to the kabbalists, formed in succession the six material worlds, or rather attempts at worlds, that preceded our own, which they say is the seventh. If, in laying aside the metaphysical-spiritual conception, we give our attention but to the religio-scientific problem of creation in "six days," over which our best biblical scholars have vainly pondered so long, we might perchance be on the way to the true idea underlying the allegory. The ancients were philosophers, consistent in all things. Hence they taught that each of these departed worlds, having performed its physical evolution and reached—through birth, growth, maturity, old age, and death—the end of its cycle, had returned to its primitive subjective form of a spiritual earth. Thereafter it had to serve through all eternity as the dwelling of those who had lived on it as men, and even animals, but were now spirits. This idea, were it even as incapable of exact demonstration as that of our theologians relating to Paradise, is at least a trifle more philosophical.

Like man and every other living thing upon it, our planet has had its spiritual and physical evolution. From an impalpable, ideal thought under the creative Will of Him of whom we know nothing, and but dimly conceive in imagination, this globe became fluidic and semispiritual, then condensed itself more and more, until its physical development—matter, the tempting demon—compelled it to try its own creative faculty. Matter defied Spirit, and the earth, too, had its "Fall." The allegorical curse under which it labors is that it only procreates, it does not create. Our physical planet is but the handmaiden, or rather the maid-of-all-work, of the spirit, its master. "Cursed be the ground . . . thorns and thistles shall it bring," the Elohim are made to say. "In sorrow thou shalt bring forth children." The Elohim say this both to the ground and the woman. And this curse will last until the minutest particle of matter on earth has outlived its days, until every grain of dust has, by gradual transformation through evolution, become a constituent part of a "living soul," and until the latter shall reascend the cyclic arc and finally stand—its own Metatron, or Redeeming Spirit—at the foot of the upper step of the spiritual worlds, as at the first hour of its emanation. Beyond that lies the great "Deep"—a MYSTERY!

It must be remembered that every cosmogony has a trinity of workers at its head: Father, spirit; Mother, nature, or matter; and the manifested universe, the Son or result of the two. The universe, also, as well as each planet which it comprehends, passes through four ages like man himself. All have their infancy, youth, maturity, and old age, and these four added to the other three make the sacred seven again.

The introductory chapters of Genesis were never meant to present even a remote allegory of the creation of our earth. They embrace a metaphysical conception of some indefinite period in the eternity, when successive attempts were being made by the law of evolution at the formation of universes. This idea is plainly stated in the *Zohar*: "There were old worlds, which perished as soon as they came into existence, were formless, and were called *sparks*. Thus, the smith, when hammering the iron, lets the sparks fly in all directions. The sparks are the primordial worlds which could not continue, because the Sacred Aged (Sephirah) had not as yet assumed its form (of androgyne or opposite sexes) of king and queen (Sephirah and Kadmon) and the Master was not yet at his work."[1]

The six periods or "days" of Genesis refer to the same metaphysical belief. Five such ineffectual attempts were made by the Elohim, but the sixth resulted in worlds like our own (i.e., all the planets and most of the stars are inhabited worlds, though not like our earth). Having formed this world at last in the sixth period, the Elohim rested in the seventh. Thus the "Holy One," when he created the present world, said: "This pleases me; the previous ones did not please me" (*Bereshith Rabbah* parsha 9). And the Elohim "saw everything that he had made, and behold it was very good. And the evening and the morning were the sixth day" (Genesis 1.31).

The reader will remember that an explanation was given of the "day" and "night" of Brahma. The former represents a certain period of cosmical activity, the latter an equal one of cosmical repose. In the one, worlds are being evolved, and are passing through their allotted four ages of existence; in the latter, the "inbreathing" of Brahma reverses the tendency of the natural forces; everything visible becomes gradually dispersed; chaos comes; and a long night of repose reinvigorates the cosmos for its next term of evolution. In the morning of one of these "days" the formative processes are gradually reaching their climax of activity, and in the evening imperceptibly diminishing the same until the pralaya arrives, and with it "night." One such morning and evening do, in fact, constitute a cosmic day; and it was a "day of Brahma" that the kabbalistic author of Genesis had in mind each time when he said: "And the evening and the morning were the first (or fifth or sixth or any other) day." Six days of gradual evolution, one of repose, and then—evening! Since the first appearance of man on our earth there has been an eternal Sabbath or rest for the Demiurge.

The cosmogonical speculations of the first six chapters of Genesis are shown in the races of "sons of God," "giants," etc., of chapter 6. Properly speaking, the story of the formation of our earth, or "creation," as it is very improperly called, begins with the rescue of Noah from the deluge.

The successive existence of an incalculable number of worlds before the subsequent evolution of our own was believed and taught by all the ancient peoples.

The Hindu doctrines teach of two pralayas or dissolutions; one universal, the maha-pralaya, the other partial, or the minor pralaya. This does not relate to the universal dissolution which occurs at the end of every "Day of Brahma," but to the geological cataclysms at the end of every minor cycle of our globe. A partial cataclysm occurs at the close of every "age" of the world, they say, which does not destroy the latter, but only changes its general appearance. New races of men and animals and a new flora evolve from the dissolution of the precedent ones.

But if such a universal cataclysm had ever taken place within man's memory, surely some of the monuments of the Egyptians, of which many are of such tremendous antiquity, would have recorded that occurrence. But till now there has not been found the remotest allusion to such a calamity. On the other hand, the Chaldeans preserved the tradition, as we find Berosus testifying to it, and the ancient Hindus possess the legend. But the Egyptians, whose first settlers had evidently come from southern India, had less reason to record the cataclysm, since it had perhaps never affected them except indirectly.

We are prepared to maintain that Egypt owes her civilization, commonwealth, and arts—especially the art of building—to pre-Vedic

India, and that it was a colony of the dark-skinned Aryans, or those whom Homer and Herodotus term the eastern Ethiopians, i.e., the inhabitants of southern India, who brought to it their ready-made civilization in the ante-chronological ages, what Bunsen calls the pre-Menite, but nevertheless epochal history.

To the present moment, with all the controversies and research, history and science remain as much as ever in the dark as to the origin of the Jews. They may as well be the exiled Chandalas, or Pariahs, of old India, the "bricklayers" mentioned by Vina-Snati, Veda-Vyasa, and Manu, as the Phoenicians of Herodotus, or the Hyksos of Josephus, or descendants of Pali shepherds, or a mixture of all these.

There is no real history in the Old Testament, and the little historical information one can glean is only found in the indiscreet revelations of the prophets. The book, as a whole, must have been written at various times, or rather invented as an authorization of some subsequent worship, the origin of which may be very easily traced partially to the Orphic Mysteries, and partially to the ancient Egyptian rites, in familiarity with which Moses was brought up from his infancy.

The exoteric plan of the Bible was made to answer also to four ages. Thus they reckon the Golden Age from Adam to Abraham; the Silver, from Abraham to David; Copper, from David to the Captivity; and thence forward, the Iron. But the secret computation is quite different and does not vary at all from the zodiacal calculations of the Brahmans. We are in the Iron Age, or Kali-Yuga, but it began with Noah, the mythical ancestor of our race.

Nearly all the prophecies about Christ are credited to the patriarchs and prophets. If a few of the latter may have existed as real personages, every one of the former is a myth. We will endeavor to prove it by the hidden interpretation of the zodiac and the relations of its signs to these antediluvian men.

If the reader will keep in mind the Hindu ideas of cosmogony, he will better understand the relation between the biblical antediluvian patriarchs and that puzzle of commentators—"Ezekiel's wheel." Thus, let it be remembered: (1) The universe is not a spontaneous creation, but an evolution from preexistent matter. (2) It is only one of an endless series of universes. (3) Eternity is pointed off into grand cycles, in each of which twelve transformations of our world occur, following its partial destruction by fire and water, alternately, so that when a new minor period sets in, the earth is so changed, even geologically, as to be practically a new world. (4) Of these twelve transformations, the earth after each of the first six is grosser, and everything on it—man included—more material, than after the preceding one, while after each of the remaining six the contrary is true, both earth and man growing more and more refined and spiritual with each terrestrial change. (5) When the apex of the cycle is reached, a gradual dissolution takes place, and every living and objective form is destroyed. But when that point is reached, humanity has become fit to live subjectively as well as objectively. And not humanity alone, but also animals, plants, and every atom. After a time of rest, say the Buddhists, when a new world becomes self-formed, the astral souls of animals and of all beings, except such as have reached the highest Nirvana, will return on earth again to end their cycles of transformations, and become men in their turn.

This stupendous conception the ancients synthesized for the in-struction of the common people into a single pictorial design—the zodiac, or celestial belt. Instead of the twelve signs now used, there were originally but ten known to the general public, viz.: Aries, Taurus, Gemini, Cancer, Leo, Virgo-Scorpio, Sagittarius, Capricornus, Aquarius, and Pisces. These were exoteric. But in addition there were two mystical signs inserted, which none but initiates comprehended, viz.: at the middle or junction point where Libra now stands and at the sign now called Scorpio, which follows Virgo. When it was found necessary to make them exoteric, these two secret signs were added under their present appellations as blinds, to conceal the true names which gave the key to the whole secret of creation and divulged the origin of "good and evil."

The deluge then, in this sense, points to that final struggle between the conflicting elements which brought the first great cycle of our planet to a close. These periods gradually merged into each other, order being brought out of chaos, or disorder, and the successive types of organism being evolved only as the physical conditions of nature were prepared for their appearance; for our present race could not have breathed on earth during that intermediate period, not having as yet the allegorical coats of skin.

And is there no possibility that there was a period, perhaps several periods, when man *existed* and yet was not an organic being—therefore could not have left any vestige of himself for exact science? Spirit leaves no skeletons or fossils behind, and yet few are the men on earth who doubt that man can live both objectively and subjectively. At all events, the theology of the Brahmans, hoary with antiquity, which divides the formative periods of the earth into four ages and places between each of these a lapse of 1,728,000 years, agrees far more with official science and modern discovery than do the absurd chronological notions promulgated by the Councils of Nice and Trent.

NOTE

1. *Idrah Zutah* 10.421–30. The Supreme consulting with the Architect of the world—his Logos—about creation.

24

The Devil Myth

The Devil is the patron genius of theological Christianity. This dogma of the Devil and redemption seems to be based upon two passages in the New Testament: "For this purpose the Son of God was manifested, that he might destroy the works of the Devil" (1 John 3.8). "And there was war in heaven; Michael and his angels fought against the Dragon; and the Dragon fought, and his angels, and prevailed not; neither was their place found any more in heaven. And the great Dragon was cast out, that old serpent called the Devil and Satan, which deceiveth the whole world" [Revelation 12.7–9]. Let us, then, explore the ancient theogonies, in order to ascertain what was meant by these remarkable expressions.

The first inquiry is whether the term *Devil*, as here used, actually represents the malignant deity of the Christians, or an antagonistic, blind force—the dark side of nature. By the latter we are not to understand the manifestation of any evil principle that is *malum in se*, but only the shadow of the Light, so to say. The theories of the kabbalists treat of it as a force which is antagonistic, but at the same time essential to the vitality, evolution, and vigor of the good principle. Plants would perish in their first stage of existence if they were kept exposed to a constant sunlight; the night alternating with the day is essential to their healthy growth and development. Goodness, likewise, would speedily cease to be such, were it not alternated by its opposite. In human nature, evil denotes the antagonism of matter to the spiritual, and each is accordingly purified thereby. In the cosmos, the equilibrium must be preserved; the operation of the two contraries produces harmony, like the centripetal and centrifugal forces, which are necessary to each other. If one is arrested, the action of the other will immediately become destructive.

This personification, denominated *Satan*, is to be contemplated from three different planes: the Old Testament, the Christian Fathers, and the ancient gentile attitude. He is supposed to have been represented by the Serpent in the Garden of Eden; nevertheless, in the Hebrew sacred writings the epithet of *Satan* is nowhere applied to that or any other variety of snake.

The temptation, or probation, of Jesus is the most dramatic occasion in which Satan appears. As if to prove the designation of Apollo, Aesculapius, and Bacchus, *Diobolos*, or son of Zeus, he is also styled *Diabolos*, or accuser. The scene of the probation was the wilderness. In the desert around the Jordan and Dead Sea were the abodes of the "sons of the prophets" and the Essenes (Pliny, *Nat. Hist.* 5.16). These ascetics used to subject their neophytes to probations, analogous to the tortures of the Mithraic rites, and the temptation of Jesus was evidently a scene of this character. But the Diabolos, or Devil, is in this instance evidently no malignant principle, but one exercising discipline. In this sense the terms *Devil* and *Satan* are repeatedly employed (see 1 Corinthians 5.5; 2 Corinthians 11.14; 1 Timothy 1.20).

The story of Satan in the Book of Job is of a similar character. He is introduced among the "Sons of God," presenting themselves before the Lord as in a mystic initiation. The Lord counsels with Satan and gives him carte blanche to test the fidelity of Job. The latter is stripped of his wealth and family and smitten with a loathsome disease. In his extremity, his wife doubts his integrity, and exhorts him to worship God, as he is about to die. His friends all beset him with accusations, and finally the Lord, the chief hierophant Himself, taxes him with the uttering of words in which there is no wisdom and with contending with the Almighty. In all these scenes there is manifested no such malignant diabolism as is supposed to characterize "the adversary of souls."

The allegory of Job, if correctly understood, will give the key to this whole matter of the Devil, his nature, and his office and will substantiate our declarations. Let no pious individual take exception to this designation of allegory. Myth was the favorite and universal method of teaching in archaic times. Paul, writing to the Corinthians, declared that the entire story of Moses and the Israelites was typical,[1] and in his Epistle to the Galatians asserted that the whole story of Abraham, his two wives, and their sons was an allegory.[2] Indeed, it is a theory amounting to certitude that the historical books of the Old Testament were of the same character. We take no extraordinary liberty with the Book of Job when we give it the same designation which Paul gave the stories of Abraham and Moses.

But perhaps we ought to explain the ancient use of allegory and symbology. The symbol expressed some abstract quality of the Deity which the laity could easily apprehend. Its higher sense terminated there, and it was employed by the multitude thenceforth as an image in idolatrous rites. But the allegory was reserved for the inner sanctuary, when only the elect were admitted. Hence the rejoinder of Jesus when his disciples interrogated him because he spoke to the multitude in parables. "To you," said he, "it is given to know the mysteries of the Kingdom of Heaven, but to them it is not given. For whosoever hath, to him shall be given, and he shall have more abundance; but whosoever hath not, from him shall be taken away even that he hath" [Matthew 13.11–12].

The whole allegory of Job is an open book to him who understands the picture language of Egypt as it is recorded in the Book of the Dead. In the scene of Judgment, Osiris is represented sitting on his throne, holding in one hand the symbol of life, "the hook of attraction," and in the other the mystic Bacchic fan. Before him are the sons of God, the forty-two assessors of the dead. An altar is immediately before the throne, covered with gifts and surmounted with the sacred lotus flower, upon which stand four spirits. By the entrance stands the soul about to be judged, whom Thmei [Maat], the genius of Truth, is welcoming to this conclusion of the probation. Thoth, holding a reed, makes a record of the proceedings in the Book of Life. Horus and Anubis, standing by the scales, inspect the weight which determines whether the heart of the deceased balances the symbol of truth or the latter preponderates. On a pedestal sits a bitch—the symbol of the Accuser.

Initiation into the Mysteries, as every intelligent person knows, was a dramatic representation of scenes in the underworld. Such was the allegory of Job.

Several critics have attributed the authorship of this book to Moses. But it is older than the Pentateuch. Jehovah is not mentioned in the poem itself; and if the name occurs in the prologue, the fact must be attributed to either an error of the translators, or the premeditation exacted by the later necessity to transform polytheism into a monotheistic religion. The plan adopted was the very simple one of attributing the many names of the Elohim (gods) to a single god. So in one of the oldest Hebrew texts of Job (12.9) there stands the name of Jehovah, whereas all other manuscripts have "Adonai." But in the original poem Jehovah is absent. In place of this name we find *Al, Aleim, Ale, Shaddai, Adonai*, etc. Therefore, we must conclude that either the prologue and epilogue were added at a later period, which is inadmissible for many reasons, or that it has been tampered with like the rest of the manuscripts.

Satan is called in it a "Son of God," one of the council which presents itself before God, who leads him into tempting Job's fidelity. In this poem, clearer and plainer than anywhere else, we find the meaning of the appellation *Satan*. It is a term for the office or character of *public accuser*. Satan is the Typhon of the Egyptians, barking his accusations in Amenti, an office quite as respectable as that of the public prosecutor, in our own age; and if, through the ignorance of the first Christians, he became later identical with the Devil, it is through no connivance of his own.

The Book of Job is a complete representation of ancient initiation and the trials which generally precede this grandest of all ceremonies. The neophyte perceives himself deprived of everything he valued and afflicted with foul disease. His wife appeals to him to adore God and die; there was no more hope for him. Three friends appear on the scene by mutual appointment: Eliphaz, the learned Temanite, full of the knowledge "which wise men have told from their fathers . . . to whom alone the earth was given"; Bildad, the conservative, taking matters as they come, and judging Job to have done wickedly because he was afflicted; and Zophar, intelligent and skillful with "generalities" but not interiorly wise. Job boldly responds:

> If I have erred, it is a matter with myself. You magnify your-
> selves and plead against me in my reproach; but it is God who has
> overthrown me. . . . Why do you persecute me and are not satisfied
> with my flesh thus wasted away? But I know that my Champion
> lives, and that at a coming day he will stand for me in the earth; and
> though, together with my skin, all this beneath it shall be destroyed,

224

yet without my flesh I shall see God. . . . Ye shall say: "Why do we molest him?" for the root of the matter is found in me! [19.4–6, 22, 25–28]

This passage, like all others in which the faintest allusions could be found to a "Champion," "Deliverer," or "Vindicator," was interpreted into a direct reference to the Messiah; but in the Septuagint [Job 19.25–27] this verse is translated thus:

> For I know that He is eternal
> Who is about to deliver me on earth,
> To restore this skin of mine which endures these things.

In the King James version, the translation has no resemblance whatever to the original. The crafty translators have rendered it, "I know that *my Redeemer liveth*," etc. And yet Septuagint, Vulgate, and Hebrew original are all considered as the inspired Word of God. Job refers to his own immortal spirit, which is eternal and which, when death comes, will deliver him from his putrid earthly body and clothe him with a new spiritual envelope. In the Mysteries of Eleusinia, the Egyptian Book of the Dead, and all other works treating on matters of initiation, this "eternal being" has a name. With the Neoplatonists it was the *Nous*, the *Augoeides*; with the Buddhists it is *Agra*; and with the Persians, *Feroher*. All of these are called the "Deliverers," the "Champions," the "Metatrons," etc. In the Mithraic sculptures of Persia, the Feroher is represented by a winged figure hovering in the air above its "object" or body. It is the luminous Self—the Atman of the Hindus, our immortal spirit, who alone can redeem our soul and will, if we follow him instead of being dragged down by our body. Therefore, in the Chaldean texts, the above reads, "My deliverer, my restorer," i.e., the Spirit who will restore the decayed body of man, and transform it into a clothing of ether. And it is this Nous, Augoeides, Feroher, Agra, Spirit of himself that the triumphant Job shall see without his flesh—i.e., when he has escaped from his bodily prison—and that the translators call "God."

Instead of offering consolations, the three friends of the suffering Job seek to make him believe that his misfortune must have come in punishment of some extraordinary transgressions on his part. Hurling back upon them all their imputations, Job swears that while his breath

225

is in him he will maintain his cause. Then he asserts his sympathy for the unfortunate, his chastity, his integrity, his probity, his strict justice, his charities, his moderation, his freedom from the prevalent sun worship, his tenderness to enemies, his hospitality to strangers, his openness of heart, his boldness for the right, though he encountered the multitude and the contempt of families; and he invokes the Almighty to answer him and challenges his adversary to write down of what he had been guilty.

To this there was not, and could not be, any answer. The three had sought to crush Job by pleadings and general arguments, and he had demanded consideration for his specific acts. Then appeared the fourth: Elihu, the son of Barachel the Buzite, of the kindred of Ram.

Elihu is the hierophant; he begins with a rebuke, and the sophisms of Job's false friends are swept away like the loose sand before the west wind.

> And Elihu, the son of Barachel, spoke and said: "Great men are not always wise. . . . There *is* a spirit in man; the spirit within me constraineth me. . . . God speaketh once, yea twice, yet man perceiveth it not. In a dream, in a vision of the night, when deep sleep falleth upon man, in slumberings upon the bed, then he openeth the ears of men and sealeth their instruction. O Job, hearken unto me: hold thy peace, and I shall teach thee wisdom." [32.8, 9, 18; 33.14–16, 33]

The sore-eaten, afflicted Job, who in the face of the official clergy— offering for hope only the necessarianism of damnation—had in his despair nearly wavered in his patient faith, answered:

> What ye know, the same do I know also; I am not inferior unto you. . . . Man cometh forth like a flower and is cut down: he fleeth also as a shadow and continueth not. . . . Man dieth and wasteth away, yea, man giveth up the ghost, and where is he? . . . If a man die, shall he live again? . . . When a few years are come then I shall go the way whence I shall not return. . . . O that one might plead for a man with God, as man pleadeth for his neighbor! [13.2; 14.2, 10, 14; 16.21–22]

Job finds one who answers his cry of agony. He listens to the wisdom of Elihu, the hierophant, the perfected teacher, the inspired philosopher. From his stern lips comes the just rebuke for his impiety in charging upon the Supreme Being the evils of humanity. "God," says Elihu, "is excellent in power, and in judgment, and in plenty of justice; He will not afflict" [37.23].

As long as the neophyte was satisfied with his own worldly wisdom and irreverent estimate of the Deity and His purposes, and as long as he gave ear to the pernicious sophistries of his advisers, the hierophant kept silent. But when this anxious mind was ready for counsel and instruction, his voice is heard, and he speaks with the authority of the Spirit of God.

Job hearkens to the words of wisdom and then the "Lord" answers Job "out of the whirlwind" of nature, God's first visible manifestation: "Stand still, O Job, stand still! and consider the wondrous works of God; for by them alone thou canst know God. 'Behold, God is great, and we know him not,' Him who maketh small the drops of water; but they pour down rain according to the vapor thereof" (Job 36.26–27; 37.14; 38.1).

"Who is this that darkeneth counsel by words without knowledge?" speaks the voice of God through His mouthpiece, nature.

> Where wast thou when I laid the foundations of the earth? Declare, if thou hast understanding. Who hath laid the measures thereof, if thou knowest? When the morning stars sang together, and all the sons of God shouted for joy? . . . Wast thou present when I said to the seas, "Hitherto shalt thou come, but no further; and here shall thy proud waves be stayed?" . . . Knowest thou who hath caused it to rain on the earth, where no man is; on the wilderness, wherein there is no man. . . . Canst thou bind the sweet influences of Pleiades, or loose the bands of Orion? . . . Canst thou send lightnings, that they may go and say unto thee, "Here we are"? [Job 38]

"Then Job answered the Lord." He understood His ways, and his eyes were opened for the first time. The Supreme Wisdom descended upon him; and if the reader remains puzzled before this final Petroma of initiation, at least Job, or the man "afflicted" in his blindness, then realized the impossibility of catching "Leviathan by putting a hook into his nose." Leviathan is occult science, on which one can lay his hand but "do no more" (Job 41.2, 8), whose power and "comely proportion" God wishes not to conceal.

Job recognized his "Champion" and was assured that the time for his vindication had come. Immediately the Lord said to Job's "friends": "My wrath is kindled against thee and against thy two friends; for ye have not spoken of me the thing that is right, as my servant Job hath." So "the Lord turned the captivity of Job," and "blessed the latter end of Job more than his beginning" [42.7, 10].

In the [Egyptian] judgment the deceased invokes four spirits who preside over the Lake of Fire and is purified by them. He then is conducted to his celestial house and is received by Hathor and Isis, and stands before Atum,[3] the essential God. He is now Turu, the essential man, a pure spirit, and henceforth On-ati, the eye of fire, and an associate of the gods.

It will be perceived from these extended illustrations that the Satan of the Old Testament, the Diabolos or Devil of the Gospels and Apostolic Epistles, were but the antagonistic principle in matter, necessarily incident to it, and not wicked in the moral sense of the term. The Jews, coming from the Persian country, brought with them the doctrine of two principles. They could not bring the Avesta, for it was not written. But they—we mean the Asidians [Chasidim] and Pharsi—invested Ormazd with the secret name of Jehovah, and Ahriman with the name of the gods of the land, Satan of the Hittites, and Diabolos, or rather Diobolos, of the Greeks. The early Church—at least the Pauline part of it—the Gnostics, and their successors further refined their ideas; and the Catholic Church adopted and adapted them, meanwhile putting their promulgators to the sword.

We ought, perhaps, to make a brief notice of the European Devil. He is the genius who deals in sorcery, witchcraft, and other mischief. The Fathers, taking the idea from the Jewish Pharisees, made devils of the pagan gods, Mithras, Serapis, and the others. The Roman Catholic Church followed by denouncing the former worship as commerce with the powers of darkness. The *malefeci* and witches of the Middle Ages were thus but the votaries of the proscribed worship. Magic in all ancient times had been considered as divine science, wisdom, and the knowledge of God. The healing art in the temples of Aesculapius, and at the shrines of Egypt and the East, had always been magical.

All was now changed. Ignorance was enthroned as the mother of devotion. Learning was denounced, and savants pursued the sciences in peril of their lives. They were compelled to employ a jargon to conceal their ideas from all but their own adepts and to accept opprobrium, calumny, and poverty.

The votaries of the ancient worship were persecuted and put to death on charges of witchcraft. The Albigensians, descendants of the Gnostics, and the Waldensians, precursors of the Protestants, were hunted and massacred under like accusations. Martin Luther himself was accused of companionship with Satan in proper person. The whole Protestant world still lies under the same imputation. There is no distinction in the judgments of the Church between dissent, heresy, and witchcraft. And except where civil authority protects, they are all capital offenses.

It hardly seems credible that, of all the various nations of antiquity, there was never one which believed in a personal devil more than liberal Christians in the nineteenth century, and yet such is the sorrowful fact. Neither the Egyptians, whom Porphyry terms "the most learned nation of the world" (*De abstinentia* 2.5), nor Greece, its faithful copyist, were ever guilty of such a crowning absurdity. We may add at once that none of them, not even the ancient Jews, believed in hell or an eternal damnation any more than in the Devil, although our Christian churches are so liberal in dealing it out to the heathen. Wherever the word "hell" occurs in the translations of the Hebrew sacred texts, it is unfortunate. The Hebrews were ignorant of such an idea.

In the Old Testament the expressions "gates of death" and the "chambers of death" simply allude to the "gates of the grave," which are specifically mentioned in the Psalms and Proverbs. Hell and its sovereign are both inventions of Christianity, coeval with its accession to power and resort to tyranny. They were hallucinations born of the nightmares of the St. Anthonys in the desert. Before our era the ancient sages knew the "Father of Evil" and treated him no better than an ass, the chosen symbol of Typhon, "the Devil." Sad degeneration of human brains!

Ophios and Ophiomorphos, Apollo and Python, Osiris and Typhon, Christos and the Serpent are all convertible terms. They are all Logoi, and one is unintelligible without the other, as day could not be known if we had no night. All are regenerators and saviors, one in a spiritual, and the other in a physical sense. One insures immortality for the Divine Spirit; the other gives it through regeneration of the seed. The Savior of mankind has to die, because he unveils to humanity the great secret of the immortal ego; the serpent of Genesis is cursed because he said to matter, "Ye shall not die." In the world of paganism the counterpart of the "serpent" is the second Hermes, the reincarnation of Hermes Trismegistus.

The great dissimilarity which exists between the various conceptions of the Devil is really often ludicrous. While bigots will invariably endow him with horns, tail, and every conceivable repulsive feature, even including an offensive human smell, Milton, Byron, Goethe, Lermontov, and a host of French novelists have sung his praise in flowing verse and thrilling prose. Milton's Satan and even Goethe's Mephistopheles are certainly far more commanding figures than some of the angels, as represented in the prose of ecstatic bigots.

Notes

1. 1 Corinthians 10.11: "All these things happened unto them for types."
2. Galatians 4.22, 24: "It is written that Abraham had two sons, the one by a bondmaid, the other by a freewoman . . . which things are an allegory."
3. Atum, or At-mu, is the Concealed God, at once Ptah and Amon, Father and Son, Creator and thing created, Thought and Appearance, Father and Mother.

25

Comparative Results of
Buddhism and Christianity

Whatever the faith, if the worshiper is sincere, it should be respected in his presence. If we do not accept Jesus as God, we revere him as a man. Such a feeling honors him more than if we were to attribute to him the powers and personality of the Supreme, and credit him at the same time with having played a useless comedy with mankind, as, after all, his mission proves scarcely less than a complete failure; 2,000 years have passed, and Christians do not comprise one-fifth of the population of the globe, nor is Christianity likely to progress any better in the future. No, we aim but at strict justice, leaving all personality aside.

No orthodox Brahmans and Buddhists would deny the Christian incarnation; but they understand it in their own philosophical way. How could they deny it? The very cornerstone of their religious system is periodical incarnations of the Deity. Whenever humanity is merging into materialism and moral degradation, a Supreme Spirit incarnates himself in his creature selected for the purpose. The "Messenger of the Highest" links itself with the duality of matter and soul, and the triad being thus completed by the union of its Crown, a savior is born who helps restore humanity to the path of truth and virtue.

The early Christian Church, imbued with Asiatic philosophy, evidently shared the same belief—otherwise it would have neither erected into an article of faith the second advent, nor cunningly invented the fable of Anti-Christ as a precaution against possible future incarnations. Neither could they have imagined that Melchisedek was an avatar of Christ. They had only to turn to the Bhagavad Gita to

231

find Krishna or Bhagavat saying to Arjuna: "He who follows me is saved by wisdom and even by works. . . . As often as virtue declines in the world, I make myself manifest to save it" [3.4].

Indeed, it is difficult to avoid sharing this doctrine of periodical incarnations. Has not the world witnessed, at rare intervals, the advent of such grand characters as Krishna, Sakyamuni, and Jesus? Like the two latter personages, Krishna seems to have been a real being, deified by his school at some time in the twilight of history and made to fit into the frame of the time-honored religious program. Compare the two Redeemers, the Hindu and the Christian, the one preceding the other by some thousands of years; place between them Siddhartha Buddha, reflecting Krishna and projecting into the night of the future his own luminous shadow, out of whose collected rays were shaped the outlines of the mythical Jesus, and from whose teachings were drawn those of the historical Christos; and we find that under one identical garment of poetical legend lived and breathed three real human figures. The individual merit of each of them is brought out in stronger relief by this same mythical coloring, for no unworthy character could have been selected for deification by the popular instinct, so unerring and just when left untrammeled. *Vox populi, vox Dei* was once true, however erroneous when applied to the present priest-ridden mob.

Kapila, Orpheus, Pythagoras, Plato, Basilides, Marcion, Ammonius, and Plotinus founded schools and sowed the germs of many a noble thought, and disappearing left behind them the refulgence of demigods. But the three personalities of Krishna, Gautama, and Jesus appeared like true gods, each in his epoch, and bequeathed to humanity three religions built on the imperishable rock of ages. That all three, especially the Christian faith, have in time become adulterated, and the latter almost unrecognizable, is no fault of any of the noble reformers. Purify the three systems of the human dogmas and the pure essence remaining will be found identical.

The Wheel of the Law has the following: "Buddhists believe that every act, word, or thought has its consequence, which will appear sooner or later in the present or in the future state. Evil acts will produce evil consequences, . . . good acts will produce good consequences: prosperity in this world, or birth in heaven . . . in some future state" [(London, 1871), 45].

This is strict and impartial justice. This is the idea of a Supreme Power which cannot fail and therefore has neither wrath nor mercy, but leaves every cause, great or small, to work out its inevitable effects. "With what measure you mete, it shall be measured to you again" (Matthew 7.2) points neither by expression nor implication to any hope of future mercy or salvation by proxy. Cruelty and mercy are finite feelings. The Supreme Deity is infinite, hence it can only be just, and Justice must be blind. The ancient pagans held on this question far more philosophical views than modern Christians, for they represented their Themis blindfolded.

We have often wondered at the extraordinary ideas of God and His justice that seem to be honestly held by those Christians who blindly rely upon the clergy for their religion, and never upon their own reason. How strangely illogical is this doctrine of the Atonement. We propose to discuss it with the Christians from the Buddhistic standpoint, and show at once by what a series of sophistries, directed toward the one object of tightening the ecclesiastical yoke upon the popular neck, its acceptance as a divine command has been finally effected and also that it has proved one of the most pernicious and demoralizing of doctrines.

The clergy say that, no matter how enormous our crimes against the laws of God and of man, we have but to believe in the self-sacrifice of Jesus for the salvation of mankind, and His blood will wash out every stain. God's mercy is boundless and unfathomable. It is impossible to conceive of a human sin so damnable that the price paid in advance for the redemption of the sinner would not wipe it out if a thousandfold worse. And, furthermore, it is never too late to repent. Though the offender waits until the last minute of the last hour of the last day of his mortal life before his blanched lips utter the confession of faith, he may go to Paradise; the dying thief did it, and so may all others as vile. These are the assumptions of the Church.

But if we step outside the little circle of creed and consider the universe as a whole balanced by the exquisite adjustment of parts, how all sound logic, how the faintest glimmering sense of justice revolts against this vicarious atonement! If the criminal sinned only against himself, and wronged no one but himself, and if by sincere repentance he could cause the obliteration of past events, not only from the memory of man, but also from that imperishable record, which no deity—not even the Supremest of the Supreme—can cause to disappear, then this dogma might not be incomprehensible. But to maintain that one may wrong his fellow man, kill, disturb the equilibrium of society and the natural order of things, and then—through cowardice, hope, or compulsion, it matters not—be forgiven by believing that the spilling of one blood washes out the other blood spilt—this is preposterous!

Can the results of a crime be obliterated even though the crime itself should be pardoned? The effects of a cause are never limited to the boundaries of the cause, nor can the results of crime be confined to the offender and his victim. Every good as well as evil action has its effects, as palpably as the stone flung into calm water. The simile is trite, but it is the best ever conceived, so let us use it. The eddying circles are greater and swifter as the disturbing object is greater or smaller, but the smallest pebble, nay, the tiniest speck, makes its ripples. And this disturbance is not alone visible and on the surface. Below, unseen, in every direction—outward and downward—drop pushes drop until the sides and bottom are touched by the force. More, the air above the water is agitated, and this disturbance passes, as the physicists tell us, from stratum to stratum out into space forever and ever; an impulse has been given to matter and is never lost, so can never be recalled!

So with crime, and so with its opposite. The action may be instantaneous, the effects are eternal. When, after the stone is once flung into the pond, we can recall it to the hand, roll back the ripples, obliterate the force expended, restore the etheric waves to their previous state of nonbeing, and wipe out every trace of the act of throwing the missile, so that Time's record shall not show that it ever happened, then, *then* we may patiently hear Christians argue for the efficacy of this Atonement.

The present volumes have been written to small purpose if they have not shown (1) that Jesus, the Christ-God, is a myth concocted two centuries after the real Hebrew Jesus died; (2) that therefore he never had any authority to give Peter, or any one else, plenary power; (3) that even if he had given such authority, the word *petra* (rock) referred to the revealed truths of the Petroma, not to him who thrice denied him; and that besides, the apostolic succession is a gross and palpable fraud; and (4) that the Gospel according to Matthew is a fabrication based upon a wholly different manuscript. The whole thing, therefore, is an imposition alike upon priest and penitent.

But putting all these points aside for the moment, it suffices to ask these pretended agents of the three gods of the Trinity how they reconcile it with the most rudimental notions of equity: why, if the power to pardon sinners for sinning has been given to them, they did not also receive the ability by miracle to obliterate the wrongs done against person or property. Let them restore life to the murdered, honor to the dishonored, property to those who have been wronged, and force the scales of human and divine justice to recover their equilibrium. Then we may talk of their divine commission to bind and loose.

But all are silent: no answer, no reply, and still the inexorable unerring Law of Compensation proceeds on its unswerving path. If we but watch its progress, we will find that it ignores all creeds, shows no preferences, but its sunlight and its thunderbolts fall alike on heathen and Christian. No absolution can shield the latter when guilty, no anathema hurt the former when innocent.

The Gospels being "divine revelation," doubtless Christians will regard their testimony as conclusive. Do they affirm that Jesus gave himself as a voluntary sacrifice? On the contrary, there is not a word to sustain the idea. They make it clear that he would rather have lived to continue what he considered his mission, and that he died because he could not help it, and only when betrayed. Before, when threatened with violence, he had made himself invisible by employing over the bystanders the mesmeric power claimed by every Eastern adept, and escaped. When finally he saw that his time had come, he succumbed to the inevitable. But see him in the garden, on the Mount of Olives, writhing in agony until "his sweat was, as it were, great drops of blood," praying with fervid supplication that the cup might be removed from him, exhausted by his struggle to such a degree that an angel from heaven had to come and strengthen him; and say if the picture is that of a self-immolating hostage and martyr. To crown all, and leave no lingering doubt in our minds, we have his own despairing words, "Not my will, but thine, be done!" (Luke 22.42).

The precepts of Hillel appear rather as quotations than original expressions in the Sermon on the Mount. Jesus taught the world nothing that had not been taught as earnestly before by other masters.

235

He begins his sermon with certain purely Buddhistic precepts that had found acceptance among the Essenes and were generally practiced by the Orphikoi and the Neoplatonists. He tries to imbue the hearts of his audience with a scorn for worldly wealth, a fakir-like unconcern for the morrow, and love for humanity, poverty, and chastity. He blesses the poor in spirit, the meek, the hungering and the thirsting after righteousness, the merciful and the peacemakers, and, Buddha-like, leaves but a poor chance for the proud castes to enter into the kingdom of heaven. Every word of his sermon is an echo of the essential principles of monastic Buddhism. The ten commandments of Buddha, as found in an appendix to the *Pratimoksha Sutra* (Pali-Burmese text), are elaborated to their full extent in Matthew. If we desire to acquaint ourselves with the historical Jesus, we have to set the mythical Christ entirely aside and learn all we can of the man in the first Gospel. His doctrines, religious views, and grandest aspirations will be found concentrated in his sermon.

There is quite enough in the four gospels to show what was the secret and most fervent hope of Jesus, the hope in which he began to teach and in which he died. In his immense and unselfish love for humanity, he considers it unjust to deprive the many of the results of the knowledge acquired by the few. This result he accordingly preaches—the unity of a spiritual God, whose temple is within each of us and in whom we live as He lives in us, in spirit.

There were even those among the highest *epoptai* of the greater Mysteries who knew nothing of their last and dreaded rite—the voluntary transfer of life from hierophant to candidate. In *Ghost-Land*[1] this mystical operation of the adept's transfer of his spiritual entity, after the death of his body, into the youth he loves with all the ardent love of a spiritual parent is superbly described. As in the case of the reincarnation of the lamas of Tibet, an adept of the highest order may live indefinitely. His mortal casket wears out, notwithstanding certain alchemical secrets for prolonging youthful vigor far beyond the usual limits. Yet the body can rarely be kept alive beyond ten or twelve score of years. The old garment is then worn out, and the spiritual Ego who is forced to leave it, selects for its habitation a new body, fresh and full of healthy vital principle.

The High Hierophant alone knew how to perform this solemn operation by infusing his own vital life and astral soul into the adept, chosen by him as his successor, who thus became endowed with a double life.[2]

"Verily, verily, I say unto thee, except a man be born again, he cannot see the kingdom of God" (John 3.3). Jesus tells Nicodemus, "That which is born of the flesh is flesh; and that which is born of the spirit is spirit."

This allusion, so unintelligible in itself, is explained in the *Satapatha-Brahmana*. It teaches that a man striving after spiritual perfection must have three births: (1) physical, from his mortal parents; (2) spiritual, through religious sacrifice (initiation); (3) his final birth into the world of spirit at death. Though it may seem strange that we should have to go to the old land of the Punjab and the banks of the sacred Ganges for an interpreter of words spoken in Jerusalem and expounded on the banks of the Jordan, the fact is evident. This second birth, or regeneration of spirit, after the natural birth of that which is born of the flesh might have astonished a Jewish ruler. Nevertheless, it had been taught 3,000 years before the appearance of the great Galilean prophet, not only in old India but to all the *epoptai* of the pagan initiations, who were instructed in the great mysteries of life and death.

This secret of secrets, that soul is not knit to flesh, was practically demonstrated in the instance of the Yogis, the followers of Kapila. Having emancipated their souls from the fetters of *Prakriti*, or *Mahat* (the physical perception of the senses and mind—in one sense, creation), they so developed their soul-power and will-force that they actually enabled themselves, while on earth, to communicate with the supernal worlds and to perform what is bunglingly termed "miracles." Men whose astral spirits have attained on earth the *naihsreyasa*, or the *mukti*, are half-gods; they reach Moksha or Nirvana as disembodied spirits, and this is their second spiritual birth.

Buddha teaches the doctrine of a new birth as plainly as Jesus does. Desiring to break with the ancient Mysteries, to which it was impossible to admit the ignorant masses, the Hindu reformer, though generally silent upon more than one secret dogma, clearly states his thought in several passages. Thus he says: "Some people are born again; evil-doers go to Hell; righteous people go to Heaven; those who are free from all worldly desires enter Nirvana" (*Dhammapada*126). Elsewhere Buddha states that it is better to believe in a future life in which happiness or misery can be felt; for if the heart believes therein, "it will abandon sin and act virtuously; and even if there is no resurrection, such a life will bring a good name and the regard of men. But those who believe in extinction at death will not fail to commit any sin that they may choose, because of their disbelief in a future" (*The Wheel of the Law* 42).

That there are fearful secrets in nature may well be believed when, as in the case of the Russian *znachar'*, the sorcerer cannot die until he has passed the word to another, and the hierophants of White Magic rarely do so. It seems as if the dread power of the "Word" could only be entrusted to one man of a certain district or body of people at a time. When the Brahmatma was about to lay aside the burden of physical existence, he imparted his secret to his successor, either orally or by a writing placed in a securely fastened casket which went into the latter's hands alone. Moses "lays his hands" upon his neophyte, Joshua, in the solitudes of Nebo and passes away forever. Aaron initiates Eleazar on Mount Hor and dies. Siddhartha Buddha promises his mendicants before his death to live in him who shall deserve it, embraces his favorite disciple, whispers in his ear, and dies; and as John's head lies upon the bosom of Jesus, he is told that he shall "tarry" until he shall come.

Like signal fires of the olden times, which, lighted and extinguished by turns upon one hilltop after another, conveyed intelligence along a whole stretch of country, so we see a long line of "wise" men from the beginning of history down to our own times communicating the word of wisdom to their direct successors. Passing from seer to seer, the "Word" flashes out like lightning and, while carrying off the initiator from human sight forever, brings the new initiate into view. Meanwhile, whole nations murder each other in the name of another "Word," an empty substitute accepted literally by each and misinterpreted by all!

In the general spoliation of Buddhism in order to make up the new Christian religion, it was not to be expected that so peerless a character as Gautama Buddha would be left unappropriated. It was but natural that after taking his legendary history to fill out the blanks left in the fictitious story of Jesus, after using what they could of Krishna's, they should take the man Sakyamuni and put him in their calendar under an alias. This they actually did, and the Hindu Savior in due time appeared on the list of saints as Josaphat.

Let them pass on—we have devoted too much space to them and their conglomerate theology already. We have weighed both in the balance of history, of logic, and of truth and found them wanting.

As occasion required, we have reinforced our argument with descriptions of a few of the innumerable phenomena witnessed by us in different parts of the world. The remaining space at our disposal will be devoted to like subjects. Having laid a foundation by elucidating the philosophy of occult phenomena, it seems opportune to illustrate the theme with facts that have occurred under our own eye, and that may be verified by any traveler. Primitive peoples have disappeared, but primitive wisdom survives and is attainable by those who "will," "dare," and can "keep silent."

NOTES

1. *Ghost-Land; or Researches into the Mysteries of Occultism*, ed. E. Hardinge-Britten (Boston, 1876), ch. 15.
2. The atrocious custom subsequently introduced among the people of sacrificing human victims is a perverted copy of the Theurgic Mystery. The pagan priests who did not belong to the class of the hierophants carried on for awhile this hideous rite, and it served to screen the genuine purpose. Bunsen [*Egypt's Place* 1:18] shows, by the very absence of any representation of human sacrifice on the oldest monuments, that this custom had been abolished in the old Empire at the close of the seventh century after Menes.

26

Conclusions and Illustrations

It would argue small discernment on our part were we to suppose that we had been followed thus far through this work by any but metaphysicians or mystics of some sort. Were it otherwise, we should certainly advise such to spare themselves the trouble of reading this chapter; for, although nothing is said that is not strictly true, they would not fail to regard the least wonderful of the narratives as absolutely false, however substantiated.

To comprehend the principles of natural law involved in the several phenomena hereinafter described, the reader must keep in mind the fundamental propositions of the Oriental philosophy which we have successively elucidated. Let us recapitulate very briefly:

(1) There is no miracle. Everything that happens is the result of law—eternal, immutable, ever active. Apparent miracle is but the operation of forces antagonistic to what Dr. W. B. Carpenter, F.R.S.—a man of great learning but little knowledge—calls "the well-ascertained laws of nature." Like many of his class, Dr. Carpenter ignores the fact that there may be laws once "known," now unknown to science.

(2) Nature is triune: there is a visible, objective nature; an invisible, indwelling, energizing nature, the exact model of the other, and its vital principle; and, above these two, *spirit*, source of all forces, alone eternal, and indestructible. The lower two constantly change; the higher third does not.

(3) Man is also triune: he has his objective, physical body; his vitalizing astral body (or soul), the real man; and these two are brooded over and illuminated by the third—the sovereign, the immortal spirit.

240

When the real man succeeds in merging himself with the latter, he becomes an immortal entity.

(4) Magic, as a science, is the knowledge of these principles and of the way by which the omniscience and omnipotence of the spirit and its control over nature's forces may be acquired by the individual while still in the body. Magic, as an art, is the application of this knowledge in practice.

(5) Arcane knowledge misapplied is sorcery; beneficently used, true magic or Wisdom.

(6) Mediumship is the opposite of adeptship; the medium is the passive instrument of foreign influences, the adept actively controls himself and all inferior potencies.

(7) All things that ever were, that are, or that will be, having their record upon the astral light, or tablet of the unseen universe, can be known by the initiated adept, using the vision of his own spirit.

(8) Races of men differ in spiritual gifts as in color, stature, or any other external quality; among some peoples seership naturally prevails, among others mediumship. Some are addicted to sorcery and transmit its secret rules of practice from generation to generation, with a range of psychical phenomena more or less wide as the result.

(9) One phase of magical skill is the voluntary and conscious withdrawal of the inner man (astral form) from the outer man (physical body). In the cases of some mediums withdrawal occurs, but it is unconscious and involuntary. With them the body is more or less cataleptic at such times; but with the adept the absence of the astral form would not be noticed, for the physical senses are alert, and the individual appears only as though in a fit of abstraction—"a brown study," as some call it.

To the movements of the wandering astral form neither time nor space offer obstacles. The thaumaturgist, thoroughly skilled in occult science, can cause himself (that is, his physical body) to seem to disappear, or to apparently take on any shape that he may choose. He may make his astral form visible, or he may give it protean appearances. In both cases these results will be achieved by a mesmeric hallucination of the senses of all witnesses, simultaneously brought on. This hallucination is so perfect that the subject of it would stake his life that he saw a reality, when it is but a picture in his own mind, impressed upon his consciousness by the irresistible will of the mesmerizer.

241

Although the astral form can go anywhere, penetrate any obstacle, and be seen at any distance from the physical body, the latter is dependent upon ordinary methods of transportation. It may be levitated under prescribed magnetic conditions, but not pass from one locality to another except in the usual way. Hence we discredit all stories of the aerial flight of mediums in body, for such would be miracle, and miracle we repudiate. Inert matter may be, in certain cases and under certain conditions, disintegrated, passed through walls, and recombined, but living animal organisms cannot.

Swedenborgians believe and arcane science teaches that the abandonment of the living body by the soul frequently occurs, and that we encounter every day, in every condition of life, such living corpses. Various causes, among them overpowering fright, grief, despair, a violent attack of sickness, or excessive sensuality may bring this about. The vacant carcass may be entered and inhabited by the astral form of an adept sorcerer, or an elementary (an earthbound disembodied human soul), or, very rarely, an elemental. Of course, an adept of white magic has the same power, but unless some very exceptional and great object is to be accomplished, he will never consent to pollute himself by occupying the body of an impure person. In insanity, the patient's astral being is either semiparalyzed, bewildered, and subject to the influence of every passing spirit of any sort, or it has departed forever, and the body is taken possession of by some vampirish entity near its own disintegration and clinging desperately to earth, whose sensual pleasures it may enjoy for a brief season longer by this expedient.

(10) The cornerstone of magic is an intimate practical knowledge of magnetism and electricity and their qualities, correlations, and potencies. Especially necessary is a familiarity with their effects in and upon the animal kingdom and man. There are occult properties in many other minerals, equally as strange as that in the lodestone, which all practitioners of magic must know, and of which so-called exact science is wholly ignorant. Plants also have like mystical properties in a most wonderful degree, but the secrets of the herbs of dreams and enchantments are unknown to European science, except in a few marked instances, such as opium and hashish. Yet, the psychical effects of even these few upon the human system are regarded as evidences of a temporary mental disorder. The women of Thessaly and Epirus, the female hierophants of the rites of Sabazius, did not carry their secrets

away with the downfall of their sanctuaries. They are still preserved, and those who are aware of the nature of Soma know the properties of other plants as well.

To sum up all in a few words, magic is spiritual wisdom; nature is the material ally, pupil, and servant of the magician. One common vital principle pervades all things, and this is controllable by the perfected human will. The adept can stimulate the movements of the natural forces in plants and animals in a preternatural degree. Such experiments are not obstructions of nature, but quickenings; the conditions of intenser vital action are given.

The adept can control the sensations and alter the conditions of the physical and astral bodies of other persons not adepts; he can also govern and employ, as he chooses, the spirits of the elements. He cannot control the immortal spirit of any human being, living or dead, for all such spirits are alike sparks of the Divine Essence, and not subject to any foreign domination.

From the remotest antiquity mankind as a whole has always been convinced of the existence of a personal spiritual entity within the personal physical man. This inner entity was more or less divine, according to its proximity to the *crown*—Chrestos. The closer the union, the more serene man's destiny, the less dangerous the external conditions. This belief is neither bigotry nor superstition, only an ever present, instinctive feeling of the proximity of another spiritual and invisible world, which, though it be subjective to the senses of the outward man, is perfectly objective to the inner ego.

Furthermore, they believed that there are external and internal conditions which affect the determination of our will upon our actions. They rejected fatalism, for fatalism implies a blind course of some still blinder power. But they believed in destiny, which from birth to death every man is weaving thread by thread around himself, as a spider does his cobweb; and this destiny is guided either by that presence some term the "guardian angel" or by our more intimate astral inner man, who is but too often the evil genius of the man of flesh. Both these lead on the outward man, but one of them must prevail; and from the very beginning of the invisible affray the stern and implacable law of compensation steps in and takes its course, following faithfully the fluctuations. When the last strand is woven, and man is seemingly enwrapped in the network of his own doing, then he finds himself completely under the empire of this self-made destiny. It then either fixes him like the inert shell against the immovable rock, or like a feather carries him away in a whirlwind raised by his own actions.

The adepts of Eastern magic are uniformly in perfect mental and bodily health, and in fact the voluntary and independent production of phenomena is impossible to any others. We have known many, and never a sick man among them. The adept retains perfect consciousness; shows no change of bodily temperature or other sign of morbidity; requires no "conditions," but will do his feats anywhere and everywhere; and instead of being passive and in subjection to a foreign influence, rules the forces with iron will. But we have elsewhere shown that the medium and the adept are as opposed as the poles. We will only add here that the body, soul, and spirit of the adept are all conscious and working in harmony, and the body of the medium is an inert clod, and even his soul may be away in a dream while its habitation is occupied by another.

The medium need not exercise any will power. It suffices that she or he shall know what is expected by the investigators. The medium's "spiritual" entity, when not obsessed by other spirits, will act outside the will or consciousness of the physical being, as surely as it acts when within the body during a fit of somnambulism. Its perceptions, external and internal, will be acuter and far more developed, precisely as they are in the sleepwalker. And this is why "the materialized form sometimes knows more than the medium," for the intellectual perception of the astral entity is proportionately as much higher than the corporeal intelligence of the medium in its normal state as the spirit entity is finer than the astral entity. Generally the medium will be found cold, the pulse will have visibly changed, and a state of nervous prostration succeeds the phenomena, bunglingly and without discrimination attributed to disembodied spirits, whereas only one-third of them may be produced by the latter, another third by elementals, and the rest by the astral double of the medium himself.

While it is our firm belief that most of the physical manifestations, i.e., those which neither need nor show intelligence nor great discrimination, are produced mechanically by the scîn-lâc (double) of the medium, as a person in sound sleep will when apparently awake do things of which he will retain no remembrance, the purely subjective phenomena are but in a very small proportion of cases due to the

244

action of the personal astral body. They are mostly, and according to the moral, intellectual, and physical purity of the medium, the work of either the elementary, or sometimes very pure human spirits. Elementals have naught to do with subjective manifestations. In rare cases it is the divine spirit of the medium himself that guides and produces them.

Years ago, a small party of travelers were painfully journeying from Kashmir to Leh, a city of Ladakh (Central Tibet). Among our guides we had a Tatar shaman, a very mysterious personage, who spoke Russian a little and English not at all, and yet who managed to converse with us and proved of great service. Having learned that some of our party were Russians, he had imagined that our protection was all-powerful and might enable him to safely find his way back to his Siberian home, from which, for reasons unknown, some twenty years before he had fled, as he told us, via Kyakhta and the great Gobi Desert, to the land of the *Chakhars*. With such an interested object in view, we believed ourselves safe under his guard.

To explain the situation briefly: Our companions had formed the unwise plan of penetrating into Tibet under various disguises, none of them speaking the language, although one, a Mr. K———, had picked up some Kazan Tatar, and thought he did. As we mention this only incidentally, we may as well say at once that two of them, the brothers N———, were very politely brought back to the frontier before they had walked sixteen miles into the weird land of Eastern Bod; and Mr. K———, an ex-Lutheran minister, could not even attempt to leave his miserable village near Leh, as from the first days he found himself prostrated with fever and had to return to Lahore via Kashmir. But one sight seen by him was as good as if he had witnessed the reincarnation of Buddha itself. Having heard of this "miracle" from some old Russian missionary in whom he thought he could have more faith than in Abbé Huc, it had been for years his desire to expose the "great heathen" jugglery, as he expressed it. K——— was a positivist, and rather prided himself on this antiphilosophical neologism. But his positivism was doomed to receive a deathblow.

About four days' journey from Islamabad, at an insignificant mud village, whose only redeeming feature was its magnificent lake, we stopped for a few days' rest. Our companions had temporarily separated from us, and the village was to be our place of meeting. It was there that

245

we were apprised by our shaman that a large party of lama "saints," on pilgrimage to various shrines, had taken up their abode in an old cave temple and established a temporary vihara therein. He added that, as the "Three Honorable Ones"[1] were said to travel along with them, the holy bhikshu (monks) were capable of producing the greatest miracles. Mr. K———, fired with the prospect of exposing this humbug of the ages, proceeded at once to pay them a visit, and from that moment the most friendly relations were established between the two camps.

The vihara was in a secluded and most romantic spot secured against all intrusion. Despite the effusive attentions, presents, and protestations of Mr. K———, the Chief, who was Pase-Budhu (an ascetic of great sanctity), declined to exhibit the phenomenon of the "incarnation" until a certain talisman in possession of the writer was exhibited. Upon seeing this, however, preparations were at once made, and an infant of three or four months was procured from its mother, a poor woman of the neighborhood. An oath was first of all exacted of Mr. K———, that he would not divulge what he might see or hear for the space of seven years. The talisman is a simple agate or carnelian known among the Tibetans and others as *A-yu*, which naturally possessed, or had been endowed with, very mysterious properties. It has a triangle engraved upon it, within which are contained a few mystical words.[2]

Several days passed before everything was ready; meanwhile nothing of a mysterious character occurred, except that, at the bidding of a bhikshu, ghastly faces were made to peep at us out of the glassy bosom of the lake, as we sat at the door of the vihara, upon its bank. One of these was the countenance of Mr. K———'s sister, whom he had left well and happy at home, but who, as we subsequently learned, had died some time before he had set out on the present journey. The sight affected him at first, but he called his skepticism to his aid, and quieted himself with theories of cloud shadows, reflections of tree branches, etc., such as people of his kind fall back upon.

On the appointed afternoon, the baby, being brought to the vihara, was left in the vestibule or reception room, as K——— could go no further into the temporary sanctuary. The child was then placed on a bit of carpet in the middle of the floor, and everyone not belonging to the party being sent away, two "mendicants" were placed at the entrance to keep out intruders. Then all the lamas seated themselves on the floor with their backs against the granite walls, so that each was separated from the child by a space of at least ten feet. The chief, having had a square piece of leather spread for him by the *desservant*, seated himself at the farthest corner. Alone, Mr. K——— placed himself close by the infant, and watched every movement with intense interest. The only condition exacted of us was that we should preserve a strict silence and patiently await further developments.

A bright sunlight streamed through the open door. Gradually the "Superior" fell into what seemed a state of profound meditation, while the others, after a *sotto voce* short invocation, became suddenly silent, and looked as if they had been completely petrified. It was oppressively still, and the cooing of the child was the only sound to be heard. After we had sat there a few moments, the movements of the infant's limbs suddenly ceased, and his body appeared to become rigid. K——— watched intently every motion, and both of us, by a rapid glance, became satisfied that all present were sitting motionless. The Superior, with his gaze fixed upon the ground, did not even look at the infant; but, pale and motionless, he seemed rather like a bronze statue of a Talapoin in meditation than a living being.

Suddenly, to our great consternation, we saw the child, not raise itself, but, as it were, violently jerked into a sitting posture! A few more jerks, and then, like an automaton set in motion by concealed wires, the four months old baby stood upon his feet! Fancy our consternation, and, in Mr. K———'s case, horror. Not a hand had been outstretched, not a motion made, nor a word spoken, and yet here was a baby-in-arms standing erect and firm as a man!

The rest of the story we will quote from a copy of notes written on this subject by Mr. K——— the same evening and given to us, in case it should not reach its place of destination, or should the writer fail to see anything more. "After a minute or two of hesitation," writes K———,

> the baby turned his head and looked at me with an expression of intelligence that was simply awful! It sent a chill through me. I pinched my hands and bit my lips till the blood almost came, to make sure that I did not dream. But this was only the beginning. The miraculous creature, making, as I fancied, two steps toward me, resumed his sitting posture, and, without removing his eyes from

mine, repeated, sentence by sentence, in what I supposed to be Tibetan language, the very words, which I had been told in advance, are commonly spoken at the incarnations of Buddha, beginning with "I am Buddha; I am the old Lama; I am his spirit in a new body," etc. I felt a real terror; my hair rose upon my head, and my blood ran cold. For my life I could not have spoken a word. There was no trickery here, no ventriloquism. The infant lips moved, and the eyes seemed to search my very soul with an expression that made me think it was the face of the Superior himself, his eyes, his very look that I was gazing upon. It was as if his spirit had entered the little body, and was looking at me through the transparent mask of the baby's face. I felt my brain growing dizzy. The infant reached toward me, and laid his little hand upon mine. I started as if I had been touched by a hot coal; and, unable to bear the scene any longer, covered my face with my hands. It was but for an instant; but when I removed them, the little actor had become a cooing baby again, and a moment later, lying upon his back, set up a fretful cry. The superior had resumed his normal condition, and conversation ensued.

It was only after a series of similar experiments, extending over ten days, that I realized the fact that I had seen the incredible, astounding phenomenon described by certain travelers, but always denounced by me as an imposture. Among a multitude of questions that were unanswered, despite my cross-examination, the Superior let drop one piece of information which must be regarded as highly significant. "What would have happened," I inquired, through the shaman, "if, while the infant was speaking, in a moment of insane fright at the thought of its being the 'Devil,' I had killed it?" He replied that, if the blow had not been instantly fatal, the child alone would have been killed. "But," I continued, "suppose that it had been as swift as a lightning flash?" "In such case," was the answer, "you would have killed me also."

Both in western and eastern Tibet, as in every other place where Buddhism predominates, there are two distinct religions, the same as in Brahmanism—the secret philosophy and the popular religion. The former is that of the followers of the doctrine of the sect of the Sautrantikas.[3] They closely adhere to the spirit of Buddha's original teachings, which show the necessity of intuitional perception and all deductions therefrom. These do not proclaim their views or allow them to be made public.

"All compounds are perishable," were the last words uttered by the lips of the dying Gautama, when preparing under the Sala tree to enter into Nirvana. "Spirit is the sole, elementary, and primordial unity, and each of its rays is immortal, infinite, and indestructible. Beware of the illusions of matter." Buddhism was spread far and wide over Asia and even farther by Dharmasoka. He was the grandson of the miracle worker Chandragupta, the illustrious king who rescued the Punjab from the Macedonians—if they ever were at Punjab at all—and received Megasthenes at his court in Pataliputra. Dharmasoka was the greatest King of the Maurya dynasty. From a reckless profligate and atheist, he had become Priyadarsin, the "beloved of the gods," and the purity of his philanthropic views was never surpassed by any earthly ruler. His memory has lived for ages in the hearts of the Buddhists, and has been perpetuated in the humane edicts engraved in several popular dialects on the columns and rocks of Allahabad, Delhi, Gujarat, Peshawar, Orissa, and other places. His famous grandfather had united all India under his powerful scepter. When the Nagas, or serpent worshipers of Kashmir, had been converted through the efforts of the apostles sent out by the Sthaviras of the third council, the religion of Gautama spread like wildfire. Gandhara, Kabul, and even many of the Satrapies of Alexander the Great accepted the new philosophy. The Buddhism of Nepal being the one which may be said to have diverged less than any other from the primeval ancient faith, the Lamaism of Tartary, Mongolia, and Tibet, which is a direct offshoot of this country, may thus be shown to be the purest Buddhism; for, we repeat, Lamaism properly is but an external form of rites.

The Upasakas and Upasikas, or male and female semi-monastics and semi-laymen, like the lama monks themselves have to strictly abstain from violating any of Buddha's rules and must study *Meipo* and every psychological phenomenon. Those who become guilty of any of the "five sins" lose all right to congregate with the pious community. The most important of these rules is not to curse upon any consideration, for the curse returns upon the one that utters it, and often upon his innocent relatives who breathe the same atmosphere with him. To love each other, and even our bitterest enemies; to offer our lives even for animals, to the extent of abstaining from defensive arms; to gain the greatest of victories by conquering one's self; to avoid all vices; to practice all virtues, especially humility and mildness; to be obedient to superiors, to cherish and respect parents, old age, learning, and virtuous and holy men; to provide food, shelter, and comfort for men and animals; to plant trees on the roads and dig wells for the comfort of travelers—such are the moral duties of Buddhists. Every ani or bikshuni (nun) is subjected to these laws.

Numerous are the Buddhist and Lama saints who have been re-nowned for the unsurpassed sanctity of their lives and their "miracles." Contrary to the prevailing idea, few of these saints are *Hubilgans*, or shaberons (reincarnations).

Some of the female nuns possess marvelous psychological powers. We have met some of these women on their way from Lhasa to Kandi, the Rome of Buddhism, with its miraculous shrines and Gautama's relics. To avoid encounters with Muslims and other sects, they travel by night alone, unarmed and without the least fear of wild animals, for these will not touch them. At the first glimpse of dawn, they take refuge in caves and viharas prepared for them by their coreligionists at calculated distances; for, notwithstanding the fact that Buddhism has taken refuge in Ceylon, and nominally there are but few of the denomination in British India, yet the secret Byauds (brotherhoods) and Buddhist viharas are numerous, and every Jain feels himself obliged to help, indiscriminately, Buddhist or Lamaist.

Ever on the lookout for occult phenomena, hungering after sights, one of the most interesting that we have seen was produced by one of these poor traveling bhikshus. It was years ago and at a time when all such manifestations were new to the writer. We were taken to visit the pilgrims by a Buddhist friend, a mystical gentleman born at Kashmir, of Katchi parents, but a Buddha-Lamaist by conversion, who generally resides at Lhasa.

"Why carry around this bunch of dead plants?" inquired one of the bhikshunis, an emaciated, tall, and elderly woman, pointing to a large nosegay of beautiful, fresh, and fragrant flowers in the writer's hands.

"Dead?" we asked, inquiringly. "Why, they just have been gathered in the garden!"

"And yet they are dead," she gravely answered. "To be born in this world, is this not death? See how these herbs look when alive in the world of eternal light, in the gardens of our blessed Foh?"

Without moving from the place where she was sitting on the ground, the ani took a flower from the bunch, laid it in her lap, and began to draw together, by large handfuls as it were, invisible material from the surrounding atmosphere. Presently a very, very faint nodule of vapor was seen, and this slowly took shape and color, until, poised in midair, appeared a copy of the bloom we had given her. Faithful to the last tint and the last petal it was, and lying on its side like the original, but a thousandfold more gorgeous in hue and exquisite in beauty, as the glorified human spirit is more beauteous than its physical capsule. Flower after flower to the minutest herb was thus reproduced and made to vanish, reappearing at our desire, nay, at our simple thought. Having selected a full-blown rose we held it at arm's length, and in a few minutes our arm, hand, and the flower, perfect in every detail, appeared reflected in the vacant space about two yards from where we sat. But while the flower seemed immeasurably beautified and as ethereal as the other spirit flowers, the arm and hand appeared like a mere reflection in a looking glass, even to a large spot on the forearm, left on it by a piece of damp earth which had stuck to one of the roots.

The religion of the lamas has faithfully preserved the primitive science of magic, and produces feats as great now as it did in the days of Kublai Khan and his barons. The ancient mystic formula of the King Song-tsen Gampo, the "Aum mani padme hum,"[4] effects its wonders now as well as in the seventh century.

Within the cloisters of Tashi-lhunpo and Si-dzang, these powers, inherent in every man but called out by so few, are cultivated to their utmost perfection. Who in India has not heard of the Panchen Rimpoche, the *Hutuktu* of the capital of Higher Tibet? His brother-hood of Khe-lan was famous throughout the land; one of the most famous "brothers" was a *Peh-ling* (an Englishman) who had arrived one day during the early part of this century from the West, a thor-ough Buddhist, and after a month's preparation was admitted among the Khe-lans. He spoke every language, including the Tibetan, and knew every art and science, says the tradition. His sanctity and the phenomena produced by him caused him to be proclaimed a shaberon after a residence of but a few years. His memory lives to the present day among the Tibetans, but his real name is a secret with the shaberons alone.

251

The shamans of Siberia are all ignorant and illiterate. Those of Tartary and Tibet—few in number—are mostly learned men in their own way and will not allow themselves to fall under the control of spirits of any kind. The former are mediums in the full sense of the word; the latter, magicians.

We have mentioned a kind of carnelian stone in our possession which had such an unexpected and favorable effect upon the shaman's decision. Every shaman has such a talisman, which he wears attached to a string and carries under his left arm.

"Of what use is it to you, and what are its virtues?" was the question we often offered to our guide. To this he never answered directly, but evaded all explanation, promising that as soon as an opportunity was offered and we were alone, he would ask the stone to answer for himself. With this very indefinite hope, we were left to the resources of our own imagination.

But the day on which the stone "spoke" came very soon. It was during the most critical hours of our life, at a time when the vagabond nature of a traveler had carried the writer to far-off lands, where neither civilization is known nor security can be guaranteed for one hour. One afternoon, as every man and woman had left the *yurta* (Tatar tent) that had been our home for over two months to witness the ceremony of the lama exorcism of a jedker,[5] accused of breaking and spiriting away every bit of the poor furniture and earthenware of a family living about two miles distant, the shaman, who had become our only protector in those dreary deserts, was reminded of his promise. He sighed and hesitated but, after a short silence, left his place on the sheepskin and, going outside, placed a dried-up goat's head with its prominent horns over a wooden peg. Dropping down the felt curtain of the tent, he remarked that now no living person would venture in, for the goat's head was a sign that he was "at work."

After that, placing his hand in his bosom, he drew out the little stone, about the size of a walnut and, carefully unwrapping it, proceeded, as it appeared, to swallow it. In a few moments his limbs stiffened, his body became rigid, and he fell, cold and motionless as a corpse. But for a slight twitching of his lips at every question asked, the scene would have been embarrassing, nay—dreadful. The sun was setting, and were it not that dying embers flickered at the center of the tent, complete darkness would have been added to the

252

oppressive silence which reigned. We have lived in the prairies of the West and in the boundless steppes of southern Russia; but nothing can be compared with the silence at sunset on the sandy deserts of Mongolia; not even the barren solitudes of the deserts of Africa, though the former are partially inhabited, and the latter utterly void of life. Yet there was the writer alone with what looked no better than a corpse lying on the ground. Fortunately, this state did not last long.

"Mahandu!" uttered a voice, which seemed to come from the bowels of the earth, on which the shaman was prostrated. "Peace be with you. . . . What would you have me do for you?"

Startling as the fact seemed, we were quite prepared for it, for we had seen other shamans pass through similar performances. "Whoever you are," we pronounced mentally, "go to K——, and try to bring that person's *thought* here. See what that other party does, and tell —————— what we are doing and how situated."

"I am there," answered the same voice. "The old lady (cucoana)[6] is sitting in the garden. . . . She is putting on her spectacles and reading a letter."

"The contents of it, and hasten," was the hurried order while preparing notebook and pencil. The contents were given slowly, as if, while dictating, the invisible presence desired to afford us time to put down the words phonetically, for we recognized the Walachian language of which we know nothing beyond the ability to recognize it. In such a way a whole page was filled.

"Look west . . . toward the third pole of the yurta," pronounced the Tatar in his natural voice, though it sounded hollow and as if coming from afar. "Her *thought* is here."

Then with a convulsive jerk, the upper portion of the shaman's body seemed raised, and his head fell heavily on the writer's feet, which he clutched with both his hands. The position was becoming less and less attractive, but curiosity proved a good ally to courage. In the west corner was standing, lifelike but flickering, unsteady and mistlike, the form of a dear old friend, a Romanian lady of Walachia, a mystic by disposition but a thorough disbeliever in this kind of occult phenomena.

"Her thought is here, but her body is lying unconscious. We could not bring her here otherwise," said the voice.

We addressed and supplicated the apparition to answer, but all in vain. The features moved, and the form gesticulated as if in fear and agony, but no sound broke forth from the shadowy lips; only we imagined—perchance it was a fancy—hearing as if from a long distance the Romanian words, *Non se póte* (it cannot be done).

For over two hours, the most substantial, unequivocal proofs that the shaman's astral soul was traveling at the bidding of our unspoken wish were given to us. Ten months later, we received a letter from our Walachian friend in response to ours, in which we had enclosed the page from the notebook, inquiring of her what she had been doing on that day and describing the scene in full. She was sitting, she wrote, in the garden on that morning[7] prosaically occupied in boiling some conserves; the letter sent to her was word for word the copy of the one received by her from her brother; all at once—in consequence of the heat, she thought—she fainted, and remembered distinctly dreaming she saw the writer in a desert place, which she accurately described, sitting under a "gypsy's tent," as she expressed it. "Henceforth," she added, "I can doubt no longer!"

But our experiment was proved still better. We had directed the shaman's inner ego to the same friend heretofore mentioned, the Katchi of Lhasa, who travels constantly to British India and back. We know that he was apprised of our critical situation in the desert, for a few hours later came help, and we were rescued by a party of twenty-five horsemen who had been directed by their chief to find us at the place where we were, which no living man endowed with common powers could have known. The chief of this escort was a shaberon, an adept whom we had never seen before, nor did we after that, for he never left his *süme* (lamasery), and we could have no access to it. But he was a personal friend of the Katchi.

The above will of course provoke naught but incredulity in the general reader. But we write for those who will believe, who, like the writer, understand and know the illimitable powers and possibilities of the human astral soul. In this case we willingly believe, nay, we know, that the "spiritual double" of the shaman did not act alone, for he was no adept but simply a medium. According to a favorite expression of his, as soon as he placed the stone in his mouth, his "father appeared, dragged him out of his skin, and took him wherever he wanted" at his bidding.

Traveling from one tribe to the other, we passed some time in company with the Kurds. As our object is not autobiographical, we omit all details that have no immediate bearing upon some occult fact, and even of these, we have room for only a few. We will then simply state that a very expensive saddle, a carpet, and two Circassian daggers, richly mounted and chiseled in gold, had been stolen from the tent, and that the Kurds, with the chief of the tribe at the head, had come, taking Allah for their witness that the culprit could not belong to their tribe. We believed it, for it would have been unprecedented among these nomadic tribes of Asia, as famed for the sacredness in which they hold their guests as for the ease with which they plunder and occasionally murder them once they have passed the boundaries of their *aûl*.

A suggestion was then made by a Georgian belonging to our caravan to resort to the light of the *kudian* (sorcerer) of their tribe. This was arranged in great secrecy and solemnity, and the interview was appointed to take place at midnight, when the moon would be at its full. At the stated hour we were conducted to the tent described above.

A large hole, or square aperture, was managed in the arched roof of the tent, and through it poured in vertically the radiant moonbeams, mingling with the vacillating triple flame of the little lamp. After several minutes of incantations addressed to the moon, as it seemed to us, the conjurer, an old man of tremendous stature, whose pyramidal turban touched the top of the tent, produced a round looking glass, of the kind known as "Persian mirrors." Having unscrewed its cover, he then proceeded to breathe on it for over ten minutes, wiping off the moisture from the surface with a package of herbs and muttering incantations all the while *sotto voce*. After every wiping, the glass became more and more brilliant, till its crystal seemed to radiate refulgent phosphoric rays in every direction.

At last the operation was ended; the old man, with the mirror in his hand, remained as motionless as if he had been a statue. "Look, Hanoum . . . look steadily," he whispered, hardly moving his lips. Shadows and dark spots began gathering, where one moment before nothing was reflected but the radiant face of the full moon. A few more seconds, and there appeared the well-known saddle, carpet, and daggers, which seemed to be rising as from a deep, clear water and becoming with every instant more definitely outlined. Then a still

255

darker shadow appeared hovering over these objects, which gradually condensed itself and then came out, as visibly as at the small end of a telescope, as the full figure of a man crouching over them.

"I know him!" exclaimed the writer. "It is the Tatar who came to us last night, offering to sell his mule!"

The image disappeared, as if by enchantment. The old man nodded assent, but remained motionless. Then he again muttered some strange words, and suddenly began a song. The tune was slow and monotonous, but after he had sung a few stanzas in the same unknown tongue, without changing either rhythm or tune, he pronounced, recitative-like, the following words, in his broken Russian:

"Now, Hanoum, look well whether we will catch him—the fate of the robber—we will learn this night," etc.

The same shadows began gathering, and then, almost without transition, we saw the man lying on his back, in a pool of blood across the saddle, and two other men galloping off at a distance. Horror-stricken and sick at the sight of this picture, we desired to see no more. The old man, leaving the tent, called some of the Kurds standing outside, and seemed to give them instructions. Two minutes later, a dozen horsemen were galloping off at full speed down the side of the mountain on which we were encamped.

Early in the morning they returned with the lost objects. The saddle was all covered with coagulated blood.

The story they told was that, upon coming in sight of the fugitive, they saw disappearing over the crest of a distant hill two horsemen, and upon riding up, they found the Tatar thief dead upon the stolen property, exactly as we had seen him in the magical glass. He had been murdered by the two banditti, whose evident design to rob him was interrupted by the sudden appearance of the party sent by the old sorcerer.

By those who have followed us thus far, it will naturally be asked to what practical issue this book tends; much has been said about magic and its potentiality, much about the immense antiquity of its practice. Do we wish to affirm that the occult sciences ought to be studied and practiced throughout the world? Would we replace modern spiritualism with the ancient magic? Neither. The substitution could not be made, nor the study universally prosecuted, without incurring the risk of enormous public dangers.

We would have neither scientists, theologians, nor spiritualists turn practical magicians, but all to realize that there was true science, profound religion, and genuine phenomena before this modern era. We would that all who have a voice in the education of the masses should first know and then teach that the safest guides to human happiness and enlightenment are those writings which have descended to us from the remotest antiquity and that nobler spiritual aspirations and a higher average morality prevail in the countries where the people take their precepts as the rule of their lives. We would have all realize that magical, i.e., spiritual, powers exist in every man, and have those few practice them who feel called to teach and are ready to pay the price of discipline and self-conquest which their development exacts.

There being but one Truth, man requires but one church—the Temple of God within us, walled in by matter but penetrable by anyone who can find the way; the pure in heart see God. The trinity of nature is the lock of magic, the trinity of man the key that fits it. Within the solemn precincts of the sanctuary, the Supreme had and has no name. It is unthinkable and unpronounceable; and yet every man finds in himself his god.

Besides, there are many good reasons why the study of magic, except in its broad philosophy, is nearly impracticable in Europe and America. Magic being what it is—the most difficult of all sciences to learn experimentally—its acquisition is practically beyond the reach of the majority of white-skinned people, whether their effort is made at home or in the East. Probably not more than one man in a million of European blood is fitted—either physically, morally, or psychologically—to become a practical magician, and not one in ten million would be found endowed with all these three qualifications as required for the work.

Civilized Western nations lack the phenomenal powers of endurance, both mental and physical, of the Easterners; the temperamental idiosyncrasies of the Orientals are utterly wanting in them. In the Hindu, the Arabian, and the Tibetan, an intuitive perception of the possibilities of occult natural forces in subjection to human will comes by inheritance; and in them, the physical senses as well as the spiritual are far more finely developed than in the Western races. Notwithstanding the notable difference of thickness between the skulls of a European and a southern Hindu, this difference, being a purely climatic result due to the intensity of the sun's rays, involves no psychological principles.

Furthermore, there would be tremendous difficulties in the way of training, if we can so express it. Contaminated by centuries of dogmatic superstition, by an ineradicable—though quite unwarranted—sense of superiority over those whom the English term so contemptuously "niggers," the white European would hardly submit himself to the practical tuition of either Copt, Brahman, or Lama. To become a neophyte, one must be ready to devote himself heart and soul to the study of mystic sciences. Magic—most imperative of mistresses—brooks no rival. Unlike other sciences, a theoretical knowledge of formulas without mental capacities or soul powers is utterly useless in magic. The spirit must hold in complete subjection the combativeness of what is loosely termed educated reason, until facts have vanquished cold human sophistry.

Our examination of the multitudinous religious faiths that mankind, early and late, have professed most assuredly indicates that they have all been derived from one primitive source. It would seem as if they were all but different modes of expressing the yearning of the imprisoned human soul for intercourse with supernal spheres. As the white ray of light is decomposed by the prism into the various colors of the solar spectrum, so the beam of divine truth, in passing through the three-sided prism of man's nature, has been broken up into varicolored fragments called religions. And as the rays of the spectrum, by imperceptible shadings, merge into each other, so the great theologies that have appeared at different degrees of divergence from the original source have been connected by minor schisms, schools, and offshoots from one side or the other. Combined, their aggregate represents one eternal truth; separate, they are but shades of human error and the signs of imperfection. It needs only the right perception of things objective to finally discover that the only world of reality is the subjective.

What has been contemptuously termed paganism was ancient wisdom replete with Deity; and Judaism and its offspring, Christianity and Islam, derived whatever inspiration they contained from this ethnic parent. Pre-Vedic Brahmanism and Buddhism are the double source from which all religions spring; Nirvana is the ocean to which all tend.

For the purposes of a philosophical analysis, we need not take account of the enormities which have blackened the record of many of the world's religions. True faith is the embodiment of divine charity; those who minister at its altars are but human. As we turn the blood-stained pages of ecclesiastical history, we find that, whoever may have been the hero and whatever costumes the actors may have worn, the plot of the tragedy has ever been the same. But the Eternal Night was in and behind all, and we pass from what we see to that which is invisible to the eye of sense. Our fervent wish has been to show true souls how they may lift aside the curtain and, in the brightness of that Night made Day, look with undazzled gaze upon the Unveiled Truth.

NOTES

1. These are the representatives of the Buddhist trinity, Buddha, Dharma, and Sangha, or Fo, Fa, and Sengh, as they are called in Tibet.
2. These stones are highly venerated among Lamaists and Buddhists. They are found in the Altai Mountains and near the river Yarkhun. Our talisman was a gift from the venerable high-priest, a *Gelong*, of a Kalmuck tribe. Treated as apostates from their Lamaism, these nomads maintain friendly intercourse with their brother Kalmucks, the Khoshuts of eastern Tibet and Kokonor, and even with the Lamaists of Lhasa. The ecclesiastical authorities, however, will have no relations with them.
3. From the compound word *sutra*, maxim or precept, and *antika*, close or near.
4. *Aum* (mystic Sanskrit term of the Trinity), *mani* (holy jewel), *padme* (in the lotus, *padma* being the name for lotus), *hum* (be it so). The six syllables in the sentence correspond to the six chief powers of nature emanating from Buddha (the abstract deity, not Gautama), who is the seventh, the Alpha and Omega of being.
5. An elemental daemon, in which every native of Asia believes.
6. Lady, or Madam, in Moldavian.
7. The hour in Bucharest corresponded perfectly with that of the country in which the scene had taken place.

Index

abortion, reincarnation and, 88
Abraham, 180, 218, 223, 230
Abrasax, 170, 171
Adam, 3, 4, 15, 34, 66, 102, 124, 191, 192, 218
    as androgyne, 68, 70
    composition of, 69
    fall of, 70, 74, 191
Adam-Kadmon, 25, 68, 69, 170, 178, 189, 191
Adam Primus, 69, 180
Adi Buddha, 163
Adonai, 178, 224
ages of man, 13–14, 31–32, 66–67, 190, 218
Ahriman, 228
akasa, 32, 96, 130, 151
Akhamôth, 172
Akkadians, 124–125
Albigensians, 229
alchemy, 30–31, 47, 71–72, 111
Aleim, 124
Alexander Severus, 98
Alexander the Macedonian, 7, 14, 125
Alexandria, 138, 139, 143–144
Alexandrian library, 113, 144
alkahest, 30, 37
alligators, fakirs and, 93
Amenti, 136
Ammonius Saccas, 104, 143, 183, 232
Amphitheatrum Sapientiae Aeternae, 78
anastasis, 192
Anata, 170

Andhera, 136
anima mundi, 50, 63
animals,
    fascination in, 32, 49
    instincts of, 102, 103
    spirits of, 22–23, 81
Anti-Christ, 231
Anu, 170, 171
Apollonius of Tyana, 10, 90, 103, 110, 145, 159, 165
Aporrheta, 149, 174
apostasia, 192
apostles, 90, 110, 155
Apuleius, 204
archons, 146
Arhats, 63, 87, 199
Aristotle, 7, 11, 72, 97, 98, 140
Artemis, 162
Ashmole, Elias, 202
Asidians, 228
Asoka, King, 142, 157
astral body, 43, 50, 58, 59, 240
    after death, 80, 101, 107–108
    as matter, 62
    phenomena and, 241, 244–245
    return to physical body of, 108
    as soul, 43
    travel in sleep by, 42
    see also astral soul
astral light, 30, 33, 47, 53, 83, 84, 94, 112
    elementals and, 59
    future and past in, 41, 44, 241
    pregnant women and, 96–97

prophecies from, 46
thoughts and actions in, 41, 96–97
will and, 32
see also ether
astral soul, 6, 50
after death, 79, 80, 101, 205
annihilation of, 62, 75, 77
disembodied, 64
as intermediary, 71
levitation by, 45
and location of spirit, 74
as matter, 62
and physical body, 44, 79
separation from body of, 104–105
travel by, 254
see also astral body
astral spirit, 38–39, 42, 79, 130
see also spirit; divine spirit
astronomical bodies, 38–39, 51
ancients and, 55, 57
Egyptians and, 118
evolution of, 95–96
influences of, 73–74
magnetism of, 38, 40, 48–49, 58
movement of, 59, 67
Asvattha, 35–36
Atlantis, 119, 120, 127–128
Atman, 225
atonement, doctrine of, 75–76, 141, 142, 233–234
attraction and repulsion, 32, 43, 49, 58, 83
see also magnetism
Atum, 228, 230
augoeides, 6, 50, 71, 74, 101
Augustine, St., 66, 104
Aum mani padme hum, 251, 259
Avatars, 163, 189–191, 201
Azoth, 112

Babylonian captivity, 124, 162, 203, 218
Babylonians, 118, 119, 124, 125, 128
Balder, 136
Basilideans, 169, 182
Basilides, 155, 163, 168, 232
Bel, 171
Berosus, 16, 30, 83, 88, 190, 217

Bertrand, A. J. F., 40
Bhagavad Gita, 190, 231
Bible, 103, 110, 147, 175, 204, 205
ages of, 218
allegory and fact in, 123, 124, 211–212
early Christian sects and, 147, 169, 172
evolution and, 35
gehenna in, 89, 137
Masons and, 207
"master builder" in, 146
non-Christian religions and, 194
Peter in, 110, 147
see also New Testament; Old Testament
Bin, 171
Binah, 178
black magic, 79
Blavatsky, Helena, phenomena witnessed by, 92–93, 246–248, 250–251, 252–254, 255–256
body, physical, 38–39, 50, 60
density of, 66
magnetism and, 40
périsprit and, 44
phenomena and, 242
purity of, 58
Book of Concealed Mystery see Sifra di-Tseniuta
Book of Numbers, Chaldean, 13, 124, 149
Book of the Dead, Egyptian, 205, 223, 225
Brahma, 25, 27–28, 30, 63, 169, 170, 171, 191
days and nights of, 181, 187, 188–189, 216–217
Brahman-Dyaus, 170, 189
Brahmanas, 213–214
Brahmanism, 35, 61, 130, 150, 164, 204, 213, 218, 220, 248, 258
avatars of, 189–190, 191
Buddhism and, 155, 158, 168, 169–170, 200
Christianity and, 231
cosmogony of, 179, 181, 213
days and nights of Brahma in, 181, 187, 188–189, 216–217
Rishis of, 27
Trimurti of, 170–171

see also Hinduism
Brahmans, 9, 64, 104, 125
Brahmatma, 149, 238
Brihaspati, 12
Bruchion, 137
Bruno, G., 25–26
Buddha (diety), 196, 200, 259
Buddha, Gautama, 14, 110, 158, 165, 169, 200, 238
   incarnations of, 63–64, 189
   Jesus and, 157, 167, 192, 198–199, 200, 232, 238
   teachings of, 61, 62, 63, 86, 87, 150, 155, 198–199, 248–249
Buddhas, 63, 111, 200
Buddhism, 61–65, 77, 86–88, 135, 162, 225, 248–249
   annihalation in, 62, 63, 64
   Brahmanism and, 168, 169–170
   cause and effect in, 232
   commandments of, 167, 236
   cycles of chronology of, 12
   doctrines of, 150, 152, 163, 168, 177, 181, 187, 190, 204, 219, 231
   early Christianity and, 155, 164, 238
   Essenes and, 142, 157, 168
   four truths of, 62, 199
   Gnosticism and, 169–170
   illusion in, 62, 164
   initiations of, 151
   Jainism and, 200
   pre-Vedic, 155, 158, 258
   Pythagorean philosophy and, 61, 63, 87
   reincarnation in, 86–87
   rules of, 249–250
   Sermon on Mount and, 236
   as source of other religions, 155, 176, 258
   trinity of, 259
builder, as title, 207–208
   Master-, 146, 208
Bunsen, Christian C. J., 13, 116, 131, 218, 239
Bythos, 170, 171

Caesar, 137
Cain, race of, 128
carnelian stones, 246, 252, 259
Carpenter, W. B., 116, 240
Cassandrus, 82
Catholic Church, 135, 193, 206, 207, 228
cause and effect, 232–234
Celsus, 143, 144
Ceres-Demeter, 150
Chaldean Oracles, 41
Chaldean philosophy, 136, 162, 186, 225
   cosmogony of, 30
   despiritualization of man in, 34
   doctrine of emanations in, 170–171, 181
Chaldeans, 124, 130, 146, 148, 157, 158, 203, 211, 217
Chandragupta, 249
chaos, 29, 31, 34, 83–84, 91, 179
Charybdis, 119
Cherubim, 178
Christianity, 130, 138
   Asian origins of, 61, 155, 175, 231, 238
   atonement in, 141–142, 233–234
   devil and hell in, 136, 137, 221–222, 224, 228, 229
   emblems of, 185–186
   heathen/pagan origins of, 35, 69, 136, 141–142, 142–143, 147, 152–153, 182–183, 184–185, 212, 258
   immortality in, 75–76
   Judaism and early, 165–166
   misdirection of, 66, 139–140, 182, 211–212, 232, 235
   number seven in, 213
   Platonic origins of, 139, 140, 141, 143, 150, 174, 184
   sects of early, 155, 156–158, 160, 162–165, 172–174, 182, 193
   see also under names of individual sects
   trinity of, 56, 140
Christians, destruction and persecution by, 98, 103–104, 113, 137, 140, 141, 143, 163, 182, 185
Christos, 63, 156, 164–165, 171, 172, 174, 195, 196, 201, 229, 232

Chthonia-Vesta, 55
circle of necessity, 86, 87
Clement Alexandrinus, 6, 16, 69, 155, 165
Cleopatra, 137, 138
climate, change of, 11–12
"coats of skin," 4, 34, 66, 67, 191, 219
Codex Nazaraeus, 157, 197
Coleman, Charles, 16
compensation, law of, 77, 235, 243
Confucius, 165
conscience, 71, 79
Constantine, 103
Copts, 138, 175, 194
Corinthians, 145–146, 222
cosmogony(ies), 100, 170–172, 177–182, 214–219
  of Brahmanism, 181, 213, 216–217
  Chaldean, 170–171
  doctrine of emanations and, 170–172, 177–179, 181–182
  Egyptian, 25, 34
  Elohim in, 214–215, 216, 217
  ether and chaos in, 83–84
  evolution and, 31
  of Genesis, 124, 180, 181, 212, 216
  Hindu, 25, 170–171, 179, 218–219
  of the Kabbala, 177–179, 181–182
  Ophite, 170–172
crime, 233–234
Crookes, William, 18, 110
cross, as symbol, 112–113, 185–186, 206, 208
cycles,
  of earth, 11–13, 16, 82, 217, 218–219, 220
  of mankind, 3–4, 5, 11–13, 53–54, 66–67, 70, 186–187, 191, 204, 218–219
Cyril, 143, 184

Dagon, 30, 186
Darwin, Charles, 60, 66, 100–101
Davis, S., 12
de Beaumont, Élie, 111
de Jussieu, Antoine L., 39

de Payens, Hugues, 206
de Saint-Adhémar, Geoffroy, 206
death, 26, 76, 80–81, 101
  half-, 104–105
  occurrence of, 106–108
  resuscitation after, 107–109
  spiritual, 76–77
Demiurge, 19, 55–56, 68, 163, 205, 214, 217
Democritus, 19, 97
demons, 90
d'Eslon, Charles, 39
destiny, 243–244
Devanaguy, 189
Devil, 105, 136, 221, 222, 224, 228, 229, 230
Dharma, 259
Dharmasoka, 249
Dhyani Buddhas, 163
Diabolos, 222, 228
Diocletian, 98
Diodorus, 98
Disciples of St. John, 193, 194
divine spirit, 43, 50, 51, 64, 68, 76
  of Christos, 165
  desertion of man by, 59, 75, 79–80, 101
  knowledge of, 71
  location of, 74
  in matter, 6, 102
Draper, John W., 67
dreams, 42, 105
Druids, 9
Druzes, 175, 193, 194–197
Du Potet, J., 33, 40
Dvapara-yuga, 12, 190

Earth,
  circulation system of, 111
  cycles of, 11–13, 16, 82, 217, 218–219, 220
  evolution of, 81, 215
Ebers Papyrus, 10, 118
Ebionites, 156, 173, 174
Eddas, 30
Eden, garden of, 124
ego, 75, 101, 199

Egypt, 7, 24, 98, 115–119, 121, 194, 229
    advancement of ancient, 115–119
    cosmogony of ancient, 25, 34
    human sacrifices in, 239
    and India, 24, 115, 126, 217–218
    judgement allegories of, 223, 228
    Mysteries of, 117, 118, 142, 148,
       204–205, 218
    mythology of ancient, 30
    records of, 98, 209, 217
    Sacred Books of, 16
    snake charmers in, 92–93
Eikon, 170
El Hay, 178
elemental spirits, 83, 84, 88, 110, 242, 259
    classes of, 72–73, 77–78
    evolution of, 59–60
    human spirits becoming, 132
    inhabiting either, 59
    phenomena by, 21, 22, 26–27, 73, 78,
       85, 131, 244, 245
elements, 47, 84–85, 91, 113
Elisha, 108–109
Eloah, 178
Elohim, 69, 70, 124, 126, 178, 205,
       214–215, 216, 224
Elohim-Tsabaôth, 178
Elysium, 159
emanations, doctrine of, 140, 170–171,
       178–179, 181–182
Emepht, 33
emotions *see* feelings
EN-SOF, 7, 57, 64, 170, 177, 179, 180
Ennoia, 170, 171, 172
Ephesus, 162
Epiphanius, 165
epopteia, 146, 149, 150, 151
Essenes, 7, 110, 7, 110, 148, 156, 158, 160,
       162, 167, 205, 222
    Jesus and, 157, 158, 159, 236
    origins of, 142, 157, 168
ether, 29–31, 53, 59, 62, 83–84, 91
    see also astral light
Ethiopians, 98, 115, 218
Euhemarus, 212
Eulamius, 104

Eusebius, 98, 163, 173
Eve, 66, 109, 175
evolution, 35, 68, 70–71, 100–101, 212
    ancient knowledge of, 31–32, 35–36,
       60
    avatars and, 190, 191
    double, 51, 191
    individual cycles of, 95–96
    missing links in, 6, 27, 60, 192
    spiritual, 27, 35, 60, 68, 70–71, 81, 89,
       191, 212

Fa, 259
faith, 52
fakirs, 93, 110, 147, 151
fascination, 32, 49
feelings, 49, 59, 94
Feroher, 225
fetuses,
    development of, 94–95
    impact of mothers on, 94, 96–97
    and reincarnation, 89
Ficino, Marsilio, 94, 98–99
fish, as symbol, 186
Fo, 62, 259
force(s), 34
    antagonistic or contrary, 111, 221
    and matter, 45, 100, 199
    sidereal, 38
    and will, 19, 45, 59, 199
Fragment of Hermias, 84
Freemasons see Masons
French Academy of 1784, 39
Frigga, 136

Gabriel, Angel, descent of, 161
Galileans, 158, 160
gan-dunias, 124, 131
Geburah, 178
gehenna, 80, 89, 137
Genesis, 30, 68, 128, 212, 213, 230
    as allegory, 123–124, 180
    "coats of skin" of, 34, 66
    cosmogony of, 179, 180, 181, 216, 217
    Kabbala and, 102
    natural selection and, 70

geometry, 84
  Egyptian knowledge of, 10, 117
  of God, 19, 111, 112, 113
Ghengis Khan, tomb of, 129
Ghost-Land, 236
giants, race of, 35, 70, 128
Gibbon, Edward, 87, 139
Giles, Chauncey, 76
Gnosis, 140, 160, 162, 164, 208
Gnostics, 142, 148, 196, 205, 211, 228
  doctrines of, 6, 162, 163, 164–165,
    169–172, 182, 184, 196, 201
  Druzes and, 195, 196
  early Christianity and, 103, 140, 141,
    143, 163–164, 167, 173, 174, 175,
    182, 184, 185
  Jesus and, 162, 172, 174
Gobi Desert, 129, 204
gods, men as, 160–161, 165
Goethe, J. W. von, 230
Gogard, 69
Greece, ancient, 117, 118, 120, 126, 229
Gymnosophists, 24–25, 194

Hades, 77, 80, 89, 136, 159, 168
Hakim, 195
half-death, 104
H'amza, 195, 196
Hanuman, 189, 192
harmony, law of, 44, 76, 81, 88
Hathor, 25
Haug, M., 27
healing, 52–53
  in ancient Egypt, 118–119
  imagination in, 94
heliacal year, 12
hell, 136, 229
  see also Hades
Heptaktys, 214
Herakles, 69
Hermeias, 104
Hermes, 7, 25, 112, 230
  on death, 107
  writings of, 13, 16, 98, 104, 112, 118,
    152, 169, 179, 204
Hermetic philosophy, 79, 110–111

astral light in, 112
cosmogony of, 83, 179
of cycles of mankind, 3, 67
of man and matter, 3
man's triune nature in, 204
philosopher's stone in, 71–72
Herodotus, 5, 116, 117, 118, 218
Hesed, 178
Hibil-Ziwa, 161
hierophants, 110, 124, 126, 148, 149, 238,
    242
  of Atlantis, 127, 128
  atonement of, 142
  doctrines of, 64, 67, 158
  Gymnosophists and, 24
  powers of, 45
  transfer of life by, 236–237
Higgins, Godfrey, 12, 13, 152
Hillel, 160, 235
Hinduism, 24, 35, 36, 130, 136, 167, 177,
    178, 195, 205, 212, 225
  avatars of, 189–190, 191
  chronology of, 190, 191, 217
  cosmogony of, 25, 179
  initiation in, 147–148, 151
  reincarnation in, 86
  ten virtues of, 147–148
  see also Brahmanism
Hinnom, 137
Hoa, 171
Hod, 178
Hokhmah, 178
Homer, 119, 218
Horace, 212
Hovelacque, A.-A., 192
Hypatia, 143–144, 183, 184

Iamblichus, 16, 79, 98, 103, 110, 145, 165
idiocy, reincarnation and, 88, 89
Ilu, 170
imagination, 94
immortality, 75–76, 79, 101, 107, 198,
    199, 204
India, 120, 138, 141, 158, 203, 213, 249,
    250
  ancient, 125–126

Egypt and, 24, 115, 126, 217–218
fakirs of, 93, 110
Mysteries of, 147
spirit communication in, 151
individuality, 74–76, 79, 101
infants, reincarnation and, 88–89
initiations, 117, 147, 148, 149, 152, 154, 156, 174, 185, 225
atonement in, 142
common systems of, 148, 151
of Druzes, 195–196
Hindu, 147–148, 151
Job as allegory of, 223, 224, 227
Paul and, 146
Plato on, 150–151
insanity, 242
instinct, 101–103
intuition, 102–103
Irenaeus, 139, 140, 143, 147, 155, 156, 163, 164, 165
Isaiah, 123
Ishmonia, 139
Isis, 7, 228
veil of, 7, 78, 122
Islam, 130, 258

Jacolliet, L., 110, 125, 131
Jainism, 200
Jakatas, 63–64
James, 192, 199
Jannes, 203
Jehovah, 25, 166, 167, 178, 194, 228
in *Job*, 223–224
Jervis, J., 156
Jesuits, 203
Jesus, 14, 130, 137, 146, 186, 194, 197, 231, 237, 238
Buddha and, 157, 192, 198–199, 200, 232, 237, 238
Buddhism and, 155, 156, 167, 236
casting out of demons by, 90
disciples view of, 173, 174
early Christian sects and, 157, 158, 159, 162, 163, 164–165, 172, 174, 195, 196

exoteric and esoteric teachings of, 159, 223
God and, 166, 167
Krishna and, 232
Masons and, 206, 207
misrepresentation of, 103, 139–140, 182, 233, 234, 235
as reformer, 157, 159–160, 166, 167, 183, 200
Sermon on Mount of, 158, 166, 235–236
temptation of, 222
use of parables by, 158–159, 223
Job, 30, 213, 222–228
Joel, 130
John, 159, 174, 186, 238
Gospel of, 4, 175, 198, 221
John the Baptist, 156, 157, 160, 194, 195, 206, 207
Josaphat, St., 238
Josephus, 157, 159, 167, 218
Joshua, 142, 238
Judaism, 8, 228, 229
Christianity and, 165, 166, 167, 212
origins of, 155, 180, 203, 211, 218, 258
Jupiter, 57
Justinian, 103, 104
Kabbala, 33, 99, 139, 140, 170, 177–182, 186
on Genesis, 102
Jewish, 8, 102, 208, 211, 212
Oriental, 8, 126, 140, 141, 177, 208, 213
kabbalistic doctrine, 48, 66, 156, 163, 205
antagonistic forces in, 221–222
Christianity and, 175
of cycles, 87–88, 95–96
death in, 107, 108
of emanations, 170, 177–179, 181–182
EN-SOF in, 7, 177–178, 179, 180
future in, 44
Genesis in, 123–124
gods in, 160–161
Hades in, 80
human development in, 94–95
law of harmony in, 76, 221–222

number seven in, 213, 214–215
of permutation, 160
powers of nature in, 106
spirit and matter in, 83
trinities of, 177–178
Kali, 190
Kali-yuga, 12, 190, 218
Kalki, 189–190, 191
Kalmucks, 259
kalpas, 12
Kaneya, 189
Kapila, 27, 232, 237
karma, 87, 199
Kenrick, J, 116
Kether, 178
Khe-lan, brotherhood of, 251
Khunrath, Henry, 78
King, C. W., 152, 157, 168, 176, 185
Kircher, A., 48, 49
Kneph, 30
Knight, R. Payne, 152, 175
Knights-Templars, 206–207
    see also Masons
Koinobioi, 194
Krishna, 165, 189, 190, 200, 232, 238
Krita-yuga, 12, 190
Kurma-Avatar, 189

Lamaism, 249, 259
Lao-Tzu, 165
laws of nature see natural law
Legatus, 139, 161
Lévi, Éliphas, 42
    on astral light, 32, 53
    on law of reciprocal influences, 73–74
    on physical death, 107, 108
    on pregnant women, 97
    on resuscitation of dead, 108, 109
Leviathan, 227
life principle, 32, 96, 106, 107, 130
life, prolonging of, 111
Logos, 34, 63, 69, 139, 163, 170, 171, 172,
    175, 177, 179, 182, 229
Loki, 136

Magi, 11, 148, 158, 181, 194, 203

Magian religion, 10, 195
magic, 8–10, 11, 47, 54, 129–130, 207,
    228, 241, 242, 243, 256–258
magnale magnum, 51, 52
Magnes, 112
magnetism, 242
    animal, 38, 40, 48
    of celestial bodies, 38–39, 40, 48, 58
    discovery of, 23
    of feelings, 49
    French rejection of, 38–39
    Kircher on, 48–49
    mineral, 48
    of pregnant mothers, 96–97
    transcendent, 40
Mahabharata, 190
Mahat, 237
Maitreya-Buddha, 190
Malkhuth, 178
man,
    fall of, 3, 67, 74, 190, 191
    involution of, 34, 204
    as microcosm of macrocosm, 19, 50,
        84, 89, 191
    physical development of, 95
    races of, 3–5, 27, 34, 35, 67, 68,
        69–71, 126–128,187, 191, 204, 217,
        219–220, 241
    three births of, 237
    three spirits of, 50–51
    triple nature of, 4, 19, 51, 72, 192, 204,
        240, 257
Mandaeans, 193, 194
Manes, 182
Manetho, 16, 117, 131
manifestation see under will; see
    phenomena, physical
Mantra, 214
Manu, 8, 127, 147, 167, 169, 179, 187,
    189, 218
manvanteras, 12, 16
Marcion, 165–166, 169, 232
Marcionites, 182
Martin Luther, 229
Mary Magdalene, 109
Masons, 146, 193, 205, 209, 211, 213

beliefs and practices of, 148–149,
207–208
history of, 202–203, 206–207
materializations, 21–22, 78
Matron Baubo, 149–150
Matsya-Avatar, 189
matter,
antagonism of, 221, 228
astral man as, 6, 62
conquering of, 71
in creation of woman, 68–69
as curse, 102
descent from spirit to, 60
divine spirit in, 6, 102
energizing principle of, 83, 91
eternal nature of, 80
as illusion, 62, 65, 249
increased density in involution of, 3,
34, 36, 102
in manifestation, 45
as serpent, 68–69, 102, 124
spirit and, 100
thought as, 20, 94
Matter, A. J., 162
Matthew, 163
Gospel of, 174–175, 234–235, 236
Maya, 62, 164
mediatorship, 109–110
mediumship, 20–22, 45, 78, 109–110, 241,
242, 244, 254
Melchisedek, 231
memory,
astral light and, 41, 44
elementals and, 73, 85
Menes, 98, 116, 126, 131
Mephistophiles, 230
Mesmer, Anton, 23, 38, 39, 40
Metamorphoses, 204
Metatron, 139, 161, 182, 215, 225
metempsychosis, 6, 61, 62, 94
Metis, 55, 56
Mexico, 119, 121
Milman, H. H., 174
Milton, J., 230
minerals, 81, 106, 242
miracles, 131, 136, 237, 240

Mithras, 228
modern science, 131
ancient allegories and, 55, 57
archaeological finds of, 4–5
astral light and, 112
evolution and, 35
and God, 7
ignorance of, 33
and life principle, 106
Moeris, lake, 116
Moksha, 190, 237
monad, 51, 56, 63, 111, 163, 170
astral, 88, 89
Mongolia, 126, 249
monotheism,
of ancients, 10–11, 181
of Plato, 61
Moses, 90, 103, 156, 165, 180, 203, 218,
222, 223
on creation of life, 30, 95
as god on earth, 160, 161
Jesus and, 167
Joshua and, 142, 238
on Mt. Sinai, 188
wrath of, 128
mothers, impact on fetuses of, 94, 96–97
Müller, Max, 136
Multimamma, 162
music, reptiles and, 92–93
Mylitta, 171
Mysteries, 7, 60, 153, 185, 236
Bacchic, 148, 185
Buddha and, 237
Egyptian, 117, 118, 142, 148, 204–205,
218
Eleusinian, 146, 148, 159, 185
Hindu, 147, 148
human sacrifice and, 239
initiation into, 142, 147, 148, 149–150,
151, 152, 154, 159, 174, 223, 225
Jesus and, 159
Job and, 223, 225
Nazireate, 156, 225
Paul and, 146
Plato and, 61

Nabathaeans, 156
Nara, 170, 179
Nara-Sinha, 189
Narada, 131
Narayana, 179
Nari, 170, 171
Nasera, 156
natural law, 19, 57, 77, 111, 130, 240
natural selection, 66, 70
nature,
    powers of, 106
    triune, 240, 257
nature spirits see elemental spirits
Nazareans, 193, 194
Nazarenes, 156–157, 158, 160, 161, 162,
    173, 174, 182
Nazaria, 156
nazars, 146, 156, 158
necromancy, 47, 79
Neoplatonists, 98, 148, 158, 176, 236
    augoeides of, 74, 225
    Christianity and, 140, 141, 142–143
    last of, 104
    triad of, 56
nephesh, 204
neroses, 12, 16
Netzah, 178
New Testament, 60, 80, 90, 137, 141, 167,
    170, 221
    see also Bible
    see also under names of individual books
    of the New Testament
Nicolini, G. B., 203
Nile, diversion of, 116
Nirvana, 62–63, 64, 87, 190, 192, 195,
    198, 199, 219, 237, 258
    temporary, 88
Noah, 128, 217, 218
Nous, 19, 163, 192, 196, 225
Nozari, 156
numerals, 212–213, 214

Oannes, 30, 88
occultism, 8, 47, 256
    Leviathan as, 227
    powers of, 53, 129–130

psychomatics of, 86
Od, 33, 128
Odin, 9
Old Testament, 60, 165, 167, 170, 218,
    222, 223, 228, 229
    see also Bible
    see also under names of individual books
    of the Old Testament
On-ati, 228
Ophiomorphos, 229
Ophios, 229
Ophis, 171
Ophites, 169, 182, 193, 195
    doctrine of emanations of, 170–172
Origen, 6, 69, 75, 90, 143
Ormazd, 228
Orpheus, 82, 232
Orphic theology, 55–56, 83
Orphikoi, 236
Osiris, 25, 223, 229
Osirism, 152
Osthanes, 203
Ozarim, 161

Pa'had, 178
pain, Buddhism and, 63
Panchen Rimpoche, 251
Pandora, 109
Pantheism, 35
Paracelsus, Theophrastus, 31, 40, 48,
    73–74, 202
    on astral travel, 42
    healing by, 52
    and magnetism, 23, 38
    on three spirits of man, 50
Parasu-Rama, 189, 191
Parsiism, 152
Paul, 26, 162, 172
    Peter and, 145, 172
    as initiate, 145–146, 159
    writings of, 145, 165, 192, 197, 198,
    222–223
Pausanias, 22
Perfection of Wisdom see Prajña Paramita
périsprit, 44, 62
permutation, doctrine of, 160

Persia, 126, 193, 194, 225
personality, 74–75
Peter, 110, 147, 163, 174, 234
  Paul and, 145, 172
Pharisees, 87, 157, 173, 174, 200, 228
Pharsi, 228
phenomena, physical,
  accounts of witnessed, 246–248,
    250–251, 252–254, 255–256
  by adepts, 151–152, 241–242, 243, 244
  of animation of inert matter, 130–131
  Crookes theories on, 18
  dangers of, 53
  genuineness of, 78
  of materialization, 21–22, 78
  science and, 18–19
  by spirits, 20, 21–23, 26–27
Philalethes, 72
Philalethians, 183, 208
Philo Judeas, 4, 11, 36, 139, 179
philosopher's stone, 48, 71, 72, 111, 112
Phoenicians, 119, 218
Phronêsis, 163
Pimander, 25, 69, 171, 177
pitris, 87, 151
plants,
  attraction and repulsion in, 49
  mystical properties of, 106, 242–243
  reproduced in spirit, 250–251
  spirits of, 81
Plato, 27, 36, 59, 84, 98, 104, 111, 113,
    140, 156, 165, 173, 184, 192, 204,
    232
  on ancient races, 4, 68, 69
  Atlantis and, 127
  esoteric writing of, 5, 14, 60–61
  on external influences on man, 58–59
  on fertile and barren periods, 53
  on Mysteries, 61, 149, 150, 151, 153
  on prayer, 103
  on prophets, 46
  on soul after death, 26, 79, 80
  trinity of, 139
  on visible out of invisible, 19
Pleasonton, A. J., 48, 58
Pliny, 9, 10, 157, 203

Plotinus, 56, 65, 103, 110, 145, 150, 165,
    184, 232
Plutarch, 184
Pluto, 136
Pneuma, 171
Polier, M. E. de, 25
Popol Vuh, 30, 127, 128
Porphyry, 23, 55, 56, 65, 103, 130, 145,
    176, 229
Porta, G. Baptista della, 47–48
possession, 46, 90, 109, 110
Prajña Paramita, 63
Prakriti, 237
pralayas, 217
Pratimoksha Sutra, 236
prayer, 103
pregnancy, fetus during, 94–97
Proclus, 51, 55, 56, 78, 101, 130, 149, 151
Prometheus, 69, 130
prophecies, 46
Protestantism, 135, 229
Psellus, 78
Ptah, 33, 205, 230
Purusha, 179
pyramids, Egyptian, 5, 36, 67–68, 116, 117
Pythagoras, 36, 61, 87, 104, 153, 154, 156,
    159, 165, 173, 232
Pythagorean doctrine, 25, 103
  of cosmogony, 83
  of God as universal mind, 60–61
  Jesus and, 158, 159
  of metempsychosis, 6, 94
  of numbers, 212, 213, 214
Python, 229

Rama-Chandra, 189
Ramayana, 189
reason, 71, 88–89, 101–103
Reichenbach, Karl L., 33, 96
reincarnation, 41–42, 86–87, 88–90
religions, common truths in all, 104,
    120–121, 148, 153, 155–156, 158,
    258
reptiles, music and, 92–93
Researches on the Phenomena of Spiritualism,
    18

resuscitation of dead, 107–109
Rig-Veda, 58
Rishis, 25, 27, 194
Rosicrucian, 84
Rosicrucians, 124, 202, 205–206, 209
ruins, ancient, 8, 121, 127, 128

sacrifices, human, 239
Sadducees, 160, 173, 200
Saint Germain, Count, 124
Sakyamuni, 157, 158, 167, 189, 198, 232, 238
Samas, 171
Sanchoniathon, 83, 190
Sangha, 259
sannyasis, 147, 151
Sanskrit literature, 125
Santanelli, I., 40
sars, 11, 16
Satan, 222, 224, 228, 229, 230
Satapa-tha-Brahmana, 237
Saturn, 57, 180
Sautrantikas, 248
Sayer, Anthony, 202
Schleicher, 192
Schopenhauer, A., 19
secrecy and ancient wisdom, 5–6, 14, 61, 120, 148–149, 197, 238
Secret Doctrine, 35, 80, 101, 104, 106, 113, 123, 124, 174, 203, 208
secret societies, 121, 193–197, 202–203, 205–209
Selecus, 98
Sengh, 259
Sephirah, 56, 57, 178, 179, 181, 216
Septuagint, 225
Serapeion, 185
Serapis, 228
Sermon on the Mount, 158, 235–236
serpent(s), 36
    charming of, 92–93, 109
    in Egyptian cosmogony, 30, 34
    in Genesis, 68–69, 102, 124, 128, 230
    as Satan, 222, 229
    symbolizing matter, 68–69, 102, 124
seven, as sacred number, 212–213, 214

Shekînah, 170, 178
Shimon ben-Yohai, 160
Siddharta *see* Buddha, Gautama
Sifra di-Tseniuta, 3
Sigê, 171
Simon Magnus, 145
Simon the Cyrenian, 163
Sin, 171
Siva, 136, 171
sleep, 42, 105
Smyth, Charles Piazzi, 117
snakes *see* serpents
Socrates, 6, 26, 79, 197
Solomon, 180
Song-tsen Gampo, King, 251
sons of God, 4, 34, 69, 70, 126, 127
Sophia, 163, 170, 171, 172, 174, 175
sossus, 16
soul(s), 57, 191–192, 195
    abandonment of body by, 242
    Egyptian philosophy of, 204–205
    immortality and, 75–76, 199, 204
    in physical body, 150, 168, 204
    second death of, 205
    and spirit, 43
    two of man, 6, 65
    see also astral body; astral soul
sound, impact of, 214
Spinoza, Benedictus de, 25–26
spirit(s), 243
    immortality of, 199, 204
    in *Job*, 225
    and matter, 100
    names for, 225
    and soul, 43
    three of man, 50
    union with man of, 160–161, 165, 180, 240–241
    see also astral spirit; divine spirit
spirits, human,
    becoming elementals, 132
    communication with, 151
    as demons, 89–90
    diversity of, 85–86
    evocation and attraction of, 22, 78–79, 84

forms of, 64
phenomena by, 20–21, 26–27, 78, 131
spiritualism, 18, 21–22, 47, 76
Sufis, 194
sun, 48–49, 57–58
central spiritual, 48, 51, 57–58, 84, 110
Svabhavat, 187
Svabhavikas, 26, 181, 187
Svayambhu, 179, 181
Swedenborg, E., 75, 76
Swedenborgians, 242
Sybils, books of, 143
sympathy, 49

talismans, 246, 252, 259
Talmud, 8, 137, 156, 186
Tannaim, 161, 162, 174, 181, 202
Tartary, 126, 129, 138, 249, 252
Tau, 185–186
Taylor, Thomas, 150–151
Temple of Solomon, 207
temples, allegorical, 207–208
terrestrial spirits, 72, 77–78
Tertullian, 73, 155, 164, 165
Tetragrammaton, 186
Tetraktys, 56, 111, 172
Thales, 31
Theodas, 137, 138
Theon of Smyrna, 149
Theophilus, 143
theopoiia, 130
Therapeutae, 110, 156, 194
Thevatat, King, 128
Thomson, A. Todd, 11
Thoth, 104, 223
thought, 20, 41, 43, 97
Thouret, M. A., 39
Tibet, 126, 129, 236, 245, 248, 249, 251, 252
Tiphereth, 178
Tirthankara, 200
Tophet, 137
transmigration, 86, 87, 195
Treta-yuga, 12, 190
Trimurti, 170, 178
trinity(ies), 51, 56, 84, 113, 216

Chaldean, 170–171
Christian, 56, 140
Indian, 170–171
kabbalistic, 177–178
Ophite, 170–171
Platonic, 130–140
Turu, 228
Typhon, 229

Unseen Universe, The, 80, 96
Uranus, 57

Vaivasvata, 128
Valentinians, 182
Vamana, 189
vampirism, 90, 105
Van Helmont, B., 40, 51
Varaha, 189
vatus, 147, 151
Vedas, 8, 35, 104, 197, 211, 213–214
vicarious atonement *see* atonement, doctrine of
Viraj, 171
Vishnu, 171, 189–190
Volney, C. F., 11
Voltaireans, 27

Waldensians, 229
Wheel of the Law, 232
Wilder, Alexander, 104, 128, 131, 159, 175
Wilkinson, J. G., 116, 118
will, 19–20, 26, 32–33
of Creator, 51
force and, 19, 45, 59, 199
in healing, 52
manifestation of, 19–20, 32–33, 45, 94, 130
Wisdom Religion, 140–141, 152, 158, 180, 193, 207
witchcraft, 90, 109, 228, 229
woman, in Genesis, 68–69, 102, 124
writings, ancient, 98–99
destruction of, 98, 113, 137, 163
of Hermes, 13, 16, 98, 104, 112, 118, 152, 169, 179, 204

preservation of, 137–138, 143
Sanskrit, 125

Xisuthros, 128

Yâh, 178
Yava Aleim, 124, 126
Yehovah-Tsabaôth, 178

Yesod, 178
yugas, 12, 66

Zeruan, 180
Zeus, 55–56
zodiac, 218, 219
Zohar, 141, 177, 188, 192, 216
Zoroaster, 10, 41, 156, 203